HABITS UNLEASHED

The Ultimate Guide to Transforming Bad Habits into Positive Power

By

Dr. Hesham Mohamed Elsherif

About the Author

Dr. Hesham Mohamed Elsherif stands at the forefront of library management and research, boasting an impressive 22-year tenure in the field. Holding dual doctoral degrees, one in Management and Organizational Leadership and the other in Information Systems and Technology, Dr. Elsherif brings a unique blend of knowledge to any intellectual endeavor.

An expert in Empirical research methodology, Dr. Elsherif specializes particularly in the Qualitative approach and Action research. This specialization has not only strengthened his research endeavors but has also allowed him to contribute invaluable insights and advancements in these areas.

Over the years, Dr. Elsherif has made significant contributions to the academic world not only as a professional researcher but also as an Adjunct Professor. This multifaceted role in the educational landscape has further solidified his reputation as a thought leader and pioneer.

Furthermore, Dr. Elsherif's expertise isn't confined to one region. He has served as a consultant to numerous educational institutions on an international scale, sharing best practices, innovative strategies, and his deep insights into the ever-evolving realms of management and technology.

Combining a passion for education with an unparalleled depth of knowledge, Dr. Elsherif continues to inspire, educate, and lead in both the library and academic communities.

Preface

As I reflect on the journey that led me to write this book, I am reminded of a time when my own habits felt like an unbreakable chain, binding me to a version of myself that I desperately wanted to change. Mornings began with the snooze button, afternoons slipped away in procrastination, and evenings were a haze of mindless distractions. I knew I wasn't living up to my potential, yet the patterns persisted, as if controlled by an unseen force.

It wasn't that I lacked desire or ambition. Like many, I had dreams and goals that stirred excitement within me. I wanted to be healthier, more productive, to cultivate meaningful relationships, and to contribute something valuable to the world. But day after day, I found myself slipping back into the same routines, each one a tiny thread woven into the fabric of my daily life. I began to wonder: Why is change so elusive? Why do bad habits cling so stubbornly, even when we know they're holding us back?

These questions sparked a journey of exploration and discovery. I delved into the realms of psychology, neuroscience, and behavioral science, seeking answers not just for myself but for anyone grappling with the invisible chains of habit. What I found was both enlightening and profoundly empowering: habits are not destiny. They are learned behaviors, wired into our brains through repetition, but they can be rewired. We have the power to reshape them, to transform the very patterns that define our lives.

I began experimenting with the concepts I was learning, applying techniques to identify the triggers of my habits, to understand the rewards they provided, and to consciously alter the routines in between. It wasn't an overnight transformation - change rarely is - but gradually, I started to see shifts. Mornings became opportunities rather than obstacles. Procrastination gave way to purposeful action. Distractions lost their grip as I became more present and engaged.

One of the most profound realizations was that habits are not inherently good or bad; they are simply tools our brains use to conserve energy and navigate the world efficiently. It's how we wield these tools that determines their impact on our lives. A habit of regular exercise can bolster our health and vitality, while a habit of negative self-talk can erode our confidence and happiness. By understanding the mechanics of habit formation, we gain the ability to steer our behaviors toward the life we desire.

This book is the culmination of that journey - a comprehensive guide crafted from personal experience, extensive research, and the stories of countless individuals who have successfully transformed their own habits. It is designed to be more than just a collection of theories; it is a practical roadmap that walks you through the process of identifying, understanding, and reshaping your habits to unlock your full potential.

In the chapters that follow, we will embark together on an exploration of the habit loop—the cue, routine, and reward that underlies every habitual action. We'll delve into the fascinating science of how our brains form and maintain habits, and how neuroplasticity allows us to rewire those patterns. You'll learn strategies to increase mindfulness and self-awareness, enabling you to spot the subtle triggers that set your habits in motion.

We'll tackle the challenges head-on: the emotional triggers that often lead us astray, the environmental cues that nudge us toward old patterns, and the social influences that can either support or hinder our progress. Throughout the journey, practical exercises and reflective prompts will help you apply these concepts directly to your life, making the abstract tangible and the theoretical practical.

Perhaps most importantly, we'll address the reality that change is seldom linear. There will be obstacles and setbacks, moments when old habits resurface, and progress seems stalled. But within these moments lie valuable lessons and opportunities for growth. Together, we'll develop strategies to navigate these challenges with resilience and grace, ensuring that temporary setbacks do not become permanent roadblocks.

Writing this book has been a deeply personal endeavor. It has reinforced my belief in the incredible capacity we all possess to change and grow. I've been inspired by the resilience of the human spirit, the stories of transformation that emerge when people commit to taking control of their habits and, by extension, their lives.

My hope is that "Habits Unleashed" serves as a catalyst for your own journey of transformation. Whether you're looking to break free from habits that no longer serve you or to cultivate new ones that propel you toward your goals, this book is a companion and guide. It's an invitation to take that first step, to embrace the discomfort of change, and to discover the profound impact that mastering your habits can have on every aspect of your life.

As you turn the pages, I encourage you to approach this journey with an open mind and a willing heart. Change is rarely easy, but it is always possible. Remember that every habit, no matter how ingrained, started somewhere - and so can its transformation. The power lies within you, waiting to be unleashed.

Thank you for allowing me to be a part of your journey. I am honored to walk alongside you as we explore the boundless potential that emerges when we take control of our habits and, ultimately, our destinies.

Sincerely,

Dr. Hesham Mohamed Elsherif

Who Should Read This Book?

Imagine waking up each morning with a sense of purpose, feeling fully in control of your actions, and knowing that each step you take is leading you closer to your goals. This vision isn't a distant dream - it's a reality that begins with understanding and mastering your habits. "The Habit Revolution: Transform Bad Habits into Positive Power" is a journey crafted for anyone who recognizes that their habits are the foundation of their life's trajectory and is eager to harness that power for positive change.

If you've ever felt trapped by routines that no longer serve you, this book is your guide to liberation. Perhaps you're a professional feeling the weight of procrastination, watching opportunities slip by as you grapple with distractions. You might be a student overwhelmed by the demands of academia, seeking effective strategies to manage your time and focus. Maybe you're someone striving for a healthier lifestyle, yet find yourself caught in cycles of unhealthy eating or inactivity.

This book is for individuals who:

Feel Stuck in Negative Patterns: You recognize that certain habits are holding you back - be it in your career, relationships, health, or personal growth - but you're unsure how to break free. This book offers the tools to dismantle those patterns and replace them with empowering behaviors.

Desire Personal Growth: You're committed to self-improvement and are looking for a comprehensive approach to understand and optimize your habits. The insights in this book will deepen your self-awareness and provide actionable steps toward continuous development.

Seek Greater Productivity and Focus: In an age of constant distractions, maintaining focus is a challenge. If you're aiming to enhance your productivity, manage your time more effectively, and achieve your goals with greater efficiency, this book provides the strategies to get there.

Want to Improve Relationships: Habits extend beyond personal routines - they impact how we interact with others. This book explores how transforming your habits can lead to more meaningful connections and healthier relationships.

Are Facing Life Transitions: Whether you're starting a new job, entering a different life stage, or seeking a fresh start, changing your habits can ease transitions and set the foundation for success in new endeavors.

Feel Overwhelmed by Stress: If stress and emotional triggers often derail your intentions, this book offers techniques to manage your responses and maintain control, even in challenging situations.

Aspire to Lead and Inspire Others: Leaders, coaches, educators, and parents will find valuable insights into how habits shape behaviors in groups and individuals. By mastering your own habits, you become better equipped to guide and influence others positively.

But beyond these specific scenarios, "The Habit Revolution" is for anyone who believes that change is possible. It's for those who have tried to alter their habits before and found themselves slipping back, as well as for those embarking on this journey for the first time. It's for skeptics who question whether they can truly change, offering evidence-based approaches that demystify the process and make transformation attainable.

This book doesn't require you to be an expert in psychology or neuroscience. It is written for real people living real lives, filled with complexities and challenges. The stories, examples, and exercises are designed to resonate with diverse experiences, ensuring that the guidance is relatable and applicable.

If you're ready to take responsibility for your actions, to move from intention to action, and to transform your habits into a source of positive power, then this book is for you. It's not about perfection but progression - a journey toward becoming the best version of yourself.

Embarking on the habit revolution means stepping into a proactive role in your life story. It's about recognizing that while you can't control everything that happens, you can control how you respond, the habits you cultivate, and the person you become. This book is your companion on that journey, offering support, insights, and the assurance that you're not alone in your quest for change.

So, whether you're at the beginning of your self-improvement path or looking to deepen and reinforce the progress you've already made, "The Habit Revolution" welcomes you. Together, we'll explore the profound impact that transforming your habits can have—not just on your own life, but on the lives of those around you. The revolution starts within, and its ripples extend far beyond.

Why This Book Is an Essential Read

In a world that moves at an unprecedented pace, where distractions are abundant and time feels ever fleeting, understanding the mechanisms that drive our daily actions has never been more crucial. " Habits Unleashed: The Ultimate Guide to Transforming Bad Habits into Positive Power" is not just another self-help book; it is a transformative journey into the very core of human behavior. This book is essential reading because it tackles the foundational elements that shape our lives - our habits - and offers a tangible roadmap to harnessing them for profound personal change.

At some point, we all find ourselves questioning why certain patterns persist despite our best intentions. Perhaps you've set New Year's resolutions that faded by February, or you've attempted to break a habit only to find yourself back where you started. This isn't a reflection of a lack of willpower or motivation; it's a testament to the incredible power of habits and the subconscious grip they hold over us. This book demystifies that power, pulling back the curtain on the psychological and neurological processes that make habits so enduring.

One of the reasons this book is indispensable is its grounding in both scientific research and real-life application. It bridges the gap between theory and practice, providing insights from psychology, neuroscience, and behavioral economics in a way that is accessible and engaging. You'll not only learn *what* to change but *why* change is often so challenging and *how* to make it lasting. By understanding the habit loop - the cue, routine, and reward - you'll gain the tools to dissect your own behaviors and reconstruct them in ways that align with your deepest goals.

Moreover, the book recognizes that habits are not formed in isolation. Our environment, social circles, emotional states, and even societal norms play significant roles in shaping our behaviors. " Habits Unleashed: The Ultimate Guide to Transforming Bad Habits into Positive Power" delves into these external influences, offering strategies to create a supportive ecosystem that fosters positive habit formation. It's an essential read for understanding how to design your surroundings - both physical and social - to make good habits not only possible but inevitable.

Another compelling aspect of this book is its emphasis on mindfulness and self-awareness. In a society often fixated on external achievements, we sometimes overlook the internal landscapes that dictate our actions. This book invites you to pause and reflect, to become an observer of your own life. Through mindfulness practices and self-assessment techniques, you'll learn to recognize the subtle triggers and underlying needs that drive your habits. This heightened awareness is a critical step toward meaningful change, allowing you to address the root causes rather than just the symptoms.

" Habits Unleashed: The Ultimate Guide to Transforming Bad Habits into Positive Power" is also essential because it doesn't promise a quick fix; instead, it offers a sustainable approach to transformation. It acknowledges that setbacks are a natural part of the journey and provides strategies to navigate them with resilience. This realistic perspective ensures that you're prepared for the challenges ahead, reducing the likelihood of discouragement and abandonment of your goals. The book becomes a steadfast companion, guiding you through the ebbs and flows of personal growth.

Furthermore, the impact of this book extends beyond individual benefit. As you transform your habits, you inherently influence those around you. Whether you're a parent modeling behaviors for your children, a leader inspiring your team, or a friend offering support, the positive changes you make ripple outward. By reading this book, you're not just investing in yourself; you're contributing to a larger movement toward healthier, more intentional living.

In an era where information is abundant but wisdom is scarce, " Habits Unleashed: The Ultimate Guide to Transforming Bad Habits into Positive Power" stands out as a beacon of practical knowledge and heartfelt guidance. It cuts through the noise, offering clarity in a domain often muddled by conflicting advice. The book's holistic approach ensures that you're not just changing isolated behaviors but are embarking on a comprehensive transformation that touches every facet of your life.

Lastly, consider the cost of inaction. Remaining tethered to unproductive or harmful habits doesn't just stall progress - it can lead to detrimental outcomes for your health, relationships, and overall well-being. This book equips you with the tools to break free from these constraints, empowering you to live a life of purpose and fulfillment. It's an invitation to take control, to become the architect of your destiny rather than a passive participant.

In summary, " Habits Unleashed: The Ultimate Guide to Transforming Bad Habits into Positive Power" is an essential read because it offers a profound exploration of the forces that shape us and provides actionable strategies to harness those forces for positive change. It's more than a book; it's a catalyst for transformation, a guide to unlocking your potential, and a companion on the journey to a more empowered and intentional life. By delving into its pages, you're taking the first decisive step toward a future defined not by default patterns but by deliberate choices.

Happy Reading!

Dr. Hesham Mohamed Elsherif

Table of Contents

Introduction

The Power of Habits: Shaping Your Destiny

In the introduction to *"Habits Unleashed: The Ultimate Guide to Transforming Bad Habits into Positive Power,"* the narrative centers on the profound impact habits can have on our lives, subtly yet powerfully shaping the path we walk each day. Habits, like unseen currents beneath the surface of a river, steer our actions, thoughts, and ultimately our destiny. They are the seemingly small decisions we make repeatedly, from how we start our mornings to the way we respond to challenges and setbacks.

Consider a person who, upon waking, reaches for their phone and spends precious minutes scrolling through social media. It seems insignificant, a harmless ritual to ease into the day. But, over time, this habit can influence one's mood, productivity, and even self-perception. Contrast this with someone who begins each day with a short meditation or a brisk walk—equally small actions, yet the ripple effect is unmistakably different. One habit may lead to distraction and anxiety, while the other cultivates focus and calm.

This is the power of habits: they become the architects of our future. The small routines, often unnoticed, lay the foundation for who we become. They influence our health, our relationships, and our ambitions. The habits we foster, whether consciously chosen or unconsciously adopted, have the ability to propel us forward toward our dreams or hold us back, ensnaring us in cycles of inertia and regret.

Yet, this power is not fixed - it can be harnessed, redirected, and even transformed. Just as a river can change its course with a shift in the landscape, we can alter the flow of our lives by intentionally reshaping our habits. Imagine the power in taking a habit that holds you back - procrastination, negative self-talk, mindless snacking - and transforming it into something that fuels your potential. What if, instead of delaying tasks, you developed a habit of taking immediate action? What if you replaced self-doubt with daily affirmations or swapped that afternoon sugar fix with a rejuvenating walk?

Shaping our habits is not about grand gestures or overnight transformations. It's about embracing the small, consistent actions that, over time, carve a new path forward. It's about realizing that each habit holds a hidden potential - an opportunity to unlock a better version of yourself. As you delve into this journey, you'll discover that the power of habits is not just in their ability to direct your actions, but in their capacity to reshape your destiny, one small choice at a time

Why Habits Matter More Than You Think

In the introduction of *"Habits Unleashed: The Ultimate Guide to Transforming Bad Habits into Positive Power,"* the concept of why habits matter more than we might imagine unfolds like a quiet revelation. Habits, those automatic behaviors that shape our days, often appear mundane, trivial even. But beneath their surface lies a profound influence, silently steering the course of our lives, for better or worse. Understanding this hidden power is the key to unlocking a life of purpose, fulfillment, and success.

Imagine your daily life as a mosaic, each small tile representing a habit. A single tile might not seem significant - brushing your teeth, taking a particular route to work, grabbing a cup of coffee. But as these tiles accumulate, they begin to form a pattern, one that defines the bigger picture of your life. It is within these small, repetitive actions that our true selves are forged, far more than through any one-time effort or grand resolution. Habits are the threads that weave through our days, creating a tapestry that tells the story of who we are.

For many of us, this truth comes as a surprise. We are conditioned to believe that dramatic transformations - massive changes, life-altering moments - are what shape our destinies. Yet, more often than not, it's the subtle, daily rituals that hold the most sway. Consider, for instance, the habit of how we treat our bodies. A few extra bites at every meal, a skipped workout here and there, might not seem like much. But over time, these choices compound, just like interest in a bank account, yielding results that shape our physical health, our energy levels, and even our self-esteem.

The power of habits extends beyond the physical realm into our mental and emotional landscapes. Imagine the way a simple habit, like expressing gratitude daily, can transform your outlook on life. At first, it might feel awkward or insubstantial, just a small pause to acknowledge the good in your day. But with time, this habit can recalibrate your mindset, helping you focus less on what's lacking and more on the abundance around you. In contrast, holding onto a habit of complaining, even if it's only in small doses, can darken your perspective, casting a shadow over even the brightest days.

The science behind habits reveals just how deeply ingrained they become. Our brains are wired to seek efficiency, which is why habits are formed in the first place. They help us automate behaviors so that our conscious minds can focus on more complex tasks. However, this efficiency comes at a cost:

once a habit is established, it becomes deeply entrenched, operating like a well-worn path through a forest. This is why breaking a bad habit feels so difficult - your brain has become accustomed to taking that path. But just as a forest path can be rerouted, so too can the patterns in our brains. It's challenging, but it's possible, and the rewards can be life-changing.

Why do habits matter more than you think? Because they are the invisible architects of our future. They determine not only our actions but our thoughts, our emotions, and our identity. A habit of self-doubt, for instance, doesn't just affect the things you try; it colors your self-perception, your relationships, your sense of worth. On the other hand, a habit of persistence - of always taking one more step, even when things are tough - builds resilience, shaping a person who believes in their own strength.

In essence, habits are the building blocks of character. They determine how we face adversity, how we seize opportunities, and how we interact with the world around us. They influence our happiness, our productivity, and even our relationships. Yet, despite their far-reaching impact, habits often go unnoticed, their power overlooked.

This is why understanding and harnessing the power of habits is so crucial. It is not about attempting radical change overnight but about recognizing the extraordinary potential that lies within ordinary actions. When you realize that each habit is a seed - one that can either take root and flourish or wither and hold you back - you begin to see your life with new eyes. You start to understand that every small choice matters, and that within those choices lies the power to shape your destiny.

In the pages that follow, this book aims to guide you through the process of recognizing, reshaping, and reinforcing habits that align with the life you aspire to live. By the end, you'll see that habits are not merely routines; they are the tools that can build a life of purpose, allowing you to become the architect of your own destiny. Because in the end, it is not just about the habits we keep - it's about the life they help us create.

How This Book Will Change Your Life

In the introduction of *"Habits Unleashed: The Ultimate Guide to Transforming Bad Habits into Positive Power,"* the narrative delves into the promise and potential that this book holds for every reader. This book is not just another collection of motivational quotes or a fleeting burst of inspiration. It is a guide, a roadmap, and a companion that will lead you through the transformative journey of taking control of your habits and, in turn, taking control of your life.

Imagine your life as a vast, untamed wilderness - beautiful, but filled with challenges and uncertainties. You have dreams and goals that feel like distant peaks on the horizon, yet you find yourself treading the same worn paths, held back by habits that no longer serve you. Perhaps you've tried to change before, maybe even succeeded temporarily, but found yourself slipping back into old patterns. This book is designed to change that, to help you carve new paths through that wilderness, paths that lead directly to the life you've always envisioned.

Through the pages of *Habits Unleashed*, you'll discover the truth that lasting change is not about willpower alone. It's about understanding the architecture of your own habits - how they form, how they function, and most importantly, how they can be reshaped. The book draws from cutting-edge science, time-tested wisdom, and real-life stories to offer you a blueprint for change that is both practical and profound. You'll learn to see your habits not as rigid, unchangeable parts of yourself, but as flexible elements that can be molded to serve your greatest aspirations.

But this transformation goes deeper than just replacing a few bad habits with better ones. This book will show you how to rewire the way you think about yourself and your potential. As you work through each chapter, you'll start to recognize the hidden beliefs that have been holding you back - those internal voices that say, "I'm not disciplined enough," or "I've always been this way." You'll learn how to challenge those beliefs, to rewrite the narrative you've been telling yourself. The shift in your habits will come with a shift in perspective, one that empowers you to see possibilities where before there were only barriers.

One of the most powerful aspects of this book is that it acknowledges the complexity of human behavior. It doesn't promise a quick fix or an easy shortcut because true change is rarely easy. Instead, it offers a step-by-step approach that meets you where you are, guiding you through the stages of change with patience and clarity. You'll learn how to break down daunting goals into manageable habits, how to create a supportive environment that nurtures your progress, and how to build resilience when setbacks inevitably arise.

Picture yourself a few months from now, standing at a crossroads in your life. You've developed habits that energize you, that align with your values, that bring you closer to your goals each day. You've shed the weight of unproductive routines, and in their place, you've cultivated habits that feel like second nature - habits that fuel your creativity, your health, and your sense of purpose. This book aims to bring you to that point, to be the catalyst for the change you've always known you were capable of achieving.

But the impact doesn't stop with you. The changes you make ripple outward, influencing the way you interact with others, the energy you bring into your relationships, and even the example you set for those around you. As you transform your habits, you'll find yourself becoming a source of inspiration - a living testament to the idea that change is possible, no matter how ingrained a habit might feel. You'll see how the small, daily choices you make can add up to a life that is not just different, but better, richer, and more aligned with your truest self.

Ultimately, this book is an invitation to a new way of living, one where you are no longer at the mercy of unconscious patterns. It offers the promise of freedom - the freedom to choose, the freedom to change, and the freedom to create a life that reflects your deepest values and desires. As you turn each page, you'll find yourself not just learning new strategies, but awakening to new possibilities, realizing that the power to shape your destiny has been within you all along. And when you reach the end, you won't just have read a book - you'll have begun a journey that changes your life forever.

Part I: Understanding the Mechanics of Habits
Chapter 1: Demystifying Habits

In this chapter we begin by exploring a fundamental question: What exactly are habits? At first glance, a habit might seem like a simple action - a behavior repeated so often that it becomes second nature. But beneath that simplicity lies a fascinating and intricate process, one that is woven deeply into the fabric of our daily lives.

What Exactly Are Habits?

Think of habits as the autopilot mode of your brain, guiding you through routines and tasks without needing conscious thought. From the moment you wake up, habits take over. They dictate whether you reach for your phone first thing in the morning or take a few deep breaths. They guide your choice between brewing a cup of coffee or starting the day with a glass of water. These actions, while seemingly mundane, are shaped by habits that have been reinforced over time, and they reveal just how much our lives are driven by patterns we often take for granted.

To truly understand habits, we must look at their structure. Psychologists and neuroscientists describe habits as a loop, a three-part process that begins with a cue, followed by a routine, and ending with a reward. The cue is a trigger, a signal that tells your brain to go into automatic mode and choose a behavior. It could be a time of day, a specific place, an emotional state, or even an external event. For example, walking past a bakery might trigger a craving for a sweet treat. The smell of freshly baked cookies becomes the cue.

Once the cue has fired, the routine is the behavior that follows. It's the part that you can observe, like reaching for a cookie or lacing up your shoes for a jog. It's the action itself, often so automatic that you may not even realize you're doing it. The routine is where habits become ingrained, as your brain learns to execute the behavior without needing to weigh the pros and cons each time.

Finally, there is the reward. This is the payoff that makes your brain remember the habit loop in the first place. It's the pleasurable sensation, the sense of satisfaction, or the relief from a negative emotion that reinforces the behavior. In the case of that cookie, it might be the sweet taste that your brain craves, or the comforting feeling of indulging after a long day. Over time, your brain begins to associate the cue with the reward, making the routine nearly automatic whenever the trigger appears.

But this three-step loop is just the beginning of understanding habits. What makes habits so powerful - and, at times, so difficult to change - is that they are deeply embedded in a part of the brain called the basal ganglia. This ancient part of the brain is responsible for storing and recalling routines, allowing us to perform complex behaviors with little conscious thought. It's why you can drive a familiar route or tie your shoes while thinking about something else entirely. Your basal ganglia have memorized the steps, freeing up your mind for other tasks.

This efficiency is what makes habits a double-edged sword. On one hand, it allows us to navigate the world without becoming overwhelmed by every tiny decision. Imagine how exhausting it would be if you had to think through every step of brushing your teeth or driving to work. Habits simplify our lives, turning actions into automated processes. On the other hand, this same efficiency makes bad habits incredibly resilient. The brain doesn't distinguish between a habit that's good for us and one that's not—it simply reinforces the behaviors that have been repeated often enough to become part of our routine.

Yet, even with their deeply rooted nature, habits are not set in stone. They are more like grooves carved into a riverbed—strong and persistent, but not unchangeable. With the right understanding and effort, you can redirect the flow, creating new pathways that align with your goals. This is the essence of what habits are: they are learned behaviors that shape our daily existence, but they are also malleable, open to change through deliberate effort.

When we demystify habits, we come to see them as the silent architects of our lives. They are not mystical forces beyond our control, but rather systems that we can learn to influence. Recognizing this power gives us a sense of agency, a realization that we can reshape those automatic behaviors that feel so ingrained. The habits that define your life right now - whether they involve scrolling through social media when you're bored, biting your nails when you're anxious, or reading a book before bed - are not permanent fixtures. They are simply patterns your brain has learned, and with the right knowledge, you can teach it new ones.

The Science Behind Habit Formation

Understanding the mechanics of habit formation requires us to delve into the science that underlies how habits take root in the brain. This journey into the scientific realm helps demystify the seemingly automatic nature of habits and reveals the processes that allow us to create new behaviors - or struggle to break old ones.

The Habit Loop: Cue, Routine, Reward

At the core of habit formation lies a three-step process known as the habit loop, which consists of a cue, a routine, and a reward. This concept, popularized by researchers like Charles Duhigg, is a fundamental framework for understanding why habits form and how they operate.

Cue: The cue acts as the trigger for a habit, setting the brain into motion. It can be as simple as a time of day, a location, or an emotional state. For example, feeling stressed might cue the desire to reach for a comforting snack. The brain identifies this cue as a prompt to begin a routine.

Routine: The routine is the behavior itself—the action that the cue triggers. It's what you do in response to the cue, like grabbing a cookie or going for a walk. Over time, this behavior becomes automatic, requiring little conscious thought.

Reward: The reward is the outcome that the brain craves, whether it's the sweet taste of a snack or the endorphins from a workout. This reward reinforces the behavior, creating a feedback loop that makes the habit stronger each time it's repeated.

This loop is critical to understanding habit formation because it explains how habits become ingrained over time. When the brain experiences a reward, it releases dopamine, a neurotransmitter associated with pleasure and reinforcement. This chemical surge encourages the brain to remember the loop, making the behavior easier to repeat the next time the cue appears.

The Role of the Basal Ganglia

The science behind habits is not just about behavior—it's also about biology. Deep within the brain lies a structure called the basal ganglia, which plays a pivotal role in habit formation. This part of the brain is responsible for controlling patterns of movement and behavior, and it is here that habits are stored, almost like automated scripts.

Basal Ganglia as the Habit Center: The basal ganglia helps conserve mental energy by automating routine behaviors. This is why you can perform habitual actions like driving a familiar route or tying your shoes without needing to consciously think about each step. The basal ganglia frees up the rest of the brain to focus on more complex tasks.

Neural Pathways and Repetition: As a behavior is repeated, the neural pathways associated with that habit become stronger. Think of these pathways like trails in a forest: the more you walk along a certain path, the more defined it becomes, making it easier to follow next time. This is why repeating a behavior consistently is key to habit formation - the brain literally wires itself to make the habit easier to perform.

Neuroplasticity: The Brain's Ability to Change

One of the most fascinating aspects of habit science is the concept of neuroplasticity—the brain's ability to reorganize itself by forming new neural connections throughout life. This adaptability means that even deeply ingrained habits can be reshaped with time and effort.

Breaking Old Habits: When you try to break a habit, you are attempting to weaken the old neural pathways that have become ingrained in the basal ganglia. This process takes time because the brain must learn to bypass the old, well-worn path. It's like letting a trail in the forest become overgrown while forging a new path nearby.

Building New Habits: Neuroplasticity also makes it possible to create new habits. As you repeat a new behavior, the brain strengthens the neural connections related to that habit, gradually making it easier and more automatic. This process is why consistency is so crucial in building new habits - each repetition reinforces the new pathway.

The Power of Dopamine in Motivation

Dopamine plays a critical role in habit formation, acting as a motivator that propels us toward certain behaviors. The brain's reward system, which releases dopamine when it anticipates or experiences pleasure, can both create and sustain habits.

Craving and Anticipation: Dopamine is not just released when a reward is experienced; it is also released in anticipation of a reward. This is why habits can become so compelling. For example, if you associate a certain time of day with having a coffee, your brain may release dopamine just at the thought of that afternoon ritual, driving you to seek out the experience even before you've had the first sip.

The Role in Habit Addiction: This same mechanism can make certain habits—especially those related to substances like sugar, caffeine, or nicotine—difficult to break. The brain learns to crave the dopamine hit associated with the habit, creating a sense of desire or even addiction. Understanding this dopamine-driven cycle is key to understanding why some habits feel nearly impossible to resist.

Willpower and the Prefrontal Cortex

While the basal ganglia automates habits, the prefrontal cortex, the area of the brain responsible for decision-making and self-control, comes into play when we try to change them. This part of the brain is crucial for exerting willpower, especially in the early stages of building or breaking a habit.

Limited Resource: The prefrontal cortex can only handle a limited amount of self-control at any given time, which is why willpower can feel like a finite resource. This is why starting a new habit can feel challenging - each time you resist an old habit or push yourself toward a new one, you are drawing on the prefrontal cortex's resources.

Automaticity and Habit Strength: As a new habit becomes more established, it requires less input from the prefrontal cortex. The behavior moves into the realm of the basal ganglia, becoming more automatic. This is why habits can eventually feel effortless - once the habit is ingrained, the brain conserves energy by relying less on the conscious mind and more on the habit loop.

Habits and the Evolutionary Brain

Understanding the evolutionary roots of habit formation also sheds light on why our brains are wired this way. From an evolutionary perspective, habits served a critical function in our survival.

Energy Conservation: Our ancestors needed to conserve mental and physical energy to survive, which meant that automating repetitive behaviors (like gathering food or finding shelter) was advantageous. The brain evolved to favor routines that required less cognitive effort, allowing early humans to focus on more pressing survival challenges.

Habitual Responses to Threats: This evolutionary background also explains why some habits are so strongly tied to stress responses. For example, the fight-or-flight response is a deeply ingrained habit triggered by perceived threats, even when those threats are no longer life-or-death situations. Modern habits, like stress-eating or mindlessly scrolling through social media, can be seen as extensions of these survival-oriented behaviors, triggered by the stresses of modern life.

The Science of Changing Habits

Understanding the science behind habit formation gives us the tools to change our habits more effectively. It shows us that habits are not fixed - they are patterns in our brains that can be rewired with intention and effort. By knowing how cues, routines, and rewards interact, and how the brain stores these patterns, we gain the ability to consciously design habits that align with our goals and values.

In demystifying the science of habit formation, this book aims to empower you with the knowledge that your brain's wiring is not destiny. With the right strategies, you can reshape even the most stubborn habits, transforming them from barriers into pathways that lead you to a better life. The science may be complex, but its message is simple: you have the power to change your habits, and in doing so, you have the power to change your life.

How Habits Influence Behavior and Decision-Making

A key aspect of understanding the mechanics of habits lies in exploring how they influence behavior and decision-making. Habits, often underestimated in their power, shape much of what we do daily, guiding our actions with a subtle but persistent force. This section delves into the profound impact habits have on our choices, steering our lives in ways we may not even be consciously aware of.

Habits as the Brain's Shortcut to Decision-Making

At the heart of habit formation is the brain's desire for efficiency. Making decisions requires energy, and our brains are wired to conserve this energy whenever possible. Habits act as mental shortcuts, allowing us to perform actions without the need for active decision-making each time.

Automatic Behaviors: When a behavior becomes a habit, the brain no longer engages in a deliberative thought process for each occurrence. This automaticity is why habits can feel so powerful—they operate beneath the surface of our conscious mind. For example, think about how you brush your teeth. You don't consciously decide each morning to pick up your toothbrush and apply toothpaste; your brain has learned to execute this sequence automatically. This frees up cognitive resources for other, more complex tasks.

Habitual Responses to Cues: Habits often take control when a specific cue is encountered. These cues can be anything from time of day, location, or a particular feeling. When a habit loop is triggered, the brain seamlessly shifts into autopilot mode. For instance, arriving at home might cue you to take off your shoes and relax on the couch - actions you don't actively think about but simply do. The result is a reduction in the mental energy required to navigate familiar situations.

The Role of Habits in Routine Decision-Making

Habits also shape our routine decisions, influencing not just what we do, but how we approach everyday choices. This influence can be seen in decisions that range from what we eat to how we react to stress.

Default Behaviors in Familiar Situations: Habits often dictate our default responses to common scenarios. For example, when faced with a stressful situation, someone with a habit of stress-eating might reach for a snack, while another person might automatically go for a run or practice deep breathing. These responses happen quickly, often without a conscious decision-making process, showing how habits can direct behavior in predictable ways.

Decision Fatigue and Habitual Choices: Decision fatigue occurs when we become mentally drained from making too many decisions, leading to a reliance on habitual behaviors. This is why, after a long day of making choices, you might default to easy and familiar habits like ordering takeout instead of cooking a healthy meal. Habits provide a mental shortcut that the brain can fall back on when it's too tired to deliberate.

The Influence of Habits on Long-Term Behavior Patterns

Habits extend beyond immediate decisions to shape long-term behavior patterns. The routines we establish in response to daily cues can accumulate over time, leading to significant outcomes in various areas of life.

Building Identity Through Repeated Actions: Over time, the habits we maintain become part of our identity. A person who consistently makes time for exercise, even when it's challenging, starts to see themselves as an active and health-conscious individual. In contrast, someone who habitually procrastinates on tasks may begin to view themselves as a procrastinator, even when they aspire to be more proactive.

Habits influence not just what we do, but who we perceive ourselves to be.

Compounding Effects of Small Habits: Small, seemingly insignificant habits have a compounding effect over time, leading to profound changes in behavior. For example, a habit of reading for just ten minutes before bed can add up to dozens of books read over a year, significantly expanding one's knowledge and perspective. Conversely, a habit of watching an extra episode of a show every night can add up to hours of lost productivity. These habits, small in the moment, create patterns that shape our lives in lasting ways.

Habits and Impulse Control

Habits play a critical role in managing impulses, influencing how we respond to immediate desires and temptations. This interaction between habits and impulse control can either support or undermine our ability to make decisions aligned with our long-term goals.

Strengthening Willpower Through Habits: Positive habits can serve as a buffer against impulsive behavior. For instance, a habit of planning meals ahead of time can help someone avoid the temptation of unhealthy snacks when hunger strikes. By establishing habits that align with desired outcomes, the brain can reduce the strain on willpower, making it easier to stick to decisions that support long-term goals.

Habits and Impulse Loops: On the flip side, certain habits can entrench impulsive behavior. A habit of checking your phone whenever you feel bored can create an impulse loop where the slightest hint of boredom triggers a compulsive scroll through social media. Over time, this behavior becomes automatic, and the impulse to reach for the phone becomes difficult to resist. Understanding this dynamic is key to recognizing why some habits are so hard to break - they have become the brain's default response to certain impulses.

How Habits Can Limit or Expand Possibilities

The habits we develop can either limit or expand our possibilities, influencing the trajectory of our personal and professional lives.

The Habitual Comfort Zone: Habits create a sense of comfort and predictability, which can be both a strength and a limitation. When habits keep us within a familiar comfort zone, they can prevent us from exploring new opportunities or taking risks. For example, a habit of sticking to the same routine each day might keep you from trying new activities or meeting new people, limiting personal growth.

Habits as Catalysts for Growth: Conversely, intentional habits can serve as catalysts for growth and development. A habit of daily learning, such as reading a new article each morning or practicing a new skill for fifteen minutes, can open doors to new knowledge and abilities. By intentionally shaping habits that challenge the status quo, you can create a life that is more dynamic, flexible, and aligned with your evolving goals.

Habits as Predictors of Success and Failure

The influence of habits extends beyond individual actions to become reliable predictors of future outcomes. They can determine whether we achieve our goals or fall short, based on the patterns we establish in our daily lives.

Success-Oriented Habits: Many successful people credit their achievements to a set of consistent habits. These could include habits of discipline, such as waking up early or maintaining a regular exercise routine, as well as habits of focus, like setting daily priorities or practicing mindfulness. These habits create a structure that supports long-term success, making it more likely that they will reach their goals.

Self-Sabotaging Habits: On the other hand, self-sabotaging habits can undermine progress, even when someone has the best intentions. A habit of negative self-talk, for instance, can chip away at confidence and resilience, making it harder to take bold actions. Habits of procrastination or avoidance can keep someone from seizing opportunities, causing them to miss out on potential success. Understanding the role of these habits in decision-making can help identify areas for change and growth.

The Interplay Between Habits and Environment

Lastly, the environment in which we operate has a significant impact on the habits we form, and in turn, the habits we maintain can shape how we interact with our surroundings.

Environmental Cues and Habit Triggers: The environments we inhabit often dictate which habits are triggered and how easily they become part of our routine. For example, keeping a bowl of fruit on the kitchen counter might cue a habit of choosing a healthy snack, while a cluttered workspace might cue distraction and disorganization. Adjusting your environment can be a powerful tool in shaping the habits that influence your behavior.

Habit-Driven Changes in Environment: At the same time, the habits we develop can transform our environment, making it more conducive to our goals. A habit of tidying up each evening can create a living space that feels calm and organized, while a habit of regular exercise can shape a lifestyle that values physical activity and well-being. By aligning our habits with our desired environment, we can create spaces that naturally support our best selves.

In understanding how habits influence behavior and decision-making, it becomes clear that they are far more than simple routines. Habits are the undercurrent that guides our daily lives, shaping how we respond to the world and how we navigate choices, big and small. Recognizing this influence is the first step toward reclaiming control over the habits that define our lives, allowing us to become more intentional about the paths we choose. As you explore this book further, you'll gain the tools to harness the power of habits, using them to steer your behavior and decisions toward the life you truly desire.

Chapter 2: The Habit Loop Explained

The Cue: Identifying Triggers

Understanding the habit loop begins with a critical element: the cue. The cue, often overlooked, is the trigger that sets a habit into motion, signaling to your brain that it's time to switch into automatic mode and initiate a specific behavior. Without cues, habits would struggle to form or sustain themselves. By identifying and understanding these triggers, you gain the power to reshape your habits and take control of the actions that follow.

The Role of Cues in Habit Formation

The cue is the first step in the habit loop, and it plays a fundamental role in habit formation. It is the moment that activates a sequence of behaviors—your brain's way of recognizing a familiar pattern. Cues can be subtle or obvious, but they always serve as the starting point for a habit. They act like a signal flare, alerting your brain that a particular routine is about to unfold.

Cues as the Brain's Reminder System: Think of cues as reminders that initiate the habit loop. They are the prompts that tell your brain, "It's time to do this." For example, hearing the chime of your phone might cue you to check your messages, or walking into your kitchen might trigger the habit of making a cup of coffee. These cues save mental energy by eliminating the need for conscious thought in repetitive behaviors, allowing you to rely on familiar routines.

Different Types of Cues

Cues can come in various forms, and they often fall into distinct categories that help pinpoint the triggers behind a habit. Recognizing these types can provide deeper insight into why certain habits emerge and how they can be changed.

Time-Based Cues: Many habits are tied to specific times of day. For example, you might have a habit of brushing your teeth after waking up or having a snack every afternoon at 3 p.m. The time itself becomes the cue that triggers these behaviors. Time-based cues are powerful because they create a sense of routine, embedding habits into the structure of your daily schedule.

Location-Based Cues: The environment you're in can serve as a potent cue for certain behaviors. Stepping into your office might trigger a habit of checking your email, while entering the gym might cue your body to prepare for a workout. Location-based cues work by associating a particular place with a specific behavior, turning spaces into triggers for action.

Emotional State as a Cue: Our emotions are significant drivers of habits. Feeling stressed might cue a habit of reaching for comfort food, while feeling bored could trigger the habit of scrolling through social media. These cues are often less tangible but extremely powerful, as they are tied directly to our inner experiences. Emotional cues create a direct link between how we feel and how we act.

Other People as Cues: Social cues are also influential in shaping our habits. Being around certain people can trigger behaviors, such as ordering a drink when meeting friends at a bar or adopting a certain tone of voice when talking to a specific colleague. Our habits often adapt to social environments, making the presence of others a powerful trigger for both positive and negative behaviors.

Recognizing Personal Cues

Identifying the specific cues that trigger your habits is the key to understanding why you behave in certain ways. It's a process that requires attention and reflection, but the insights gained can be transformative. To effectively change a habit, you first need to pinpoint the cue that sets it into motion.

Keeping a Cue Log: One method to identify your habit cues is to keep a cue log. This involves writing down the moment when a habit occurs and noting what was happening just before the behavior started. For example, if you're trying to understand why you frequently snack during the day, you might note the time, location, and emotional state each time you reach for food. Over time, patterns begin to emerge, revealing the consistent triggers behind your habits.

Asking the Right Questions: When analyzing your cues, ask yourself: What time did this behavior happen? Where was I? Who was around me? What was I feeling? What was I doing right before the habit started? These questions help you dig deeper into the context of your habits, uncovering the subtle triggers that you might not have noticed before.

The Power of Awareness in Identifying Cues

Awareness is a crucial first step in the process of habit change. By bringing cues into conscious focus, you disrupt the automatic nature of the habit loop. This awareness allows you to observe the exact moment when your brain shifts into habitual behavior, giving you a chance to make different choices.

Turning Off Autopilot: Many habits operate on autopilot, running in the background without our active awareness. By identifying the cues, you shift from passive participation to active observation. For instance, recognizing that the habit of checking your phone is triggered every time you sit on the couch helps you become conscious of the automatic reach for the device. This awareness creates a window of opportunity for change, where you can decide to do something different.

Mindfulness as a Tool for Recognizing Cues: Mindfulness practices, such as meditation or deep breathing, can enhance your ability to recognize cues. By slowing down and observing your thoughts and feelings, you become more attuned to the triggers that prompt habitual behaviors. This heightened awareness makes it easier to spot the precise moments when a cue sets off a habit, allowing you to interrupt the loop.

Changing Cues to Change Habits

Once you identify the cues behind your habits, you can begin the process of changing or managing those triggers. Altering the cues in your environment can be one of the most effective ways to disrupt a habit loop and create space for new behaviors.

Altering the Environment: Changing location-based cues can have a profound impact on habit formation. If you realize that you always snack while watching TV in the living room, you might try moving the snacks out of reach or changing the location where you watch TV. By altering the environment, you make it less likely that the cue will automatically trigger the habit.

Substituting Cues: Instead of trying to eliminate a cue entirely, you can substitute it with a new one that prompts a different behavior. For example, if stress cues the habit of reaching for a sugary treat, you might introduce a different cue - like a stress ball or a brief walk - to redirect the routine when stress arises. This approach allows you to replace an old habit with a more positive one by associating a new behavior with the same trigger.

Creating Positive Cues: On the flip side, you can intentionally introduce cues that help establish new, positive habits. For instance, placing your running shoes by the door can serve as a visual cue to remind you to exercise. Setting a specific time for reading each evening can create a time-based cue that gradually turns reading into a regular habit. These positive cues can serve as anchors, helping you build habits that align with your goals.

The Influence of Cues on Habit Strength

Cues not only initiate habits but also influence how strong and persistent they become. Understanding this relationship helps explain why certain habits feel nearly unbreakable while others can be reshaped more easily.

Consistency of Cues: Habits that are triggered by consistent cues - such as brushing your teeth at the same time every morning - tend to become stronger over time. The more predictable the cue, the more automatic the behavior becomes. This is why regular routines can make certain habits feel like second nature, embedding them deeply into daily life.

Intermittent Cues and Habit Resistance: On the other hand, habits with inconsistent cues may be weaker but also more resistant to change because the brain doesn't always anticipate the reward. For example, a habit of checking social media might be triggered by a variety of cues - boredom, stress, or simply the phone's presence. This makes it harder to identify and change the exact trigger, requiring a broader approach to modify the behavior.

Cues: The Key to Understanding the Habit Loop

Ultimately, cues are the starting point of every habit loop, serving as the signals that set your brain into a familiar pattern. By identifying and understanding these triggers, you unlock the ability to change the routines that follow them. The power of the cue lies in its ability to either reinforce old habits or to create opportunities for new, positive behaviors.

The Routine: The Behavior Itself

Understanding the habit loop means diving into its central component: the routine. The routine is the behavior itself - the action you take in response to a cue, which ultimately leads to a reward. While the cue triggers the habit, and the reward reinforces it, the routine is the visible part of the habit loop, the thing you do repeatedly, often without much conscious thought. By understanding what routines are and how they operate, you can begin to reshape your habits in meaningful ways.

The Routine: The Action That Defines the Habit

At its core, the routine is the habitual behavior that you perform when faced with a particular cue. It is the visible, actionable part of the habit loop—the aspect that you can observe and measure. While the cue and reward operate subtly, the routine is the moment of doing, where the habit plays out in real time.

The Nature of Routines: Routines can vary greatly in their complexity. Some routines are simple, like turning off a light when you leave a room or grabbing a snack when you're hungry. Others are more complex, involving multiple steps and actions, like a morning workout routine or the process of making your bed every morning. Regardless of their complexity, routines share one key characteristic: they become easier and more automatic with repetition.

Routines as Habitual Responses: A routine is your brain's learned response to a particular cue. When you encounter a trigger, your brain has already mapped out the behavior that should follow. For example, if you have a habit of reaching for your phone every time you sit down, the act of sitting becomes the cue, and the routine—scrolling through your social media feed—unfolds automatically. Understanding this automatic response is crucial to changing habits, as it reveals the pattern that needs to be altered.

Why Routines Feel So Automatic

The reason routines feel so automatic lies in the way the brain processes repeated behaviors. Neuroscience has shown that as you repeat a behavior, your brain becomes more efficient at performing it, creating a mental shortcut for the routine. This is why, over time, you might find yourself engaging in a habit without consciously deciding to do it.

The Role of Neural Pathways: Each time you perform a routine, the neural pathways associated with that behavior become stronger, like a trail becoming more defined with each step taken. This process occurs in the basal ganglia, a part of the brain responsible for storing habitual behaviors. As the pathways become more ingrained, the brain can execute the routine with less effort and focus, making it feel almost effortless. This is why routines become automatic—

your brain has learned the steps and can perform them with minimal conscious input.

Muscle Memory and Physical Routines: Many physical routines, like riding a bike or typing on a keyboard, become so automatic that they feel like second nature. This phenomenon, often referred to as muscle memory, is a form of learned behavior where the brain and muscles work together to execute movements without conscious thought. The routine becomes embedded in your physical response, making it feel as though your body is acting on its own. This same principle applies to smaller, everyday habits, like the way you reach for your toothbrush each night.

How Routines Impact Daily Life

Routines shape the structure of your daily life, determining how you spend your time and energy. They create patterns that dictate your productivity, your interactions with others, and even your mental and physical well-being. Understanding these patterns is essential for gaining control over your habits.

Time Efficiency Through Routines: Routines save time and mental energy by reducing the number of decisions you need to make each day. For example, a morning routine that includes getting dressed, making breakfast, and packing a bag for work allows you to start the day without having to think through each step. This efficiency is beneficial, especially in environments where time is limited, but it can also be limiting if the routine reinforces unproductive or unhealthy behaviors.

The Role of Routines in Mental Health: Routines can significantly influence mental health, either positively or negatively. Positive routines, such as regular exercise, mindfulness practices, or reading before bed, can create a sense of stability and well-being. In contrast, negative routines, like constantly checking the news or engaging in self-criticism, can contribute to feelings of anxiety and stress. The routines we engage in daily play a major role in shaping our overall outlook on life.

Changing Routines: The Key to Habit Transformation

To change a habit, you must first change the routine—the behavior that takes place between the cue and the reward. This process involves understanding what the routine is, why it occurs, and how it can be altered to support better habits.

Identifying the Routine: The first step in changing a habit is to clearly identify the routine you want to change. For example, if you find yourself reaching for a snack whenever you're bored, the routine is the act of snacking in response to the feeling of boredom. By isolating this behavior, you can focus on finding a replacement that satisfies the same underlying need.

Substituting the Routine: One of the most effective strategies for changing a habit is to replace the existing routine with a new one that leads to a similar reward. If the habit of snacking when bored is driven by a need for distraction, you might substitute the routine of reaching for a snack with going for a short walk or engaging in a brief creative activity. This way, the cue (boredom) and the reward (relief from boredom) remain the same, but the routine shifts to a healthier behavior.

Gradual Modification of Routines: For deeply ingrained habits, it may be difficult to change the routine all at once. In such cases, gradual modification can be more effective. This involves making small changes to the routine over time until it becomes something entirely new. For example, if you have a habit of drinking soda every afternoon, you might start by gradually replacing it with sparkling water, until eventually, the routine becomes drinking plain water. This gradual approach allows the brain to adjust without feeling deprived of the familiar behavior.

Why Routines Are Resistant to Change

Routines, once established, are often resistant to change. This resistance is a natural part of the brain's desire for stability and efficiency, but it can make breaking old habits challenging.

Comfort and Familiarity: Routines offer a sense of comfort and predictability, which is why they can be difficult to change. The brain prefers the familiar, even if the routine itself is not particularly beneficial. For example, even if you know that staying up late watching TV leaves you feeling tired in the morning, the comfort of the routine can be hard to resist. This is why making a conscious effort to change requires stepping outside of that comfort zone.

The Brain's Reward System: The routine is directly tied to the brain's reward system, which means that even an unhealthy habit can feel rewarding if it satisfies a need. This connection is why breaking a routine often involves dealing with cravings or withdrawal feelings. Understanding that these feelings are a natural response to changing the reward system can help you stay committed to the new routine until it becomes more familiar.

Building New Routines for Lasting Change

Creating new routines is the foundation of building better habits. By understanding how routines work, you can design behaviors that not only replace old habits but also fit seamlessly into your life, making positive change more sustainable.

Designing a Routine That Fits Your Life: A new routine is most likely to stick if it aligns with your existing lifestyle. For instance, if you want to establish a habit of daily exercise, choosing a time and type of workout that fits into your schedule increases the likelihood that the routine will become automatic. The more compatible the new routine is with your daily life, the easier it will be to repeat consistently.

Repetition and Consistency: The secret to embedding a new routine lies in repetition. Each time you perform the new behavior, you strengthen the neural pathways that make the routine easier to perform in the future. Consistency is key—performing the routine at the same time or in the same context helps the brain to associate the behavior with a specific cue, making it more automatic over time.

Using Rewards to Reinforce New Routines: While repetition is crucial, so is ensuring that the new routine leads to a reward that your brain finds satisfying. A reward reinforces the new routine, making it more appealing. If you decide to replace your habit of snacking with going for a walk, finding a reward - like listening to a favorite podcast during the walk - can make the new routine more enjoyable, helping it stick.

The Routine as the Pivot Point for Change

Ultimately, the routine is the heart of the habit loop, the part where behavior becomes reality. By focusing on understanding and altering routines, you gain the ability to reshape your habits and direct them towards your goals. It's not just about eliminating a bad routine or forcing a new one into place; it's about consciously choosing behaviors that align with the life you want to create.

The Reward: Understanding Payoffs

Understanding the habit loop requires us also to explore the final and perhaps most pivotal component: the reward. The reward is the outcome that follows the routine, the payoff that your brain craves and anticipates. It is this element that drives the formation and persistence of habits, reinforcing behaviors so that they become automatic over time. By understanding how rewards work, you gain insight into why certain habits are so compelling and how you can reshape them to align with your goals.

The Role of Rewards in Habit Formation

At its essence, a reward is the satisfaction or pleasure that follows a routine. It is the brain's way of learning what behaviors are worth repeating. Rewards provide feedback to the brain, signaling that a particular action is beneficial or enjoyable, making it more likely that you'll engage in the same behavior the next time the cue appears.

Rewards as Reinforcement: When you experience a reward after performing a routine, your brain releases dopamine, a neurotransmitter associated with pleasure and motivation. This dopamine release acts as positive reinforcement, strengthening the neural pathways that link the cue to the routine. For example, if you enjoy a sense of relaxation after eating a snack in response to stress, your brain learns to associate the relief with the act of snacking. The next time you feel stressed, the brain anticipates that same reward and encourages the behavior.

Teaching the Brain What Matters: Rewards teach the brain what to prioritize. They help distinguish between behaviors that are beneficial and those that are not. For example, the reward of feeling refreshed after a morning jog teaches your brain that this behavior is worth repeating. Similarly, a quick burst of enjoyment from checking social media reinforces the habit of reaching for your phone whenever you feel bored. Over time, the brain's desire for these rewards solidifies the habit, making it an automatic response to the initial cue.

Types of Rewards in Habits

Not all rewards are created equal, and they can vary greatly in form and effect. Understanding the different types of rewards can help you identify why certain habits are appealing and how to modify or replace them with new behaviors.

Immediate Rewards vs. Delayed Rewards: The timing of a reward plays a significant role in how strong a habit becomes. Immediate rewards are particularly powerful because they provide instant gratification, which the brain craves. For example, eating a piece of chocolate offers immediate pleasure, making it a strong reinforcer of the habit. In contrast, delayed rewards, such as the long-term benefits of exercise, can be harder for the brain to value in the moment. This is why habits that provide immediate rewards are often easier to form than those with delayed gratification.

Physical Rewards: Some rewards are physical sensations that create a direct feeling of pleasure or relief. For example, the warmth and comfort of a hot shower after a long day can be a physical reward that reinforces the habit of showering at a certain time. Physical rewards are particularly effective because they engage the body's senses, creating a direct connection between the routine and the pleasurable outcome.

Emotional Rewards: Many habits are driven by emotional rewards - feelings of relief, joy, satisfaction, or a sense of accomplishment. For example, the habit of checking off tasks on a to-do list might be reinforced by the emotional reward of feeling productive and in control. Emotional rewards can be subtle but powerful, shaping habits that align with how you want to feel. For instance, the habit of meditating may be driven by the emotional reward of inner calm, even if the physical action is simple.

Social Rewards: Social validation can be a significant reward that influences habits. A simple "like" or comment on social media can reinforce the habit of posting online, making it more likely that you'll repeat the behavior. Similarly, praise from a friend or the positive attention of a peer group can strengthen habits like going to the gym or participating in a hobby. Social rewards tap into the human desire for connection and approval, making them potent motivators.

Understanding Hidden Rewards

In many cases, the rewards that drive a habit are not immediately obvious. They can be hidden beneath the surface, operating subconsciously to reinforce behaviors. Identifying these hidden rewards is crucial for understanding why certain habits are so persistent and how to effectively change them.

The Role of Cravings in Seeking Rewards: Often, the craving for a reward is more powerful than the reward itself. For example, a person may crave the feeling of relaxation that comes from smoking a cigarette more than the actual experience of smoking. This craving creates a sense of anticipation, making the brain eager to perform the habit even before the reward is received. Recognizing this craving can help you identify what your brain truly seeks, allowing you to find healthier ways to satisfy it.

Uncovering the Real Reward Behind a Habit: To change a habit, it's essential to understand the true reward that drives it. For example, if you have a habit of snacking late at night, the reward might not be the taste of the food but rather the sense of comfort or distraction it provides. By identifying this underlying reward, you can experiment with alternative routines that offer similar benefits, such as a relaxing tea or a calming bedtime activity.

The Impact of Rewards on Habit Strength

Rewards do more than just reinforce individual behaviors—they play a pivotal role in determining the strength and persistence of a habit. The more satisfying a reward is, the more deeply ingrained the habit becomes.

Variable Rewards and the Slot Machine Effect: One of the most potent forms of reward is a variable reward—an outcome that is not entirely predictable. This is the principle behind slot machines, where the uncertainty of the outcome keeps players engaged. Variable rewards create a sense of anticipation and excitement, making habits like checking email or scrolling through social media highly addictive. The unpredictability of the reward - whether it's a new message or an interesting post - keeps the brain hooked, reinforcing the habit loop each time.

Satiation and Diminishing Rewards: Over time, some rewards lose their potency as the brain becomes accustomed to them. This is known as satiation. For example, the first bite of a dessert might be intensely pleasurable, but each subsequent bite offers diminishing returns. Understanding this phenomenon can help in breaking habits, as recognizing that the initial reward fades can motivate you to seek alternative behaviors that provide more lasting satisfaction.

How to Use Rewards to Change Habits

Changing a habit often involves re-engineering the reward component of the habit loop. By adjusting the reward, you can alter the way your brain perceives the value of the routine, making it easier to adopt new behaviors or abandon old ones.

Finding a Suitable Replacement Reward: One of the most effective strategies for changing a habit is to find a new reward that is just as satisfying as the old one. For example, if the reward for a smoking habit is the sense of relaxation, you might replace the routine of smoking with deep breathing exercises or a short walk that offers a similar sense of relief. The key is to find a reward that satisfies the same craving without reinforcing the old behavior.

Reframing the Reward Experience: Sometimes, the reward can be enhanced by changing the way you perceive it. For instance, if you're trying to build a habit of exercising, you might focus on the immediate sense of accomplishment or the post-workout endorphin rush rather than the long-term goal of fitness. By shifting your focus to the positive feelings that follow the routine, you can make the habit more appealing in the present.

Rewarding Yourself Consciously: In some cases, it can be helpful to introduce an external reward to reinforce a new habit, especially in the beginning stages. For example, you might reward yourself with a small treat or a moment of relaxation after completing a challenging task. These external rewards help to bridge the gap until the internal reward - the satisfaction of the habit itself - takes over.

The Reward: The Engine of Lasting Change

Ultimately, the reward is what keeps a habit alive, providing the motivation to repeat the behavior over and over. By understanding what rewards your brain craves, you can begin to reshape your habits in ways that align with your goals and values. Rewards are the engine of habit change - the force that can either keep you trapped in a cycle of unproductive behaviors or propel you toward the positive habits that support a fulfilling life.

<u>Case Studies: Habit Loops in Real Life</u>

Understanding the habit loop becomes more tangible when we explore real-life examples. Case studies of habit loops in action reveal how the interplay between cue, routine, and reward shapes our daily behaviors, often in ways we don't fully realize. These stories demonstrate the power of habit loops, illustrating both the challenges of breaking bad habits and the possibilities of building positive ones.

Case Study 1: The Habit Loop of a Morning Routine

Meet Sarah, a busy professional who starts each day with a cup of coffee. Her morning habit loop has become an integral part of how she begins her day, providing structure and comfort. Let's break down Sarah's habit loop to see how each element functions:

Cue: For Sarah, the cue is her alarm clock. As soon as it rings, her brain triggers a specific sequence of behaviors. The alarm signifies the start of her day, which has become closely linked with her next action—making coffee.

Routine: Sarah's routine involves heading straight to the kitchen to brew a fresh cup of coffee. She doesn't have to think about it—it's become a reflex. This routine is not just about the physical act of making coffee but the entire ritual: filling the water reservoir, measuring the grounds, and inhaling the aroma as the coffee brews. It's a series of actions that her body performs almost on autopilot.

Reward: The reward for Sarah is twofold: the immediate pleasure of the warm, comforting taste of coffee and the sense of alertness that follows. The coffee signals a transition from sleepiness to wakefulness, helping her feel ready to tackle the day. This feeling reinforces the routine, making it an automatic part of her morning.

In Sarah's case, the habit loop of her morning coffee is a positive one—providing comfort and helping her transition into the workday. Understanding the components of this loop could help her adjust it if she ever wanted to cut back on caffeine, perhaps by finding a similar reward through a different morning beverage or routine.

Case Study 2: Breaking a Bad Habit Loop: Procrastination

Now consider Mark, a college student struggling with procrastination. His habit loop revolves around avoiding his studies and engaging in more pleasurable activities instead, like watching YouTube videos. This habit loop has been holding him back academically, but understanding it offers a path to change.

Cue: Mark's cue is the sight of his laptop and his study materials. Every time he sits down at his desk to study, he feels a sense of dread or anxiety about the upcoming work. This negative emotion acts as a trigger for his procrastination habit.

Routine: Instead of opening his textbooks, Mark reaches for his laptop and types in the URL for his favorite video streaming site. Watching videos provides an easy escape from the discomfort of studying. This routine is his way of avoiding the stress associated with difficult coursework, providing a momentary distraction.

Reward: The reward Mark receives is the temporary relief from stress. The videos allow him to feel entertained and relaxed, even if only for a short time. However, this reward is short-lived, as the anxiety over unfinished work eventually returns. Still, the immediate relief is powerful enough to keep the habit loop alive, making it hard for Mark to change his behavior.

To break this habit loop, Mark needs to recognize the true nature of the reward—relief from stress—and find healthier ways to achieve it. He could substitute the routine of watching videos with a brief walk or a breathing exercise, offering a similar sense of relaxation without derailing his study time.

Case Study 3: Building a New Habit Loop: Exercise After Work

Consider Maria, who wants to establish a habit of exercising regularly after work. For years, she has struggled to maintain a consistent routine, often finding herself too tired or unmotivated at the end of the day. By understanding the habit loop, she learns to create a sustainable exercise routine.

Cue: Maria identifies her cue as arriving home from work. She sets a specific routine in motion every time she walks through the door. To make this cue more effective, she places her workout clothes and sneakers by the door, so they are the first thing she sees when she gets home.

Routine: The routine Maria aims to establish is a 20-minute jog around her neighborhood. She starts small, knowing that setting a manageable goal is crucial to forming a lasting habit. She also tries to make the routine enjoyable by listening to her favorite music or a podcast while she jogs.

Reward: The reward for Maria comes in two parts: the immediate release of endorphins after the jog, giving her a sense of accomplishment and a physical boost, and the longer-term satisfaction of seeing progress in her fitness. She pairs this routine with a small treat - a healthy smoothie - as an additional reward to reinforce the behavior.

By intentionally designing her habit loop, Maria gradually makes exercise a natural part of her daily life. The key to her success lies in choosing a cue she encounters daily, making the routine as enjoyable as possible, and ensuring the reward is satisfying enough to motivate her to continue.

Case Study 4: The Habit Loop of Smoking: Understanding Addiction

One of the most challenging habit loops to break is that of addiction. Let's examine John, who has smoked for over a decade. Despite his desire to quit, the habit loop associated with smoking has become deeply entrenched in his brain.

Cue: For John, the cues that trigger his smoking habit are varied and often emotional. Stressful situations, after meals, or even social gatherings with other smokers all act as cues that prompt his urge to light up. The cues have become so automatic that even small triggers - like seeing a pack of cigarettes - can activate the craving.

Routine: The routine is the act of smoking itself—taking out a cigarette, lighting it, and inhaling. Over the years, this routine has become a ritual that John performs without much thought, each movement as familiar as breathing. The routine is intertwined with other activities in his life, making it challenging to break.

Reward: The reward is a sense of calm and relaxation, as well as the dopamine rush that smoking provides. This reward is powerful, as it relieves the stress or boredom that initially triggered the urge to smoke. The brain learns to expect this payoff, making the habit loop self-reinforcing.

To break this habit, John must focus on disrupting the routine and finding alternative ways to achieve the same reward. He might experiment with nicotine replacements, mindfulness practices, or physical activities that provide a similar sense of relaxation, gradually weakening the habit loop's hold on his daily life.

Case Study 5: Transforming a Habit Loop: Healthy Eating

Lisa, a young professional aiming to eat healthier, finds herself struggling with a habit loop that leads to frequent unhealthy snacking. By analyzing her habit loop, she identifies ways to transform her behavior into a more positive one.

Cue: Lisa's cue is the afternoon slump she experiences around 3 p.m. Each day, as her energy levels dip, she feels a craving for a quick snack, often something sugary. This dip in energy is a predictable daily cue that triggers her snacking habit.

Routine: The routine involves walking to the office kitchen and grabbing a candy bar or a bag of chips. It's a quick way to feel better, and over time, her brain has come to associate this routine with a boost in energy.

Reward: The reward is the immediate spike in energy and the temporary satisfaction of indulging in a treat. This reward is strong enough that Lisa repeats the behavior daily, even though she knows it doesn't align with her health goals.

To change this habit loop, Lisa decides to keep a bowl of fresh fruit on her desk, making it easy to replace the routine with a healthier option. The cue (the afternoon slump) and the reward (a boost in energy) remain the same, but the routine shifts from grabbing candy to eating fruit. This small change helps Lisa align her habit loop with her desire to eat healthier.

The Power of Real-Life Habit Loops

These case studies illustrate how habit loops shape behaviors in a variety of contexts, from the simplicity of a morning routine to the complexities of overcoming addiction. They show that while habit loops can be challenging to break, they can also be deliberately crafted and reshaped to align with our goals. By understanding the interplay between cue, routine, and reward, anyone can gain the tools to transform their habits, turning everyday behaviors into powerful forces for positive change. As you explore further in this book, you'll learn how to apply these insights to your own life, building habit loops that empower you to achieve your highest potential.

Chapter 3: The Neurology of Habits

The Brain's Role in Habit Formation

The neurological processes behind habits reveal the brain's central role in shaping and sustaining our behaviors. Habits are not just patterns we consciously choose; they are deeply rooted in the brain's structure and function, transforming complex actions into automatic responses. Understanding how the brain creates, stores, and reinforces habits can provide powerful insights into how to reshape and control them.

The Habit Brain: A Symphony of Structures

The brain's role in habit formation is orchestrated by a network of regions that work together to create, sustain, and change habits. Each of these structures contributes a different piece to the puzzle, from recognizing cues to automating routines. Understanding this network is key to unlocking the mechanisms that make habits so enduring.

The Basal Ganglia: The Habit Center

At the core of habit formation lies the basal ganglia, a structure deep within the brain that plays a pivotal role in controlling automatic behaviors. Often referred to as the brain's "habit center," the basal ganglia helps convert complex sequences of actions into simple, repeatable patterns.

- **Role in Habit Storage:** The basal ganglia is responsible for taking behaviors that start as conscious actions and transforming them into automatic routines. For example, learning to drive a car initially requires intense focus, but over time, the basal ganglia stores the necessary movements, allowing the act of driving to become second nature. This transition from deliberate action to effortless habit is a hallmark of the basal ganglia's function.

o **Automation of Behavior:** The basal ganglia's ability to automate behavior allows the brain to conserve energy for other tasks. This is why once a habit is formed, it can be difficult to change—your brain has come to rely on this automatic pathway as a default response, making it less likely to engage in active decision-making about the behavior.

The Prefrontal Cortex: The Decision-Maker

While the basal ganglia is responsible for automating habits, the prefrontal cortex acts as the decision-making center of the brain. This region is involved in planning, willpower, and conscious control, playing a key role when you try to change or create a new habit.

o **Initial Habit Formation:** When you first start building a habit, such as learning a new language or developing a workout routine, the prefrontal cortex is highly active. It guides you through the steps, requiring conscious effort and self-control to repeat the behavior.

o **Inhibition of Old Habits:** The prefrontal cortex is also crucial when trying to break an old habit. It allows you to override the automatic responses generated by the basal ganglia, making conscious decisions to act differently. This is why breaking a habit requires effort—your prefrontal cortex must exert control over the brain's automatic responses, which can be tiring over time.

The Role of the Striatum: The Gatekeeper

Within the basal ganglia is the striatum, a key player in habit formation that processes feedback and determines whether a behavior should be repeated. The striatum acts as a sort of gatekeeper, reinforcing behaviors that lead to positive outcomes and suppressing those that do not.

- o **Learning Through Feedback:** The striatum helps the brain learn which behaviors are worth repeating by processing feedback from the environment. When a behavior leads to a positive reward, the striatum releases dopamine, reinforcing the action and increasing the likelihood of repeating the behavior in response to the same cue.

- o **Reinforcing Repetition:** This process of reinforcement is central to habit formation. For example, if you receive a compliment after dressing neatly, the striatum helps solidify the behavior of dressing well in the future. This feedback loop creates the neurological underpinnings that make habits resilient and hard to change.

Dopamine: The Brain's Reward Messenger

Dopamine, a neurotransmitter known as the brain's "feel-good" chemical, plays a critical role in habit formation. It is the key to understanding why habits can be so hard to break and why certain routines become addictive.

Dopamine Release and Habit Reinforcement:
Every time you experience a reward, whether it's a pleasant taste, a feeling of accomplishment, or relief from stress, your brain releases dopamine. This release signals to the brain that the behavior is beneficial, encouraging it to be repeated.

- o **Anticipation of Reward:** Interestingly, dopamine is not just released after a reward is experienced; it is also released in anticipation of a reward. For example, if you have a habit of eating a treat after dinner, your brain begins to release dopamine as soon as dinner ends, anticipating the pleasure of the treat. This anticipation makes the craving for the reward powerful, driving you toward the routine even before you receive the actual reward.

o **Creating a Feedback Loop:** Dopamine creates a feedback loop that strengthens the connection between the cue, the routine, and the reward. Each time the routine is performed and followed by the expected reward, dopamine reinforces the pathway in the brain, making the habit more automatic over time.

The Dopamine Deficit and Habit Change:
When you try to break a habit or replace it with a new one, the dopamine feedback loop is disrupted. The absence of the expected reward can create a feeling of discomfort or craving, making it challenging to stick with the new behavior. Understanding this can help you be patient with yourself during the process of habit change, knowing that your brain is adjusting to a new pattern.

Neuroplasticity: The Brain's Ability to Rewire Habits

Neuroplasticity is the brain's remarkable ability to adapt and change throughout life, including its capacity to rewire habits. This adaptability is a double-edged sword—it allows bad habits to become deeply ingrained, but it also provides the opportunity to form new, healthier habits.

How Habits Become Hardwired:
The more often a habit loop is repeated, the stronger the neural connections associated with that habit become. This is similar to a path through a forest: the more you walk it, the clearer and more defined the trail becomes. For example, the habit of checking your phone whenever you feel bored becomes more ingrained each time you reach for the device.

This is neuroplasticity at work, making the routine easier to perform and harder to break.

- o **The Challenge of Breaking Old Paths:** When trying to break a habit, you are essentially trying to let the old neural pathway grow over while forging a new path through repeated practice of a different behavior. This process takes time and persistence because the brain must weaken the old connection before the new one can become dominant. It's why change often feels slow, but it is entirely possible with consistent effort.

Forming New Pathways:
Neuroplasticity is also what makes it possible to develop new habits. Each time you perform a new routine in response to a cue, you begin to create a new neural connection. Repetition is key—just as with learning any new skill, the more often you practice the new behavior, the stronger the pathway becomes. For example, if you replace the habit of watching TV after dinner with going for a walk, the brain gradually adapts, making the walk feel more natural over time.

Habit Loops as Survival Mechanisms

From an evolutionary perspective, the brain's habit-forming abilities are designed to help us survive by automating behaviors that are beneficial. This historical context explains why habits form so easily and why they can be difficult to change.

Conserving Cognitive Energy:
The brain is always seeking to conserve energy, and habits serve this purpose by reducing the cognitive load required for everyday actions. This is why the brain prefers routines— automated behaviors allow it to focus its energy on new or more complex challenges. For instance, the habit of checking

for danger before crossing the road helps keep you safe without needing to consciously think about it each time.

o **From Survival to Everyday Habits:** While our modern lives no longer require constant vigilance for physical danger, the brain still uses these same mechanisms to form habits around everyday activities. Whether it's brushing your teeth before bed or reaching for a snack when stressed, the brain is applying an ancient system of habit formation to modern situations.

Adapting to Change:
Even though the brain is wired to prefer routine, it is also adaptable. This adaptability is what allows us to change habits when new circumstances arise. For example, moving to a new city might disrupt your daily routines, but over time, your brain will adapt to the new environment, forming habits around your new daily schedule. This flexibility is a testament to the brain's ability to balance stability with change, adapting old habit loops or creating new ones as needed.

The Brain's Role: The Blueprint for Habit Change

Understanding the brain's role in habit formation reveals why habits can feel so powerful and enduring. But it also offers a blueprint for change. By knowing how the basal ganglia automates routines, how dopamine reinforces behaviors, and how neuroplasticity allows for adaptation, you can develop strategies for reshaping your habits. It's not just about forcing yourself to act differently; it's about working with your brain's natural tendencies to create new, positive pathways that align with your goals. As you explore the next chapters, you'll learn how to leverage this neurological understanding to transform your habits and unlock your potential for lasting change.

<u>Neuroplasticity: Rewiring Your Brain for Change</u>

Understanding the concept of neuroplasticity is key to mastering habit change. Neuroplasticity, the brain's ability to reorganize itself by forming new neural connections throughout life, is the foundation of how habits can be reshaped or entirely rewritten. This capacity for change is not just a scientific curiosity; it is the mechanism that enables us to overcome deeply ingrained behaviors and replace them with new, more beneficial patterns.

What Is Neuroplasticity?

Neuroplasticity is the brain's capacity to adapt in response to new experiences, learning, and changes in the environment. Contrary to the outdated belief that the brain becomes fixed and unchangeable after a certain age, research has shown that the brain remains malleable throughout our lives. This plasticity is what allows us to learn new skills, recover from injuries, and, importantly, modify our habits.

Dynamic Reorganization: Neuroplasticity enables the brain to "rewire" itself, changing the strength and organization of its neural networks based on experience. This process is like a forest with pathways that become clearer the more they are walked. Each time you repeat a thought or behavior, you reinforce a particular pathway in the brain, making it easier to follow that path again in the future.

Hebb's Law: Neurons That Fire Together, Wire Together: A central principle of neuroplasticity is Hebb's Law, which states that "neurons that fire together, wire together." When you repeatedly perform a habit, the neurons involved in that behavior become more tightly connected, creating a stronger link between them. This is why a behavior that starts as a conscious choice can become automatic over time. Your brain learns to link the trigger (cue) with the response (routine) through repeated practice, making it easier and more natural to follow the same pattern.

How Neuroplasticity Shapes Habits

Neuroplasticity explains why habits, once formed, can feel so automatic and hard to change. The brain creates well-worn pathways that make certain routines effortless. However, this same plasticity also means that with effort and consistency, these pathways can be altered or replaced with new ones.

Forming New Neural Pathways: When you decide to adopt a new habit, like exercising every morning, you are essentially creating a new neural pathway. At first, this pathway is faint and undeveloped, requiring conscious effort to follow. You might have to remind yourself to get up and put on your running shoes. But each time you complete the new behavior, the neural connections strengthen, making the pathway more defined. Over time, what was once a struggle becomes second nature as the brain solidifies the new habit loop.

Weakening Old Pathways: Breaking a bad habit involves weakening the existing neural pathway that supports the unwanted behavior. For example, if you have a habit of biting your nails when stressed, that habit has a well-established pathway in your brain. Each time you resist the urge and choose a different response - like squeezing a stress ball instead - you begin to weaken the old pathway while building a new one. This process is gradual, as the brain learns to rely less on the old habit and more on the new one, but with persistence, the old pathway fades.

The Challenge of Habit Change: Neuroplasticity and Resistance

While neuroplasticity makes habit change possible, it also explains why the process can be difficult. The brain is naturally resistant to change, preferring the stability of existing pathways over the uncertainty of new ones.

The Effort of Conscious Change: When you first attempt to change a habit, you engage the prefrontal cortex, the part of the brain responsible for conscious thought and decision-making. This requires effort and energy, which is why new habits often feel tiring at first. It's like walking through thick brush to create a new trail in the forest—initially, the path is rough and difficult to navigate.

- **Initial Struggle:** The brain's preference for familiar pathways means that during the early stages of change, the old habit may feel stronger and more tempting. This is why someone trying to quit smoking might experience intense cravings, as their brain attempts to pull them back to the well-worn path.

Breaking the "Habit Loop" Resilience: The automatic nature of habits is due to the strong connections between the cue, routine, and reward that the brain has developed. When you try to interrupt this loop, the brain may resist because it has grown accustomed to the dopamine reward that follows the routine. For example, if you habitually check your phone whenever you feel bored, breaking this habit means denying the brain the quick hit of dopamine it expects. The resistance you feel is the brain's way of trying to maintain the status quo.

Strategies to Harness Neuroplasticity for Habit Change

To effectively leverage neuroplasticity, you must engage in practices that help rewire the brain. This involves consistency, patience, and a focus on creating positive reinforcement for new behaviors.

Repetition and Consistency Are Key: Neuroplasticity responds best to consistent practice. The more frequently you perform a new behavior, the more the brain adapts, strengthening the neural connections associated with that habit. Consistency helps accelerate the shift from conscious effort to automatic behavior.

o **Daily Practice:** Integrating a new habit into your daily routine is one of the most effective ways to harness neuroplasticity. For example, if you want to build a habit of reading before bed, make it a nightly ritual. The repeated action helps your brain recognize the pattern, making it easier to follow without thinking.

Mindfulness and Intentionality: Mindfulness can play a crucial role in rewiring the brain, as it encourages you to pay attention to your thoughts, feelings, and triggers without automatically reacting to them.

o **Mindful Interruption of Old Habits:** By being mindful of the cues that trigger your habits, you can intentionally choose a different response. For instance, if stress triggers a habit of emotional eating, mindfulness allows you to recognize the cue before reacting, giving you the opportunity to select a healthier response, like going for a walk or practicing deep breathing.

Positive Reinforcement to Strengthen New Pathways: Rewarding yourself for engaging in a new habit helps reinforce the neural pathway, making the new behavior more appealing to the brain.

○ **Dopamine and New Habits:** Dopamine plays a role in helping solidify new habits by making the brain associate the behavior with positive outcomes. If you reward yourself with a small treat or a moment of relaxation after completing a new habit, you can use dopamine to your advantage, creating a sense of pleasure that motivates the repetition of the behavior.

Neuroplasticity in Action: Real-Life Transformations

To see neuroplasticity at work, consider real-life examples of how people have successfully rewired their brains to change their habits.

From Sedentary to Active: Take Jane, who struggled with a sedentary lifestyle. She decided to start walking every morning, even though at first it felt like a chore. Each day, as she repeated the walk, her brain adapted, making the routine feel less burdensome. Over several weeks, the new habit became a source of enjoyment rather than effort, and her brain rewired to expect the walk as a natural part of her day. Jane's transformation showcases the power of neuroplasticity—what was once a struggle became an ingrained habit.

Overcoming Negative Self-Talk: Neuroplasticity is also essential in changing mental habits, such as negative self-talk. David, who had a habit of criticizing himself whenever he made a mistake, decided to replace this routine with self-compassion. Each time he caught himself in a negative thought, he practiced replacing it with a positive affirmation. At first, the process felt forced and insincere, but with time, his brain began to adopt the new way of thinking. The neural pathways supporting negative self-talk weakened, while those reinforcing self-kindness grew stronger, leading to a more positive mindset.

The Power of Neuroplasticity: Redefining What's Possible

Neuroplasticity makes it clear that habits are not set in stone - they are patterns that the brain has learned and can relearn with the right approach. While the process of rewiring the brain requires patience and effort, the potential for transformation is limitless. Whether you are trying to break a bad habit or establish a new, positive one, the brain's ability to adapt is your greatest ally.

The Basal Ganglia and Automatic Behavior

Understanding the neurological foundation of habits means delving into the role of the basal ganglia, a small yet powerful structure buried deep within the brain. The basal ganglia is at the heart of habit formation, acting as a sort of autopilot system that allows us to perform routine behaviors with minimal conscious effort. It is the brain's way of simplifying our lives, turning deliberate actions into automatic routines that can run quietly in the background while we focus on other things.

The Basal Ganglia: The Brain's Habit Center

The basal ganglia might not be as well-known as the cerebral cortex, which is responsible for complex thought, but it plays an equally crucial role in shaping our behavior. It's the part of the brain that allows you to ride a bike, tie your shoes, or brush your teeth without thinking about each individual step. It is the basal ganglia that transforms these complex tasks into sequences that you can perform on autopilot. Imagine trying to consciously think through every step of driving a car - checking mirrors, pressing the gas pedal, monitoring the road - all while holding a conversation. It would be exhausting. Instead, the basal ganglia takes over, allowing you to perform these actions smoothly, freeing up your conscious mind for other thoughts.

The basal ganglia is like a master archivist, cataloging patterns of behavior and storing them as habits. It learns to recognize the cues that signal the start of a routine and then executes the learned behavior without needing much input from the prefrontal cortex, the brain's center for decision-making and planning. This process is why habits can become so ingrained, feeling more like reflexes than choices.

The Shift from Conscious Effort to Automaticity

The process of habit formation can be seen as a journey from conscious effort to automaticity, a shift where the basal ganglia gradually takes control. In the beginning, when you're learning a new behavior, like playing a musical instrument or practicing a new yoga pose, the prefrontal cortex is heavily involved. It guides you through the steps, requiring focused attention and deliberate practice. You're acutely aware of what you're doing, and each action feels deliberate and sometimes awkward.

But as you continue to practice, the basal ganglia steps in. It begins to recognize patterns in your movements and stores them as automatic routines. Over time, the effort you once needed diminishes, and the action becomes more fluid. It's like moving from a dirt trail to a well-paved road—the more you travel down that path, the easier and smoother the journey becomes. Eventually, the basal ganglia can take over completely, and the routine becomes automatic. You might find yourself playing a piece of music without thinking about where your fingers should go, or moving through a series of yoga poses with your mind focused elsewhere. The basal ganglia has internalized the routine, allowing you to perform it effortlessly.

Why Automaticity Can Be a Double-Edged Sword

The basal ganglia's role in automating behaviors is both a blessing and a challenge. It allows us to streamline our daily lives, conserving mental energy for more complex decisions. But this efficiency comes at a cost—once a behavior is automated, it becomes deeply embedded and difficult to change. This is why bad habits, like nail-biting or mindlessly snacking, can feel impossible to break. The basal ganglia treats these behaviors the same way it treats positive habits, like driving or brushing your teeth, making no distinction between actions that are helpful or harmful.

Consider Emily, who has a habit of checking her phone whenever she feels a moment of boredom. Initially, she might have consciously decided to reach for her phone as a way to fill time. But over the months and years, the act became automatic. Now, whenever Emily experiences a lull in activity—a moment waiting in line, a quiet evening at home—her hand reaches for her phone almost by reflex. She doesn't need to think about it; the basal ganglia has taken over, executing the routine without engaging the decision-making parts of her brain. This is the power of automaticity, but it's also what makes habits so stubborn.

How the Basal Ganglia Manages Habit Loops

To understand how the basal ganglia operates, it's helpful to look at the structure of a habit loop - cue, routine, and reward. The basal ganglia doesn't initiate the loop; that job belongs to the prefrontal cortex, which recognizes the cue.

But once the cue is identified, the basal ganglia takes over, running the routine like a well-rehearsed script, until the reward is achieved.

For instance, imagine Michael, who has a habit of going for a run after work. His cue is arriving home and seeing his running shoes by the door. At that moment, his brain shifts gears. The prefrontal cortex recognizes the cue, but it is the basal ganglia that remembers the sequence - put on the shoes, grab a water bottle, stretch, and start running. Michael doesn't need to think through each step because his basal ganglia has automated the process. The routine unfolds seamlessly, providing him with a reward in the form of the runner's high and a sense of accomplishment.

This automation is incredibly efficient. It allows Michael to run without wasting mental energy on decision-making each time. But it also means that if Michael wanted to change his after-work habit - perhaps replacing the run with yoga - he would need to exert conscious effort for a while before the new routine could take root. The basal ganglia would need time to adapt, creating a new automatic pathway.

Rewiring the Basal Ganglia: The Challenge of Change

Because the basal ganglia is so effective at maintaining routines, changing a habit means essentially rewriting the brain's script. This process can be challenging, as it requires shifting control back to the prefrontal cortex for a period, reintroducing effort and conscious choice into a behavior that has become automatic.

For example, consider Alex, who wants to break his habit of having a glass of wine every evening. His cue is finishing dinner, and the routine involves reaching for the bottle, pouring a glass, and relaxing in front of the TV. The basal ganglia has streamlined this process, making it feel like a natural end to the day. But to change this habit, Alex must engage his prefrontal cortex to interrupt the automatic routine. He might choose a different activity, like making a cup of herbal tea or going for a short walk. For weeks, this change feels difficult. He has to remind himself not to reach for the wine and to follow the new routine instead.

During this period, the basal ganglia is slowly adapting, weakening the old pathway and beginning to strengthen a new one. Each time Alex successfully chooses tea over wine, the new behavior becomes a little easier. Eventually, the basal ganglia will automate this new pattern, just as it did the old one. The shift from conscious effort to automaticity is gradual, but it's also the key to making lasting changes in behavior.

The Basal Ganglia as a Gateway to Transformation

Understanding the role of the basal ganglia in habit formation is crucial for anyone looking to change their habits. It explains why some routines feel so natural and others feel like a struggle, especially in the early stages. But more importantly, it reveals that the brain's automaticity is not a fixed trait—it's a flexible process that can be guided and reshaped.

When you recognize that the basal ganglia is simply trying to be efficient, you can work with it rather than against it. By identifying the cues that trigger your habits and consciously choosing new routines, you begin the process of retraining the basal ganglia, teaching it new scripts that align with your goals. It takes time and patience, but the result is a brain that automates positive behaviors, turning the effort of self-improvement into a natural, effortless part of your daily life.

As you continue through the journey outlined in this book, you'll learn more about how to leverage the power of the basal ganglia, using it as a tool to build habits that support the life you want. It's not about fighting your brain's tendency toward automatic behavior; it's about guiding that tendency in the direction that serves you best, allowing the power of habit to work for you rather than against you.

Part II: Identifying and Assessing Your Habits
Chapter 4: Spotting Your Bad Habits

<u>Common Bad Habits and Their Impact</u>

Identifying and assessing bad habits is the first crucial step toward positive change. Many of us live with habits that, though small and seemingly insignificant, can have a profound impact on our lives. These common bad habits often develop slowly, slipping into our routines without us even noticing. Yet, over time, their cumulative effects can shape our health, mindset, productivity, and relationships. Understanding these habits and their impact can open the door to transformative change, helping us break free from the patterns that hold us back.

The Subtle Invasion of Bad Habits

Bad habits often begin as small indulgences or shortcuts. They can feel harmless or even comforting at first, providing temporary relief or satisfaction. A quick scroll through social media when you're bored, a cookie after dinner to unwind, or hitting the snooze button for just ten more minutes—these small actions don't seem like they could cause much harm. But as days turn into weeks, these behaviors become ingrained, transforming from occasional choices into automatic routines that we follow without thinking.

Take, for example, Sarah, a young professional with a demanding job. She started the habit of checking her phone whenever she felt a lull at work, thinking it would be a quick way to refresh her mind. But over time, those quick glances turned into longer sessions of scrolling through social media, eating away at her focus. What began as a way to manage stress eventually became a significant drain on her productivity, making it harder for her to complete tasks on time and increasing her overall stress levels. The habit, once a momentary escape, now traps her in a cycle of procrastination and frustration.

The Impact of Digital Distractions

One of the most common bad habits in today's world is the overuse of digital devices, particularly smartphones. Many people, like Sarah, find themselves reaching for their phones whenever they have a spare moment—on the bus, in line at the grocery store, or even during meals. This habit can lead to a scattered attention span, making it harder to focus deeply on any one task. It's not just about the time spent scrolling but about the fragmentation of thought and the inability to sustain concentration.

Beyond its impact on productivity, this habit can seep into relationships. Picture a family dinner where everyone is sitting together, but each person is absorbed in their screen. The habit of checking phones during conversations erodes the quality of interactions, creating a sense of disconnection even when people are physically present. Over time, this can lead to feelings of loneliness and a loss of deep, meaningful connections, all because a habit that seemed minor took precedence over human interaction.

The Lure of Emotional Eating

Another widespread habit with a significant impact is emotional eating. This habit often develops as a way to cope with stress, anxiety, or boredom. For many, food becomes a source of comfort—a way to fill an emotional void. When Lisa was navigating a tough period at work, she began reaching for snacks during late-night work sessions. At first, it felt like a small treat to keep her going through long hours. But as the habit persisted, it became her default response to stress.

The impact of emotional eating extends beyond weight gain. It can lead to feelings of guilt and self-criticism, especially when people realize that they're eating for reasons other than hunger. This habit can also mask deeper emotional struggles, making it harder to address the root causes of stress or anxiety. Over time, the physical effects of overeating - fatigue, digestive issues, and a lack of energy - can compound the emotional toll, creating a cycle that feels difficult to break.

The Invisible Costs of Procrastination

Procrastination is another classic example of a bad habit that often begins as a minor behavior but can have far-reaching consequences. It starts with putting off tasks that seem unappealing or difficult, telling yourself that you'll get to them later. For Mark, a university student, procrastination was a way of life. He often delayed starting assignments, choosing instead to relax or watch TV, convincing himself that he worked better under pressure.

But as deadlines approached, the pressure would mount, turning what could have been manageable projects into frantic, last-minute struggles. The stress and anxiety of rushing through work affected Mark's sleep, his academic performance, and his self-esteem. He constantly felt like he was falling short, even though he knew he was capable of more. Procrastination, which started as a way to avoid discomfort, ultimately created more of it, leaving him stuck in a cycle of stress and self-doubt.

The Seduction of Inaction: Sedentary Habits

In today's increasingly sedentary world, the habit of physical inactivity has become alarmingly common. Many people, like Tom, find themselves sitting for long periods - at their desks, in front of the TV, or during long commutes. What starts as a busy workday with little time for movement gradually becomes a lifestyle where physical activity is the exception rather than the norm.

The impact of this habit goes beyond physical health. While the obvious effects include weight gain, muscle stiffness, and a higher risk of chronic diseases, the less visible consequences can be just as damaging. Sedentary habits can contribute to low energy levels, a lack of motivation, and even feelings of depression. Tom noticed that the more time he spent sitting, the more sluggish and unmotivated he felt, even though he couldn't pinpoint exactly why. It wasn't until he began incorporating small bursts of movement into his day that he realized how much his inactivity had been draining his energy and enthusiasm for life.

The Trap of Negative Self-Talk

Not all bad habits are physical - some reside solely in our minds. Negative self-talk is one such habit that can quietly undermine confidence and well-being. It often begins with small, self-critical thoughts, like "I'm not good enough" or "I always mess things up." Over time, these thoughts become a default way of thinking, shaping a person's self-perception and limiting their potential.

For David, negative self-talk started as a way of motivating himself to do better, but it soon turned into a constant inner critic that made him doubt his abilities. Each time he faced a challenge, his mind would automatically conjure up thoughts of failure and inadequacy, making it harder for him to take risks or pursue new opportunities. This habit affected not just his career but also his relationships, as he found it difficult to trust others' praise or accept compliments. The habit of negative self-talk, while invisible, cast a shadow over every aspect of his life, making joy and satisfaction harder to grasp.

The Long-Term Effects: How Bad Habits Accumulate

The true impact of bad habits is often not felt immediately. They are like small drops of water that gradually fill a bucket. At first, you might not notice much change, but over time, the bucket fills, and the consequences become harder to ignore. Whether it's the gradual increase in stress from constant phone use, the creeping weight gain from emotional eating, or the steady erosion of self-confidence through negative self-talk, the effects accumulate until they shape the contours of our lives.

Understanding these common bad habits and their impacts is not about self-blame; it's about recognition. It's about seeing how small choices, repeated day after day, can lead to significant outcomes. It's about acknowledging where you are so that you can begin to steer your habits in a direction that serves you better. As you explore the next sections of this book, you'll learn how to assess these habits honestly and develop strategies to break free from their hold, replacing them with positive actions that can transform your life, one small step at a time.

Self-Assessment Techniques

Identifying bad habits is a pivotal step toward transformation, and it begins with self-assessment. This process is not just about recognizing behaviors that might be holding you back -

it's about cultivating an honest, compassionate understanding of yourself. Through self-assessment techniques, you can shine a light on patterns that have become so ingrained they operate almost invisibly, influencing your daily actions and decisions without your conscious awareness. By bringing these habits into focus, you gain the power to make meaningful changes.

The Art of Self-Reflection

One of the first steps in identifying your habits is learning to observe yourself without judgment. Self-reflection is a powerful technique that involves taking a step back and looking at your behaviors with curiosity rather than criticism. Imagine sitting down at the end of each day and replaying the events in your mind, paying attention to the small choices you made. Did you reach for your phone immediately upon waking up? Did you find yourself eating out of boredom rather than hunger? This daily reflection helps you notice patterns you might otherwise overlook.

For Emma, self-reflection became a nightly ritual. She would sit quietly before bed, asking herself what actions throughout the day felt automatic and which ones she wished she could change. At first, it was difficult for her to see past her hectic schedule, but over time, she began to notice recurring patterns. She realized that whenever she felt stressed at work, she would instinctively buy a sugary treat from the vending machine. This habit had become so routine that she hadn't even recognized it as a response to stress until she began this process of reflection. Self-reflection allowed Emma to see the connections between her emotions and her actions, giving her a clearer picture of the habits she wanted to change.

The Power of Journaling

Journaling is another effective technique for spotting bad habits. It provides a way to document your thoughts and behaviors, offering a tangible record of your patterns over time. Writing down what you do each day, how you feel, and what triggers certain actions can be incredibly revealing. It turns the abstract process of self-reflection into a concrete exercise, allowing you to see your habits on the page in black and white.

David, a software engineer, used journaling to identify his tendency to procrastinate. Each day, he would write down what tasks he had planned and what he actually accomplished. He started noticing a trend - every time he encountered a task he found difficult or boring, he would spend time browsing news websites instead of getting to work. By keeping a journal, David could pinpoint the exact moments when he deviated from his plans and understand what emotions or thoughts were driving him. This insight didn't come immediately; it was the accumulation of weeks of entries that made the pattern visible. Journaling helped David move from feeling frustrated by his lack of productivity to understanding the root cause of his procrastination.

Creating a Habit Log

A habit log is a focused form of journaling specifically aimed at tracking habits. This technique involves writing down each instance of a particular behavior, along with the context in which it occurred. It's like being a detective in your own life, looking for clues about when, where, and why certain habits arise. A habit log helps you gather data on your behavior, making it easier to identify triggers and routines that have become ingrained.

When Julia decided to cut down on her time spent watching TV, she created a habit log to track every time she turned on the television. She noted what time it was, what she was doing before she turned on the TV, and how she felt in that moment. After a few weeks, she noticed a clear pattern: she tended to watch TV late at night when she felt lonely or bored. The habit log helped her see that her TV watching wasn't just about entertainment; it was a way to avoid feeling lonely at the end of the day. This awareness was a breakthrough for Julia, allowing her to explore other ways to address those feelings instead of automatically reaching for the remote.

The Role of Self-Assessment Questions

Another powerful self-assessment technique involves asking yourself targeted questions to dig deeper into your habits. These questions help you challenge your automatic behaviors, bringing them into the light of conscious thought. By exploring not just what you do, but why you do it, you can begin to unravel the motivations behind your habits.

For Marcus, a young entrepreneur juggling multiple projects, self-assessment questions became a daily habit. Each morning, he would ask himself questions like: "What habits are helping me reach my goals?" and "Which habits are holding me back?" He also included more specific questions, like "Why do I reach for my phone when I'm working?" and "What am I avoiding when I put off making difficult phone calls?" These questions encouraged Marcus to confront his habits directly, turning vague feelings of dissatisfaction into actionable insights. Over time, he began to see that his habit of checking emails obsessively during the day was not just about staying on top of work - it was a way to feel productive without addressing the bigger tasks that required more focus.

Mindfulness: Observing Without Judgment

Mindfulness is another technique that can be used to spot bad habits. Unlike journaling or habit logs, mindfulness doesn't require writing anything down; it's about being present in the moment and noticing your actions as they happen. It involves paying attention to your thoughts, feelings, and physical sensations without trying to change them right away. Mindfulness helps you become aware of habits as they unfold, creating a space between impulse and action where change can begin.

Take the example of Sam, who had a habit of biting his nails whenever he felt anxious. He wasn't even aware he was doing it most of the time - his hands would reach his mouth almost without thinking. But when Sam started practicing mindfulness, he began to notice the physical sensations that accompanied his habit: the tightening in his chest, the clenching of his jaw. He noticed the thoughts that flitted through his mind just before he started biting his nails, often worries about work or relationships. By observing these moments without immediately trying to stop them, Sam gained a deeper understanding of his habit. He learned that his nail-biting was a way to cope with anxiety, and this insight gave him the power to explore healthier ways of dealing with his stress.

Creating a Personal Inventory of Habits

A more comprehensive approach to self-assessment involves creating a personal inventory of habits. This technique requires you to list out all the habits you can think of, both good and bad, and reflect on how each one affects your life. It's a way of taking stock, like cleaning out a cluttered closet and deciding what to keep and what to let go.

When Priya decided to take control of her time and energy, she sat down with a notebook and wrote out every habit she could think of, from her morning routine to how she spent her evenings. As she looked over her list, certain habits stood out - like her tendency to snack late at night, her habit of hitting the snooze button three times before getting up, and her routine of skipping her evening walk when she felt tired. By listing these habits and noting how they made her feel, Priya could see which ones contributed to her well-being and which ones took away from it. This personal inventory didn't just help her identify bad habits; it helped her see the bigger picture of how her daily choices shaped her life.

Embracing Self-Compassion in Assessment

While self-assessment can be an eye-opening process, it's important to approach it with compassion. Being honest about your habits can sometimes bring up feelings of guilt or frustration, especially when you realize how deeply a habit has affected your life. But it's crucial to remember that spotting a bad habit is not about blaming yourself - it's about understanding yourself better so that you can move forward.

For many, like Lisa, self-compassion became the key to making self-assessment a positive experience. Lisa struggled with a habit of negative self-talk, often criticizing herself whenever she made a mistake. As she began the process of assessing this habit, she realized how much her inner dialogue affected her confidence. At first, the awareness of her critical thoughts made her feel even more discouraged. But by practicing self-compassion, she learned to approach her inner critic with kindness. Instead of berating herself for having negative thoughts, she started acknowledging them and then gently reminding herself of her strengths. This shift allowed Lisa to transform her habit of self-criticism into a habit of self-encouragement, showing her that even the most deeply rooted habits can be changed with patience and understanding.

The Path to Change Begins with Awareness

Ultimately, the purpose of these self-assessment techniques is not to focus on what you're doing wrong but to shine a light on the behaviors that have become automatic. Awareness is the first step toward change because it brings habits out of the shadows and into the light of conscious choice. By taking the time to reflect, journal, observe, and ask questions, you can begin to see your habits for what they are - patterns of behavior that can be reshaped, one small change at a time.

Journaling: Keeping Track of Your Behaviors

The practice of journaling emerges as a powerful tool for identifying and understanding bad habits. While self-reflection allows us to notice habits in the abstract, journaling transforms these insights into something tangible - a written record of our behaviors, thoughts, and triggers. It's like holding up a mirror to our daily lives, capturing the moments that often pass by unnoticed. Through journaling, you can track the patterns that shape your actions, revealing the hidden motivations behind your habits and offering a pathway to change.

Journaling: A Daily Habit of Awareness

Imagine waking up each morning and taking a few minutes to jot down the habits that shape your day. For Julia, a graphic designer juggling a busy schedule, journaling became a daily ritual that helped her make sense of her routines. She started by writing down simple observations - what time she woke up, how many cups of coffee she drank, when she took breaks, and how she felt throughout the day. At first, it seemed mundane, just a series of ordinary moments strung together. But as she continued this practice over the weeks, a clearer picture began to emerge.

Julia noticed that on days when she felt overwhelmed by deadlines, she had a tendency to reach for snacks more frequently, especially in the afternoon. It wasn't just about hunger - she saw that stress was the real trigger behind her habit of mindless eating. By journaling, she was able to connect the dots between her emotional state and her actions, a connection that had eluded her before. The act of writing gave her a space to be honest with herself, to admit the habits that weren't serving her well, and to explore why they had taken root.

Turning the Spotlight on Daily Patterns

Journaling is not just about tracking behaviors; it's about turning a spotlight onto your daily patterns. When you write things down, you transform fleeting moments into a record you can revisit and analyze. This practice helps you see the habits that might otherwise slip through the cracks of your memory, especially those that occur when you're on autopilot. For David, a busy father of two, this became a revelation.

David often felt like his days were a blur of work, parenting, and chores, leaving little time for himself. He struggled with a habit of staying up late watching TV, even though he knew it left him feeling exhausted the next morning. Through journaling, he began keeping track of his evenings, noting what he did before bed, how he felt, and what led him to turn on the TV. He noticed a pattern: after a particularly stressful day at work, he craved the escape of his favorite shows, using them as a way to unwind. But he also realized that this habit wasn't truly relaxing him - it was simply postponing the inevitable need for rest.

By documenting these evenings, David gained clarity about why he stayed up late. It wasn't just a bad habit—it was a coping mechanism for dealing with stress. This insight allowed him to explore other ways to unwind, such as reading or practicing deep breathing before bed. The habit didn't change overnight, but the act of journaling gave him a new understanding of his behavior and the tools to start making a shift.

The Emotional Landscape of Habits

Journaling also allows you to capture the emotional landscape that surrounds your habits. Often, our behaviors are driven by feelings we might not fully understand—boredom, loneliness, anxiety, or even joy. By writing down not only what you do but how you feel when you do it, you can uncover the emotional triggers that lead to certain behaviors.

Take the example of Emma, who had developed a habit of scrolling through social media whenever she felt a sense of unease or boredom. She didn't realize how often she did this until she started journaling. Each time she reached for her phone, she made a note in her journal, writing down what she was feeling and what was happening around her. Over time, a pattern emerged: whenever she was in between tasks or felt uncertain about what to do next, she would seek out the comfort of her phone.

Emma's journal revealed that her habit was less about the content on social media and more about escaping the discomfort of uncertainty. This realization allowed her to experiment with new ways of handling those feelings, like taking a walk or calling a friend. The simple act of writing down her experiences gave her the awareness she needed to start making different choices.

Seeing Progress Through Your Pages

One of the most rewarding aspects of journaling is that it provides a tangible record of progress. It allows you to look back and see how far you've come, giving you the motivation to keep going even when change feels slow. Journaling turns your journey into a story - one where you can see the turning points, the small victories, and the moments of clarity.

For Raj, a software developer trying to reduce his habit of procrastination, journaling became a source of encouragement. He had always struggled with putting off difficult tasks, telling himself he would do them "later." But as he started documenting his daily activities, he noticed subtle shifts. He wrote down every time he managed to start a task without delay, and he also noted the times he fell back into old patterns. At first, the setbacks seemed more frequent than the successes, but over the weeks, he could see a shift in his journal entries. The instances of procrastination became less common, while the notes about taking action became more frequent.

This record of progress was a reminder that change doesn't happen all at once - it's a gradual process that unfolds over time. For Raj, his journal became a source of pride, a place where he could see the effort he was putting into his growth. It helped him stay committed to his goal, even on days when he felt discouraged.

The Surprising Benefits of Daily Check-Ins

Journaling also offers a way to conduct daily check-ins with yourself. These check-ins don't have to be lengthy; even a few lines each day can make a difference. By making journaling a regular habit, you create a routine of self-awareness that helps you stay in touch with your intentions and goals.

Sara, a marketing manager, found that taking just five minutes each morning to jot down her intentions for the day made a huge difference in how she approached her habits. She would write down what she wanted to focus on, what habits she wanted to be mindful of, and how she wanted to feel. Then, in the evening, she would reflect on how the day went, noting any habits that crept in and how they aligned (or didn't) with her goals. This daily practice kept her connected to her deeper motivations, helping her see her habits as part of a larger journey rather than isolated behaviors.

Through these daily check-ins, Sara noticed that her habit of checking emails first thing in the morning was setting a reactive tone for her day, making her feel anxious before she even got out of bed. She decided to experiment with a new routine, where she would spend the first 15 minutes of her morning reading a book or journaling before diving into work. The change wasn't always easy—there were mornings when she instinctively reached for her phone—but the act of journaling kept her aware of the shift she was trying to make, helping her build a new morning habit that felt more intentional and empowering.

Journaling as a Tool for Self-Compassion

Perhaps one of the most unexpected benefits of journaling is that it encourages self-compassion. Writing down your thoughts and behaviors can sometimes bring up feelings of guilt or frustration - especially when you recognize habits that you wish you could change. But as you document your journey, you also begin to see the patterns of effort and struggle, the times when you tried to do better and the moments when you fell short. This process can help you treat yourself with more kindness, understanding that change is rarely a straight line.

For Leah, who was trying to overcome a habit of self-criticism, journaling became a way to acknowledge her progress and forgive her setbacks. When she caught herself slipping into negative self-talk, she would write it down, along with a few words of encouragement to herself. Over time, her journal became a space where she could confront her inner critic and replace it with a gentler voice. It didn't happen overnight, but through her journaling practice, Leah learned to see her efforts as a journey rather than a destination.

The Journey of Self-Discovery

Journaling is more than just a way to track your habits; it's a journey of self-discovery. It invites you to explore the underlying reasons behind your actions, to become curious about your own behavior, and to see yourself with a clearer lens. Through the pages of a journal, you can capture the moments of insight, the turning points, and the small but significant changes that mark your path forward.

Chapter 5: Root Causes of Negative Habits

Psychological Factors Behind Bad Habits

Exploring the psychological factors behind negative habits is crucial for understanding why certain behaviors persist, even when we know they are harmful. Many of the habits that frustrate and hold us back are not just random quirks of behavior; they are deeply rooted in our psychological makeup, shaped by our emotions, beliefs, and past experiences. By uncovering these underlying psychological drivers, we can begin to see our habits in a new light—not as failures of willpower, but as reflections of deeper needs and struggles that need to be addressed.

The Role of Stress and Anxiety

Stress and anxiety are among the most common psychological triggers for negative habits. When life feels overwhelming, the mind often seeks ways to cope with the discomfort, turning to habits that provide a temporary escape or a sense of relief. This is why stress often manifests in behaviors like overeating, smoking, or drinking. These habits offer a quick but fleeting way to manage the tension, even if they create problems in the long run.

Consider the story of Mark, a marketing executive who developed a habit of late-night drinking. The habit began during a particularly stressful period at work, when he found himself struggling to keep up with deadlines and manage the demands of his team. At first, a glass of wine after work seemed harmless - a way to unwind after a long day. But as the pressure at work continued to mount, one glass turned into two, and then three. Before long, the habit became a nightly routine, a way to numb the anxiety that he couldn't seem to shake.

Mark didn't fully understand the psychological roots of his habit until he began talking with a therapist. It turned out that the drinking was less about the wine and more about the need to escape from feelings of inadequacy and fear of failure. He felt like he was constantly on the verge of letting his team down, and the wine became a way to quiet those thoughts, if only for a few hours. By recognizing that his habit was a response to deeper anxieties, Mark was able to start exploring healthier ways to manage his stress, such as practicing mindfulness and setting clearer boundaries at work. The habit didn't disappear overnight, but addressing the psychological root allowed him to regain a sense of control over his life.

Low Self-Esteem and the Cycle of Negative Habits

Low self-esteem can be a powerful psychological driver behind many bad habits, creating a cycle that is difficult to break. When people struggle with feelings of unworthiness or self-doubt, they often engage in behaviors that offer a temporary boost or distraction. But these habits, whether they involve excessive shopping, compulsive eating, or negative self-talk, often reinforce the very feelings they are meant to alleviate.

For Emma, a college student, this cycle was all too familiar. She had always struggled with self-confidence, feeling like she never quite measured up to her peers. To cope with these feelings, Emma developed a habit of online shopping. Whenever she felt down or insecure, she would browse through clothing and accessory websites, buying things she didn't really need. The rush of buying a new dress or a pair of shoes made her feel better for a moment, like she was taking control of her image. But the relief was short-lived, replaced by guilt when she saw the credit card bills piling up.

It wasn't until Emma began to explore the deeper reasons behind her habit that she realized how much of it was tied to her self-worth. She had convinced herself that looking a certain way would make her feel better about herself, but the habit was only masking her deeper insecurities. With the help of a counselor, Emma began to work on building her self-esteem from within, learning to appreciate herself beyond her appearance. As her confidence grew, the urge to shop compulsively began to fade, replaced by a desire to invest in experiences and relationships that truly made her feel valued.

Perfectionism and the Fear of Imperfection

Perfectionism is another psychological factor that can fuel negative habits. For many, the drive to be perfect creates an underlying fear of making mistakes, which can manifest in habits like procrastination, over-preparation, or avoiding challenges altogether. This fear can be paralyzing, leading people to put off tasks they feel they can't do perfectly or to seek comfort in routines that allow them to avoid the possibility of failure.

Take Daniel, a graphic designer who struggled with a habit of procrastinating on client projects. He would spend hours organizing his workspace, researching design trends, or even working on other, less important projects—anything to avoid starting the work he was afraid he wouldn't get right. On the surface, it looked like he was just avoiding work, but in reality, he was avoiding the possibility of not meeting his own high standards.

Daniel's habit of procrastination was rooted in a deep-seated fear of imperfection. He felt that if he didn't produce flawless work, he would be exposed as a fraud, someone who didn't deserve his success. The pressure to be perfect made starting a new project feel like stepping into a minefield. By working with a coach, Daniel learned to embrace the idea that imperfections were a natural part of the creative process. He started setting smaller, more manageable goals for each project, allowing himself to create imperfect drafts as a way to get started. As he gradually learned to accept his own limitations, the grip of his perfectionism—and the procrastination it fueled—began to loosen.

Trauma and Subconscious Coping Mechanisms

Trauma, whether from childhood experiences or more recent events, can also give rise to habits that serve as coping mechanisms. These habits often form as ways to manage the pain or confusion that the trauma has left behind. For many, the habits become a way of numbing difficult emotions or recreating a sense of control that was lost during a traumatic experience.

This was the case for Leah, a survivor of a difficult relationship who developed a habit of self-isolation. After years of feeling controlled and emotionally manipulated, she found it hard to trust others, even when they showed her kindness. She became used to spending her weekends alone, avoiding social gatherings and turning down invitations from friends. The habit of isolation became a protective shell, a way to avoid the possibility of being hurt again.

Leah didn't realize how much her habit of isolation was tied to her past trauma until she started journaling about her feelings. She noticed that every time she considered going out or meeting someone new, a wave of anxiety would flood her mind, reminding her of past betrayals. Her habit wasn't about disliking people—it was about trying to keep herself safe.

Understanding this helped Leah take small steps toward rebuilding her social life, like joining a local book club or meeting friends for coffee. It was a slow process, but each step allowed her to reclaim a bit of the trust and connection she had lost.

The Impact of Belief Systems and Mindsets

Our beliefs and mindsets form the lens through which we view the world, and they have a powerful influence on our habits. Limiting beliefs - such as "I'm not good enough" or "I'll never succeed" - can create habits that reinforce these narratives, keeping people stuck in cycles of behavior that align with their negative self-image.

For Alex, a software developer, this mindset took the form of a habit of self-sabotage. He often found himself starting new projects with enthusiasm, only to lose steam and abandon them just as they started to show promise. On some level, Alex believed that he didn't deserve to succeed, that any accomplishment would be short-lived. This belief drove him to sabotage his own efforts, giving up before he could see results.

It wasn't until Alex started working with a mentor that he began to recognize the belief system driving his habit. He realized that his fear of success was rooted in a fear of the unknown—he had become so accustomed to struggling that the idea of thriving felt foreign and unsafe. By challenging these beliefs and gradually exposing himself to small successes, Alex was able to break the cycle of self-sabotage. He learned that his habits were not fixed traits but responses to deeper fears, and that by changing his mindset, he could change his behavior.

Psychological Needs and Unmet Desires

Finally, many habits are rooted in unmet psychological needs, such as the need for connection, validation, or autonomy. When these needs go unfulfilled, people often turn to habits that offer a substitute, even if the fulfillment is only temporary.

For example, Jenna, a nurse working long shifts, developed a habit of constantly checking her social media. She would scroll through Instagram during her breaks, seeking a sense of connection through likes and comments. It wasn't until she began reflecting on her behavior that she realized how lonely she felt despite being surrounded by people all day. Her habit of seeking validation online was a way of filling the gap left by a lack of deeper, real-life connections.

This insight led Jenna to make a conscious effort to reconnect with friends and family outside of work. She started organizing small gatherings and making time for weekly calls with her sister. The habit of constantly checking her phone didn't vanish immediately, but as her need for real connection was met in more meaningful ways, the urge to seek validation online began to diminish.

Seeing the Bigger Picture of Bad Habits

Understanding the psychological factors behind negative habits allows us to see them for what they truly are— expressions of our deepest fears, desires, and needs. These habits are not simply flaws or failures of self-discipline; they are attempts to cope with the complex emotional landscape of being human. By addressing the underlying psychology, we can transform our approach to habit change, focusing not just on the behaviors themselves but on healing the root causes that drive them.

Emotional Triggers and Stress Responses

One of the most significant factors influencing our habits is the presence of emotional triggers and the way we respond to stress. These moments of heightened emotion—whether they involve anxiety, sadness, frustration, or even boredom—often lead to behaviors that feel automatic, like reaching for a snack, lighting a cigarette, or compulsively checking our phones. Understanding how emotional triggers and stress responses shape our habits is key to unraveling why certain behaviors persist despite our best efforts to change them.

The Connection Between Emotions and Habits

Human beings are inherently emotional creatures, and our habits often serve as coping mechanisms for dealing with these emotions. When life becomes overwhelming or emotions rise to the surface, the brain seeks comfort, safety, or distraction. For many people, this means turning to habits that offer a quick sense of relief, even if those habits come with negative consequences in the long run.

Take, for instance, the story of Alex, a young professional who found himself habitually eating sweets late at night. It wasn't just a craving for sugar that drove him to the kitchen - it was the loneliness and stress he felt after long, demanding days at work. The act of eating a cookie or two gave him a momentary sense of comfort, a small pleasure in the quiet hours before bed. But as the habit continued, he realized that the satisfaction was fleeting, often leaving him feeling worse about himself in the morning. It wasn't until Alex began to understand the emotional trigger behind his habit - the sense of emptiness he felt when the day's busyness faded away - that he could begin to address the deeper need his habit was trying to fulfill.

How Stress Fuels the Cycle of Negative Habits

Stress is one of the most powerful triggers for negative habits, often serving as a catalyst that pushes us toward behaviors we know aren't beneficial. When the body and mind are under stress, they enter a heightened state of arousal, where adrenaline courses through the veins and the heart races. This physiological response can create a sense of urgency, making the mind crave a way to release the tension or regain a sense of control.

For Sarah, a single mother working full-time, stress was a constant companion. Each evening, after putting her kids to bed, she would pour herself a glass of wine and settle in front of the television. At first, it felt like a well-deserved treat, a moment to unwind after the demands of the day. But as the habit continued, Sarah found herself drinking more frequently, even on nights when she didn't particularly want to. The habit became less about enjoyment and more about a need to escape the weight of her responsibilities. The wine dulled the edge of her worries, offering a temporary reprieve from the stress that seemed to loom over her like a shadow.

Sarah didn't fully understand the connection between her stress and her drinking until a friend gently pointed it out. When she took a closer look, she realized that her nightly ritual was less about the wine itself and more about the desire to numb the feelings of exhaustion and anxiety that she carried throughout the day. By recognizing stress as the root of her habit, she began exploring other ways to release that tension - like taking a warm bath or practicing gentle stretches. It wasn't an immediate transformation, but each small step helped her regain a sense of control over her evenings.

Emotional Triggers as Hidden Influences

Emotional triggers often operate beneath the surface of our awareness, subtly influencing our actions without us fully realizing it. These triggers can stem from a range of feelings, such as boredom, frustration, sadness, or even excitement. The brain becomes conditioned to respond to these emotions with specific behaviors, creating habits that feel almost automatic.

Imagine Lisa, a college student who had developed a habit of scrolling through social media whenever she felt bored or lonely. Whenever she was alone in her dorm room with nothing to do, her hand would reach for her phone almost reflexively. It wasn't that she found the endless feed of posts particularly interesting; it was that the act of scrolling provided a distraction from the uncomfortable feeling of being alone with her thoughts. The habit of turning to her phone became a way to fill the emotional void, offering a sense of connection, even if it was superficial.

Lisa's turning point came when she decided to track her screen time and noticed just how much of her day was spent online. She realized that her habit was most pronounced during moments when she felt disconnected from others. This awareness allowed her to explore the underlying emotional trigger – loneliness - and find new ways to address it. She started reaching out to friends more often, scheduling regular meet-ups, and even joined a campus club where she could connect with others face-to-face. As she began to fill her life with more meaningful interactions, the urge to reach for her phone started to fade.

The Role of the Fight-or-Flight Response

At the heart of many stress-driven habits is the fight-or-flight response, a survival mechanism that has evolved to protect us from danger. When faced with a perceived threat, the brain triggers this response, preparing the body to either confront the challenge or flee from it. While this response is invaluable in situations of real physical danger, it can also be triggered by everyday stressors, such as a difficult conversation, a looming deadline, or a financial worry.

For David, a small business owner, the fight-or-flight response played a central role in his habit of snapping at his employees during busy seasons. He didn't understand why he became so irritable when the pressure mounted, often regretting his words as soon as they left his mouth. It felt like an automatic reaction, something beyond his control.

Through therapy, David began to understand that his outbursts were a manifestation of his brain's stress response. When he felt overwhelmed by the demands of his business, his body reacted as if it were facing a threat, pumping adrenaline into his system and heightening his sensitivity to any perceived criticism or setback. His habit of lashing out was his brain's way of trying to regain a sense of control in a situation that felt chaotic.

Recognizing this connection allowed David to approach his stress differently. He started practicing breathing exercises and taking short breaks during the day to calm his nervous system. By addressing the physiological aspect of his stress, he found that he could pause before reacting, giving himself a chance to choose a more constructive response. It wasn't easy, but understanding the role of his body's fight-or-flight response helped him break the cycle of automatic reactions.

Emotional Memory and the Power of Past Experiences

Many emotional triggers are tied to past experiences, where certain situations, places, or even people become associated with specific feelings. These associations can linger long after the original experience has passed, creating habits that are deeply rooted in emotional memory.

Take the example of Carla, who struggled with a habit of avoiding social gatherings. Whenever she received an invitation to a party or a family event, she would find an excuse to stay home, even though she often felt lonely afterwards. It wasn't until she began working with a counselor that Carla realized how much her habit was tied to a difficult experience in high school, where she had been bullied by a group of peers. The memory of feeling excluded and judged had become a silent trigger that surfaced whenever she faced the prospect of being in a social setting.

Carla's habit of avoidance wasn't just about wanting to stay home; it was a protective response to the anxiety and fear that social situations triggered in her. By recognizing this, she began to slowly challenge her habit, starting with small gatherings where she felt more comfortable. She also practiced self-compassion, reminding herself that the fear she felt was rooted in past experiences, not present realities. It took time, but as she gradually built new, positive associations with socializing, her habit of avoidance began to loosen its grip.

Rewriting the Response to Emotional Triggers

Understanding the role of emotional triggers and stress responses in habit formation opens up the possibility for change. When we recognize that our habits are often attempts to cope with uncomfortable feelings, we can begin to explore healthier ways to address those emotions. This process requires self-compassion and patience, as changing a habit means challenging patterns that have become deeply ingrained over time.

For many, like Alex, Sarah, Lisa, David, and Carla, the journey to breaking free from negative habits began with the realization that their behaviors were not just random acts of self-sabotage - they were responses to real emotional needs. By addressing those needs directly, whether through mindfulness, therapy, or simply reaching out to others, they found new ways to cope that didn't rely on old, unhelpful habits.

Environmental and Social Influences

The influence of environment and social circles is often a critical but underestimated factor in understanding why certain habits take hold. The spaces we inhabit and the people we surround ourselves with can shape our behaviors in profound ways, often subtly steering us toward habits that align with the norms and cues of our surroundings. By exploring how these external factors shape our actions, we can begin to see how to reshape our environments and social interactions to foster healthier habits.

The Environment as a Silent Shaper of Habits

Our physical environment exerts a powerful influence over our behavior, often guiding our actions without us even realizing it. Think about how a bowl of candy placed on a desk can encourage frequent snacking or how the presence of a television in the bedroom might lead to a habit of watching shows late into the night. The environment provides cues that trigger automatic behaviors, and these cues can either support or undermine our efforts to develop better habits.

Take the story of Ben, a software developer who struggled with a habit of snacking while working from home. His kitchen was just a few steps away from his desk, and every time he felt even a hint of boredom or frustration, he would find himself wandering into the kitchen to grab a snack. It wasn't until he moved his workspace to a different room - one further from the kitchen - that he realized how much his environment had been driving this behavior. By simply changing the physical setup of his home, Ben found it easier to focus on his work without the constant temptation of the refrigerator.

Ben's experience highlights a key truth about habits: our environment often makes certain behaviors easier or more difficult, guiding us toward specific routines. In his case, the proximity of the kitchen made snacking a natural response to work-related stress. When he altered his environment, he removed a key trigger for his habit, giving himself the mental space to choose a different response. It's a reminder that sometimes, the path to changing a habit isn't about sheer willpower - it's about creating an environment that makes the desired behavior the path of least resistance.

Social Norms and the Influence of Community

Just as the physical environment shapes our habits, so too does the social environment - the people we interact with and the norms they uphold. Human beings are inherently social creatures, and our behaviors are often influenced by the desire to fit in with those around us. This can be a powerful force for positive change, but it can also perpetuate negative habits when they align with group norms.

Consider Maria, who started smoking in her early twenties, not because she particularly enjoyed it, but because all of her friends smoked during their social outings. It became a way to fit in, to share in the camaraderie of the group. Lighting up a cigarette felt like joining in a shared ritual, a way to belong. Even after she began to recognize the health risks and the growing discomfort she felt about her habit, Maria found it incredibly difficult to quit as long as her social circle continued the behavior.

Maria's struggle illustrates how social norms can reinforce habits, making it difficult to break free even when we know a behavior is harmful. It wasn't until one of her closest friends decided to quit smoking that Maria felt empowered to do the same. With a buddy to support her, she began to find new ways to connect with her friends that didn't revolve around smoking. It became easier to resist the old habit when she no longer felt like the odd one out, showing how powerful social influence can be in both creating and breaking habits.

How Social Pressure Shapes Our Behavior

Beyond the desire for belonging, social pressure can also play a role in shaping our habits, pushing us toward behaviors that we might not choose on our own. This pressure can come from direct expectations, like a boss who expects immediate responses to emails, or from more subtle sources, like the competitive atmosphere of a gym or workplace.

For John, a junior lawyer at a prestigious firm, the habit of overworking came from the pressure to keep up with his colleagues. Everyone at the office stayed late, and leaving early was seen as a sign of a lack of commitment. John found himself checking his email at all hours, even on weekends, because it seemed like the norm among his peers. Over time, this habit of constantly being "on" took a toll on his mental health, but breaking it felt impossible as long as he was surrounded by a culture that glorified busyness.

John's story is a common one in high-pressure environments. The habit of overworking was not just a personal choice; it was a response to the social environment that valued long hours over balance. It wasn't until John sought out a mentor outside of his immediate work circle who encouraged him to set boundaries that he began to see an alternative path. He realized that by setting an example of balance, he could slowly shift the expectations in his own team. The support of someone outside the intense work environment helped him break the habit, showing how crucial it is to sometimes look beyond our immediate social circles for guidance and support.

The Role of Family Dynamics in Habit Formation

Family dynamics often play a foundational role in shaping our habits, especially those that take root early in life. The routines, beliefs, and attitudes modeled by parents and siblings can leave a lasting imprint, influencing how we respond to stress, how we view food and exercise, and even how we manage emotions.

For Carla, who grew up in a family where stress was often dealt with through food, emotional eating became a deeply ingrained habit. Her parents would bring out ice cream after a bad day, and family gatherings always centered around large, indulgent meals. As an adult, Carla found herself turning to food whenever she felt overwhelmed, continuing the pattern she had learned as a child. It wasn't just about the taste - it was about the comfort and familiarity of those moments when food made everything feel better.

It wasn't until Carla joined a support group that she began to see how much of her habit was shaped by her upbringing. Sharing her experiences with others who had similar stories helped her understand that she wasn't alone, and it gave her the courage to redefine her relationship with food. She began to explore new ways to soothe herself, like taking up yoga and journaling about her feelings instead of turning to the pantry. By acknowledging the role her family environment had played, Carla was able to break the cycle and create new traditions that focused on connection rather than consumption.

How Changing Environments Can Transform Habits

While our environment can perpetuate negative habits, it can also be a powerful catalyst for change. Sometimes, a shift in surroundings can provide the fresh start needed to break away from old patterns and establish new routines. Moving to a new city, starting a new job, or even rearranging a familiar space can create an opportunity to redefine our behaviors.

This was the case for Tom, who had struggled with a habit of sedentary living. In his old apartment, he was surrounded by convenience - his couch and TV were within arm's reach of the kitchen, and there were few parks or walking trails nearby. But when Tom moved to a new neighborhood with beautiful walking paths and a nearby gym, he found it easier to adopt a more active lifestyle. He started taking morning walks simply because the park was so inviting, and he joined a local running club to meet people. The change in environment provided a natural cue for healthier habits, showing how a new setting can sometimes do more to shift behavior than sheer determination.

Tom's story underscores an important point: while willpower and self-discipline are part of habit change, the power of our environment should not be underestimated. Sometimes, changing the context in which a habit occurs can be the most effective way to change the habit itself.

Crafting an Environment for Positive Change

Recognizing the role that environmental and social influences play in habit formation offers a new way to approach change. It's about becoming intentional with the spaces we inhabit and the people we spend time with. For many, this might mean making small changes - like placing healthy snacks at eye level in the pantry or creating a dedicated space for relaxation that doesn't involve a screen. For others, it might involve rethinking relationships or seeking out new communities that support their goals.

For David, a musician who wanted to cut back on his habit of drinking, it meant finding a new social scene. He realized that most of his drinking took place during gigs and after-parties, where alcohol flowed freely and the expectation was always to join in. By seeking out sober events and venues where the focus was on music rather than drinking, he found that his desire to have a drink waned. The habit that had once felt inseparable from his identity as a musician began to fade as he surrounded himself with people who shared his new values.

David's experience is a reminder that sometimes, changing the people you spend time with can be just as important as changing your physical surroundings. The energy and expectations of those around us have a powerful effect on our habits, and finding a community that supports our desired changes can make the difference between struggling against old patterns and thriving in new ones.

Reclaiming Power Through Awareness

By understanding how environmental and social influences shape our habits, we can begin to reclaim a sense of agency over our behaviors. It's not about blaming our surroundings or our friends for our habits - it's about recognizing how these factors play a role so that we can make conscious choices to change them. Whether it's rearranging a space, setting boundaries in relationships, or seeking out new social circles, these changes can provide the support we need to transform our habits and, ultimately, our lives.

Chapter 6: The Cost of Bad Habits

<u>Physical and Mental Health Implications</u>

Understanding the true cost of bad habits means looking beyond their immediate effects and examining the long-term implications they have on both physical and mental health. While a bad habit may start as a small indulgence or an occasional behavior, over time, its impact can grow, silently eroding well-being in ways that are often difficult to reverse. The hidden toll of these habits can manifest in chronic health issues, mental strain, and a diminished quality of life, creating a cycle that becomes increasingly hard to break.

The Subtle Erosion of Physical Health

Bad habits often carry a physical price, even when their effects aren't immediately noticeable. Consider the habit of poor dietary choices - regularly opting for fast food over balanced meals, or consuming excessive sugar and processed snacks. Initially, these choices might seem like harmless conveniences, especially for someone with a busy lifestyle. But over time, they can lead to a host of physical health problems, from weight gain and digestive issues to more severe conditions like diabetes and heart disease.

Take John, a 35-year-old software engineer who developed a habit of grabbing takeout meals during late-night coding sessions. For John, fast food was a simple solution to the long hours and stress of meeting tight deadlines. It provided a quick hit of energy and comfort after a demanding day. But as the months turned into years, the impact of those choices began to show. John started gaining weight, which affected his stamina and made it harder to focus during the day. What began as a simple convenience soon became a contributing factor to high cholesterol and blood pressure, conditions that required medication and constant monitoring.

John's experience highlights how seemingly minor habits can gradually undermine physical health. It wasn't just about the extra pounds - it was about how those choices accumulated into something much larger, leading to serious health conditions that required significant effort and lifestyle changes to manage. The convenience of fast food had a hidden price, one that he didn't realize until it started affecting his ability to enjoy life and pursue the activities he once loved.

Sleep Deprivation and the Physical Toll of Bad Habits

Another common habit with profound physical consequences is inadequate sleep. In a world that often prioritizes productivity over rest, many people develop the habit of staying up late, whether to finish work, binge-watch a favorite show, or simply scroll through their phones. At first, missing an hour or two of sleep might not seem like a big deal, but chronic sleep deprivation can wreak havoc on the body over time.

For Sarah, a new mother balancing a demanding job and family life, staying up late became a habit she couldn't shake. The quiet hours after her children went to bed were the only time she had to herself, a time when she could catch up on shows or scroll through social media without interruption. But as her nights got shorter and her days remained packed, the effects of sleep loss started to accumulate. She found herself struggling to focus at work, catching colds more frequently, and feeling irritable with her kids.

What Sarah didn't realize was that her habit of sacrificing sleep was compromising her immune system and putting her at risk for more serious conditions like heart disease. Studies have shown that chronic sleep deprivation can lead to hormonal imbalances, increase the risk of obesity, and even impair cognitive function. For Sarah, the habit of staying up late wasn't just cutting into her rest - it was eroding her physical resilience, making it harder for her body to recover and cope with the demands of everyday life.

Mental Health: The Invisible Toll of Negative Habits

While the physical impact of bad habits can often be measured through weight gain or doctor's visits, the mental health implications are usually more insidious, quietly affecting mood, self-esteem, and overall mental well-being. Habits like procrastination, social media overuse, or excessive drinking can serve as temporary escapes from stress or anxiety, but they often leave behind a deeper sense of dissatisfaction and unease.

Consider David, a 29-year-old graphic designer who developed a habit of procrastinating on his creative projects. At first, he found comfort in the distraction of social media, losing himself in endless scrolling whenever a project felt overwhelming. But over time, the habit of avoidance began to take a serious toll on his mental health. As deadlines loomed and his work piled up, he found himself in a constant state of anxiety, caught between the pressure to deliver and the guilt of not making progress.

The habit of procrastination was more than just a time management issue for David - it became a source of chronic stress that affected his self-worth. He began to question his abilities, wondering if he was really cut out for his chosen career. The stress of procrastination spilled over into other areas of his life, affecting his sleep, his relationships, and even his physical health. What began as a way to escape momentary discomfort had become a source of deeper mental strain, creating a cycle of anxiety and self-doubt that was difficult to break.

The Role of Habits in Depression and Anxiety

Some bad habits can exacerbate or even contribute to conditions like depression and anxiety. When people turn to habits like binge-drinking, compulsive shopping, or constant social comparison, they are often seeking a way to fill an emotional void or distract themselves from pain. But rather than addressing the underlying issues, these habits can intensify feelings of emptiness or inadequacy.

For Emily, a 32-year-old teacher, social media became a double-edged sword. At first, it was a way to stay connected with friends and unwind after a long day. But gradually, she found herself spending more and more time comparing her life to the carefully curated posts of others. The habit of scrolling through photos of exotic vacations and happy families made her feel increasingly inadequate, as if she was falling behind in some unspoken race.

Over time, Emily's habit contributed to a growing sense of anxiety and isolation. She found herself withdrawing from real-life interactions, feeling as though she could never measure up to the idealized images she saw online. The habit that once offered a sense of connection had become a source of loneliness and despair, fueling a cycle of self-criticism that deepened her struggle with depression.

Addiction and the Brain's Reward System

The interplay between habits and mental health is perhaps most evident in the realm of addiction, where the brain's reward system becomes entangled with behaviors that provide short-term pleasure at the expense of long-term well-being. Substances like alcohol, nicotine, and even certain foods trigger the release of dopamine, creating a sense of pleasure and reinforcing the desire to repeat the behavior. Over time, the brain becomes wired to seek out these rewards, even when they come with significant physical and mental costs.

This was the case for Mark, who turned to alcohol after losing his job during a difficult economic downturn. At first, drinking helped him cope with the feelings of failure and loss, offering a temporary sense of relief from the pain. But as his drinking became a nightly habit, Mark found it harder to feel any pleasure without a drink in hand. His relationships suffered, and his motivation to find new work waned. The habit of drinking that once dulled his emotional pain began to isolate him further, leaving him trapped in a cycle of dependence and despair.

Addiction illustrates the powerful hold that habits can have over both mind and body. It's a reminder that habits are not just about behaviors - they are about how those behaviors change the chemistry of the brain, creating patterns that are difficult to undo. For Mark, overcoming his habit meant not just addressing the physical dependence on alcohol, but also finding new ways to cope with the emotional pain that had driven him to drink in the first place.

The Cumulative Impact on Quality of Life

The true cost of bad habits lies in their cumulative impact on our overall quality of life. As physical health deteriorates and mental well-being is compromised, it becomes harder to find joy in daily activities, pursue goals, or maintain meaningful relationships. Bad habits can create a sense of being stuck, as if life is passing by while you remain trapped in patterns that no longer serve you.

For many, like John, Sarah, David, Emily, and Mark, the journey to reclaiming their health and happiness began with recognizing the toll their habits had taken. It wasn't about shaming themselves for their behaviors - it was about understanding the deeper reasons behind those habits and finding the courage to address them. As they began to make changes, they discovered that each small step - whether it was taking a daily walk, seeking therapy, or limiting screen time - helped them rebuild the physical and mental resilience that their habits had worn down.

The Hope of Change

The cost of bad habits is real, but so is the potential for transformation. By facing the physical and mental toll head-on, we can begin to make choices that support our well-being rather than undermine it. This journey requires patience and self-compassion, but it is one that offers the promise of a better, healthier life.

<u>Relationship and Social Consequences</u>

the impact of bad habits extends beyond individual well-being and into the realm of relationships and social connections. While we often think of habits as personal choices, their effects ripple outward, influencing how we interact with others, how others perceive us, and ultimately, the quality of our relationships. Over time, these habits can either strengthen the bonds we share with those around us or slowly erode the trust and connection that are the foundation of meaningful relationships.

The Hidden Distance of Distraction

One of the most common ways that habits impact relationships is through distraction. In an age where digital devices are a constant companion, the habit of checking phones or scrolling through social media can create a sense of distance, even when people are physically present with one another. What begins as a simple habit of staying connected online can become a barrier to genuine connection in real life.

Take the story of Rachel, a busy mother who found herself checking her phone during family dinners. At first, it seemed harmless - just a quick glance to check an email or respond to a message. But over time, Rachel's habit became more intrusive, pulling her attention away from her children and their stories about the day. She didn't realize the extent of the problem until her youngest daughter, Emma, asked, "Mom, why are you always looking at your phone when we're eating?"

That simple question was a wake-up call for Rachel. She realized that her habit of distraction was sending an unintended message to her children - that the outside world was more important than the time they spent together. The habit that had started as a way to stay on top of work and social updates was quietly creating a gap between her and her family. Rachel's story is a reminder that habits like constant phone use can undermine the quality of our relationships, making those around us feel unseen or unimportant, even if that's not our intention.

Eroding Trust Through Unreliability

Certain habits can also erode trust within relationships, particularly when they lead to behaviors that others perceive as unreliable or inconsistent. This is especially true when habits like procrastination, forgetfulness, or avoidance affect commitments to friends, family, or colleagues. What may seem like a small personal struggle can create frustration and disappointment for those who rely on us, damaging the trust that holds relationships together.

For example, consider Jason, a talented graphic designer with a habit of procrastinating on tasks. This habit often meant missing deadlines, even when he had promised his friends or colleagues that he would deliver on time. At first, his friends were understanding, attributing his delays to his busy schedule. But as the missed commitments became more frequent, they began to lose confidence in Jason's reliability. Invitations to collaborate on projects or attend social gatherings became less frequent, and friends who once saw him as a trusted ally started to feel let down by his inability to follow through.

Jason's procrastination wasn't just about his own struggles with time management - it had real social consequences that affected how others perceived him. He found himself increasingly isolated, wondering why he felt so disconnected from the people he once considered close. It wasn't until a friend confronted him about his habit that he understood the impact it was having on his relationships. By addressing the root of his procrastination, he was able to start rebuilding the trust he had lost, but the journey was a reminder of how easily habits can create unintended barriers between ourselves and others.

The Strain of Emotional Withdrawal

Some habits can create distance not through physical distraction, but through emotional withdrawal. When people turn to habits like excessive drinking, overeating, or compulsive gaming to cope with stress or negative emotions, they often do so at the expense of engaging with the people around them. Over time, this can create a sense of isolation, as loved ones feel shut out and disconnected from the emotional lives of those they care about.

This was the case for Emily, who turned to alcohol as a way to manage the grief of losing her father. At first, having a glass of wine in the evenings seemed like a way to relax after a difficult day. But as the months passed, the habit became a nightly routine, and the time she spent with her husband and children began to dwindle. Instead of sharing her feelings or leaning on her family for support, Emily found herself retreating into her own world, using alcohol to numb the pain she didn't want to face.

The impact on her family was profound. Her husband, Mark, felt increasingly shut out, as if Emily was drifting further away with each passing evening. He tried to reach out, to encourage her to share what she was feeling, but Emily's habit had become a wall between them. It wasn't until Mark threatened to leave that Emily realized the cost of her habit - not just in terms of her own well-being, but in the distance it had created between her and the people she loved most. Addressing the habit meant more than just cutting back on alcohol - it meant learning to open up emotionally and reconnect with her family in a way that she hadn't done since her father's death.

The Impact of Negativity on Social Bonds

Negative habits, such as chronic complaining, gossiping, or focusing on the worst aspects of any situation, can also have a significant impact on relationships. While these habits may provide a temporary release for pent-up frustration or dissatisfaction, they can drain the energy from conversations and create a negative atmosphere that others find difficult to be around.

For David, a software engineer who frequently vented about the challenges of his job, the habit of complaining became a regular part of his interactions with friends. At first, his friends were sympathetic, offering advice and a listening ear. But as the complaints became a constant theme, they began to feel like they were shouldering David's negativity without getting much in return. The habit turned social gatherings into sessions of frustration rather than moments of joy, making his friends hesitant to spend time with him.

David didn't realize the impact his habit was having until one of his closest friends pointed out that he seemed to be more interested in venting than in truly connecting with others. It was a difficult truth to hear, but it prompted David to reflect on how his habit of complaining had shaped his relationships. He began to make a conscious effort to bring more positivity into his conversations, focusing on gratitude and asking about his friends' lives. As he shifted his approach, he noticed that his friendships began to deepen again, reminding him that habits can shape not only our internal world but also the way we connect with those around us.

Isolation Through Self-Sabotage

Some habits drive people to isolate themselves, not because of external factors, but because of a pattern of self-sabotage. These habits can make it difficult to maintain relationships, as they often involve behaviors that push others away, even when the desire for connection remains strong. Habits like withdrawing during conflict, refusing to apologize, or consistently prioritizing work over time with loved ones can slowly erode the foundation of even the strongest relationships.

Tom, a successful entrepreneur, found himself struggling with this pattern of self-sabotage. He had a habit of immersing himself in work whenever he faced challenges in his relationship with his partner, Jane. Instead of addressing issues head-on, he would spend late nights at the office, telling himself that he was just focusing on providing for their future. But Jane saw his behavior differently—she felt abandoned and unimportant, as if Tom cared more about his business than about their relationship.

The habit of using work as a way to avoid emotional intimacy created a growing rift between them. Jane became increasingly resentful, while Tom felt confused and misunderstood, believing he was doing what was best for their future. It wasn't until they started couples counseling that Tom understood how his habit was pushing Jane away. By learning to communicate more openly and to confront conflicts directly, he was able to start rebuilding the trust that his habit of avoidance had eroded. It was a long and challenging process, but it taught him that habits don't just shape our individual lives - they shape the dynamics of our closest relationships.

The Hidden Cost of Bad Habits: Losing Connection

The ultimate cost of bad habits, when it comes to relationships, is the loss of genuine connection. Habits like distraction, emotional withdrawal, negativity, and avoidance can create a sense of loneliness, even in the presence of those we care about. They can turn time together into a series of missed opportunities for understanding, support, and love. For many, like Rachel, Jason, Emily, David, and Tom, the journey to reclaiming their relationships began with recognizing the role their habits played in creating distance.

Understanding the impact of these habits is not about assigning blame; it's about recognizing the ways in which we unintentionally build walls between ourselves and others. By facing these habits honestly, we can begin to take down those walls and create new patterns that invite connection rather than push it away.

Financial and Career Impacts

The financial and career costs of bad habits often come into sharp focus, revealing how behaviors that seem small or insignificant can accumulate into significant setbacks over time. Habits that drain time, resources, and energy can have a ripple effect, influencing professional growth and financial stability. While many of these habits begin as minor indulgences or simple oversights, their long-term impact can hinder opportunities, derail goals, and create a sense of being stuck in a cycle of missed potential and mounting expenses.

The Financial Drain of Impulsive Spending

One of the most direct ways bad habits impact finances is through impulsive spending. For many, spending money on unnecessary items becomes a way of coping with stress, boredom, or the desire for instant gratification. But what starts as an occasional splurge can quickly turn into a habit that erodes savings and creates a cycle of debt.

Consider the story of Alex, a young professional who, after landing his first well-paying job, found himself indulging in regular online shopping sprees. The thrill of clicking "add to cart" and the anticipation of a package arriving on his doorstep became a comforting routine. It wasn't just about the items he bought - clothes, gadgets, or the latest tech - it was about the feeling of control and reward he got from each purchase. But as the months went by, Alex began to notice that his credit card balances were climbing, even as his bank account dwindled.

At first, he rationalized the habit, telling himself that he deserved to treat himself after working hard. But when he found himself unable to pay off his credit card in full and struggling with the interest charges, the reality set in. His habit of impulsive spending had created a financial burden that was starting to affect his ability to save for larger goals, like buying a home or traveling. The habit, which had begun as a way to reward himself, was now a source of anxiety and stress, creating a vicious cycle where financial strain led to more impulsive purchases as a way to cope.

Procrastination's Hidden Cost on Career Growth

In the professional realm, procrastination is a habit that can have far-reaching consequences. It's not just about missed deadlines or rushed work—it's about the opportunities that slip by and the trust that is eroded over time. When procrastination becomes a regular part of how someone manages their tasks, it can hinder career advancement, affect relationships with colleagues, and create a reputation for unreliability.

For Maria, a project manager at a thriving tech firm, procrastination was a habit she struggled with throughout her career. She often delayed starting key projects, waiting until the last minute before throwing herself into frantic work sessions. While she usually managed to meet her deadlines, the quality of her work often suffered, and her colleagues began to notice her last-minute scramble.

Maria's habit didn't just affect her performance - it also held her back from taking on more significant responsibilities. Her boss, who once saw potential for her to move into a senior role, began to assign high-visibility projects to others, believing that Maria couldn't handle the pressure. She watched as her peers advanced, while she remained in the same position, wondering why her career seemed to be stalling. It wasn't until a mentor pointed out that her procrastination was creating a pattern of missed opportunities that Maria realized the cost of her habit. By working to break the cycle, she began to reclaim her professional reputation, but the delay had already cost her time and growth she could never fully recover.

The Career Risks of Poor Time Management

Time management is another area where bad habits can take a serious toll on both professional success and financial stability. Habits like constantly checking emails, overcommitting to meetings, or failing to prioritize tasks can create a sense of constant busyness without meaningful progress. This can affect job performance, stress levels, and even earning potential.

David, a marketing executive, prided himself on being busy. His calendar was packed with meetings, networking events, and back-to-back calls. But despite the constant activity, he often felt like he was spinning his wheels - working late into the night without making real progress on his goals. David's habit of saying yes to every request left him with little time for strategic thinking or deep work, and his team began to notice that he was often distracted or spread too thin.

This pattern started to affect David's professional reputation. His superiors began to see him as someone who was good at staying busy but not necessarily effective in delivering results. When it came time for promotions, David was often passed over in favor of colleagues who seemed more focused and strategic. The habit of poor time management had trapped him in a cycle of working harder without advancing, creating a financial ceiling he couldn't seem to break through. It wasn't until he learned to set boundaries and focus on his highest priorities that David began to see a shift in his career trajectory.

The Financial Impact of Addictive Behaviors

Addictive behaviors like gambling, smoking, or excessive drinking can also have a direct impact on financial stability. The costs of these habits extend beyond the price of the behavior itself - like lottery tickets or packs of cigarettes - and into the broader effects on work performance, health, and relationships. These habits can drain financial resources while also undermining a person's ability to maintain steady employment or pursue career advancement.

For Tom, a successful sales manager, gambling started as a fun weekend activity with friends. But over time, what began as a casual habit turned into something more destructive. He found himself visiting the casino more frequently, often spending more money than he intended. The thrill of winning was quickly overshadowed by the losses, and Tom began dipping into his savings to cover his gambling expenses. When he started missing payments on his mortgage and struggling to keep up with bills, he realized that his habit was spiraling out of control.

The impact on his career was equally significant. Tom's habit began to affect his focus and motivation at work, and his performance started to decline. He found himself distracted during meetings, thinking about the next time he could visit the casino. Eventually, his boss noticed the drop in his sales numbers and warned him that he needed to get back on track. The habit that had started as a way to unwind was now threatening not just his financial security, but also his professional future. Seeking help and confronting the addiction was a difficult step, but it allowed Tom to begin repairing the damage and rebuilding his life.

Undermining Professional Relationships Through Habits

Certain habits can also have indirect financial impacts by damaging professional relationships and networking opportunities. For instance, habits like constant complaining, gossiping, or being consistently late to meetings can create friction with colleagues and managers, limiting opportunities for collaboration and advancement. These habits can create an atmosphere where people hesitate to work with someone, even if their skills and abilities are strong.

Sara, an accountant at a mid-sized firm, had a habit of being late to meetings. She often underestimated how long it would take to wrap up tasks or get across town for a client appointment, arriving several minutes late more often than not. While she didn't think much of it at first, her colleagues began to see her as disrespectful of their time. Over time, this habit started to affect her standing within the firm. She noticed that she was no longer invited to certain strategic planning sessions, and her input was sought out less frequently for important decisions.

The cost of this habit wasn't just a matter of missed meetings - it was about the opportunities that slipped away as her colleagues' perception of her changed. When a chance for a partnership role opened up, Sara found herself out of the running, with feedback that her reliability was a concern. It wasn't until she made a concerted effort to address her habit and prove her commitment to punctuality that she began to repair her reputation, but the delay had already cost her a step forward in her career.

The Long-Term Cost: Missed Investments and Savings

Bad habits can also undermine long-term financial goals, such as saving for retirement, investing in education, or building an emergency fund. Habits like spending on small luxuries - daily coffees, dining out, or buying the latest gadgets - might not seem significant in the moment, but their cumulative impact can be substantial. These habits can prevent people from building the financial security that allows them to weather unexpected challenges or take advantage of new opportunities.

Rebecca, a nurse who dreamed of buying a home, found herself constantly struggling to save enough for a down payment. Each month, she planned to set aside a portion of her paycheck, but her habit of dining out and treating herself to new clothes would often get in the way. She told herself that each purchase was a reward for her hard work, but as the months turned into years, she realized that her savings account was barely growing.

Rebecca's habit wasn't just about overspending - it was about the missed opportunities that came with it. When the real estate market offered a rare dip in prices, she found herself unprepared to take advantage of it, while some of her friends were able to buy their first homes. It was a painful realization that her habit of small indulgences had cost her a chance to achieve a dream she had held for years. By working with a financial advisor and setting stricter limits on her discretionary spending, Rebecca was eventually able to turn things around, but the lesson stayed with her: even small habits can have a big impact on long-term financial health.

Reclaiming Control Over Finances and Career

The financial and career impacts of bad habits often become apparent only after they have already created significant challenges. But by understanding these impacts, it becomes possible to take action, reclaim control, and turn things around. Whether it's breaking the cycle of impulsive spending, addressing procrastination, or setting better time management practices, the journey to financial and career stability often starts with recognizing the role that habits play.

For many, like Alex, Maria, David, Tom, Sara, and Rebecca, the path to overcoming these challenges began with a moment of clarity - a realization that their habits were costing them more than they had imagined. Addressing these habits wasn't always easy, but it allowed them to rebuild their professional reputations, regain financial stability, and start moving toward the goals they had once thought were out of reach.

Part III: Taking Control of Your Habits
Chapter 7: Mindfulness and Self-Awareness

<u>The Importance of Being Present</u>

The journey toward breaking free from negative patterns often begins with the practice of mindfulness and self-awareness, particularly through the power of being present. At its core, being present means engaging fully with the current moment, experiencing life as it unfolds without being trapped in thoughts of the past or worries about the future. This seemingly simple shift in focus can have a profound impact on how we understand and manage our habits, offering a path to greater control and a deeper connection with our inner selves.

Rediscovering the Present Moment

For many people, daily life can feel like a whirlwind of tasks, thoughts, and responsibilities. It's easy to become caught in a cycle of autopilot, where routines take over, and days blur into one another without a sense of true awareness. This is where the power of being present comes in—it offers a way to slow down and reconnect with the sensations, thoughts, and emotions that make up each moment. By cultivating presence, we can begin to notice the subtle triggers and reactions that drive our habits, providing an opportunity to make different choices.

Consider Emily, a marketing executive who found herself constantly distracted. Her habit of checking emails and social media throughout the day made it difficult for her to focus on her work, leaving her feeling frazzled and unproductive by the end of each day. She would often wonder where the time had gone, frustrated that she had so little to show for her hours of effort. It wasn't until a friend introduced her to mindfulness practices that she began to see how her lack of presence was fueling her habits.

Emily started by dedicating just a few minutes each morning to a simple mindfulness exercise - closing her eyes, taking deep breaths, and tuning into the sensations of her body. At first, it felt strange and uncomfortable; her mind would wander, and she struggled to sit still. But as she continued the practice, something shifted. She began to notice how often her mind drifted during the day, how frequently she reached for her phone whenever she felt a hint of boredom or anxiety. The habit of distraction that had once felt automatic now appeared as a choice - one that she could accept or let go of.

This newfound awareness transformed how Emily approached her workday. Instead of letting her thoughts pull her into a spiral of distractions, she started to practice bringing her attention back to the task at hand, taking a few mindful breaths whenever she felt the urge to check her phone. Being present didn't eliminate the habit overnight, but it gave her the power to see it for what it was - a response to discomfort - and to choose a different path.

How Presence Creates Space for Choice

One of the most powerful aspects of being present is that it creates a space between impulse and action—a moment of awareness that allows us to see our habits clearly before we act on them. This space is where change becomes possible. When we are not fully present, we tend to react to situations in habitual ways, driven by old patterns and automatic responses. But when we bring our attention to the present moment, we can interrupt those automatic reactions and make conscious choices.

For David, a high school teacher with a habit of snapping at his students when he felt stressed, this realization was life-changing. He had always prided himself on being a patient teacher, but in recent years, he noticed that his frustration would boil over more quickly, especially on difficult days. It was as if his stress took control, leaving him feeling guilty and disappointed in himself after each outburst. He knew he wanted to change, but he didn't know how to stop himself in the heat of the moment.

It wasn't until David attended a mindfulness workshop that he began to understand the power of being present. The instructor taught a simple technique: when you feel an emotion rising, pause and take three deep breaths, focusing fully on the sensation of the air moving in and out. David began to practice this technique, and the next time he felt himself getting frustrated with a disruptive student, he remembered to pause. Those three breaths didn't eliminate his frustration, but they created a moment of calm where he could choose how to respond. Instead of raising his voice, he was able to address the student more calmly, turning what could have been a tense moment into an opportunity for connection.

The practice of being present helped David reclaim control over his reactions, reminding him that he had the power to choose how he responded to his emotions. It showed him that his habit of lashing out wasn't inevitable - it was a pattern that he could change, one mindful moment at a time.

Deepening Self-Awareness Through Mindful Presence

Being present isn't just about changing external behaviors; it's also about deepening our understanding of ourselves. When we are fully present, we can observe the thoughts, emotions, and physical sensations that accompany our habits. This awareness allows us to explore why certain habits have taken root in our lives and what needs or desires they are trying to fulfill.

For Sarah, a writer who struggled with a habit of overeating, this self-awareness became a key part of her healing process. Sarah had always turned to food for comfort, especially when she felt anxious or lonely. She had tried diets and exercise routines, but nothing seemed to change her relationship with food. It wasn't until she began practicing mindful eating that she discovered how much of her habit was driven by emotional hunger rather than physical need.

Sarah started by simply paying attention to each bite, noticing the taste, texture, and smell of her food. At first, it felt tedious, but soon she realized that she often ate without really tasting her meals, using food as a way to distract herself from uncomfortable feelings. By bringing her full presence to the act of eating, she began to notice when she was truly hungry and when she was eating to fill an emotional void. This awareness allowed her to explore other ways to address those feelings - like journaling or taking a walk - rather than automatically turning to food.

The process wasn't always easy, and there were still times when Sarah found herself slipping into old patterns. But the practice of being present gave her a new understanding of her habit, one that was rooted in compassion rather than self-judgment. It taught her that change was not about denying herself but about learning to listen more deeply to her own needs.

The Ripple Effect of Presence in Daily Life

The practice of being present doesn't just impact specific habits - it can transform the way we experience life as a whole. When we are truly present, we become more attuned to the beauty and richness of each moment, whether it's the warmth of the sun on our face, the sound of a friend's laughter, or the simple pleasure of a quiet cup of tea. This shift in perspective can bring a sense of gratitude and contentment that makes it easier to let go of habits that no longer serve us.

For Michael, a corporate executive with a habit of constant work, learning to be present helped him reconnect with his life outside the office. He had spent years chasing professional success, always focused on the next goal or milestone. But as he practiced mindfulness, he realized how much of his life he had been missing - the joy of playing with his kids, the quiet moments with his partner, the peaceful walks in the park. By learning to be fully present, he began to find satisfaction in the simple, everyday moments that he had once overlooked.

This new perspective didn't just make Michael happier - it also made it easier for him to break his habit of overworking. He started setting boundaries around his work hours, allowing himself to truly disconnect at the end of the day. The need to constantly prove himself through work began to fade as he discovered a deeper sense of worth in the time he spent with his family. Being present showed him that the life he had been striving for was already there, waiting for him to notice.

The Power of Presence in Transforming Habits

The importance of being present lies in its ability to shift the way we relate to our habits. It allows us to move from a place of mindless reactivity to a space of intentional action. By cultivating presence, we can observe our habits with clarity, understand the needs they are trying to meet, and choose new behaviors that align with our true values.

For many, like Emily, David, Sarah, and Michael, the journey toward breaking free from negative habits began with small moments of awareness - a breath, a pause, a deeper look at what was driving their behavior. These moments became the foundation for lasting change, helping them reclaim control over their actions and reconnect with the present moment.

Techniques to Increase Mindfulness

Mindfulness is a key tool for gaining control over habits that seem to operate beyond our conscious awareness. But mindfulness is not just a state of being - it's a skill that can be cultivated through specific techniques. These practices allow us to tune into the present moment, observe our thoughts and feelings without judgment, and create the space needed to make different choices. As mindfulness deepens, it transforms the way we interact with our habits, helping us to break free from automatic reactions and foster a greater sense of self-awareness.

Mindful Breathing: Finding Calm in the Chaos

One of the simplest and most powerful techniques for increasing mindfulness is mindful breathing. This practice involves paying close attention to the rhythm of your breath, feeling the air as it moves in and out of your body. While it may sound basic, mindful breathing can have a profound

136

effect on your ability to focus and center yourself, especially when you're feeling overwhelmed or caught up in the cycle of a bad habit.

Consider Mark, a manager at a bustling retail store, who often found himself stressed and reactive during the busy holiday season. His habit of snapping at employees and rushing through tasks left him feeling guilty and disconnected from his team. A colleague suggested he try mindful breathing as a way to calm down before difficult conversations. Skeptical at first, Mark decided to give it a try.

He started by taking just a few minutes before each shift to sit quietly in his office, closing his eyes and focusing on his breath. He noticed how his thoughts would wander - worrying about customer complaints or anticipating the next task - but he gently brought his focus back to the sensation of breathing. As he continued this practice, he found that he was able to carry this sense of calm into his workday. When stressful moments arose, he used the technique to ground himself, taking a deep breath before responding.

The practice of mindful breathing didn't eliminate stress from Mark's life, but it helped him approach challenges with greater composure. He found that by pausing to focus on his breath, he could step back from the urgency of his reactions, creating a moment of choice where he could respond more thoughtfully. This simple technique became a cornerstone of his journey toward managing his stress and building healthier interactions with his team.

Body Scan Meditation: Listening to the Wisdom of the Body

Another technique for cultivating mindfulness is the body scan meditation, which involves directing your attention to different parts of your body, noticing any sensations, tension, or areas of relaxation. This practice helps you become more attuned to the physical manifestations of stress, anxiety, or discomfort that often accompany bad habits.

For Jenna, a writer who struggled with chronic anxiety, the body scan became a transformative practice. She noticed that whenever she sat down to write, she would tense her shoulders and clench her jaw without even realizing it. This tension made writing feel like a battle, adding to her habit of procrastination. Through body scan meditation, Jenna learned to recognize these subtle signs of stress before they overwhelmed her.

Each morning, she would lie down on her yoga mat and slowly move her attention from her toes to the top of her head, noticing where she held tension. She discovered that by simply acknowledging the tightness in her shoulders or the fluttering in her stomach, she could begin to release those sensations. This awareness spilled over into her writing sessions - when she felt herself tensing up, she would pause, take a deep breath, and gently relax her muscles.

The body scan meditation taught Jenna to listen to the signals her body was sending, helping her to break the cycle of stress that had fueled her procrastination. It became a way for her to connect more deeply with herself, transforming her writing process from a source of anxiety into an opportunity for mindfulness.

Mindful Walking: Bringing Awareness to Everyday Movements

Mindfulness doesn't have to be confined to sitting meditation or quiet moments - it can also be practiced through movement, like mindful walking. This technique involves paying attention to the sensations of each step, feeling the ground beneath your feet, and noticing the rhythm of your movements. It's a way to bring mindfulness into everyday life, turning something as simple as walking into an opportunity for presence.

For Tom, a busy entrepreneur who rarely had time for meditation, mindful walking became his preferred mindfulness practice. He started by taking short walks during his lunch breaks, focusing on the feeling of his feet hitting the pavement and the sound of the wind rustling through the trees. At first, his mind raced with thoughts of emails to answer and projects to complete, but he gently guided his attention back to the act of walking.

As he practiced, Tom found that these walks became a refuge from the demands of his work. He began to look forward to the quiet time, using it as a way to reset his mind and return to his office with a clearer head. Mindful walking helped him become more aware of the tension he carried in his body and the way his thoughts affected his mood throughout the day.

The practice of mindful walking showed Tom that mindfulness didn't have to be an added burden on his already full schedule. Instead, it became a way to bring a sense of calm and awareness into the flow of his daily life, helping him manage stress and approach his work with greater focus.

Observing Thoughts Without Judgment: The Power of Non-Reactivity

One of the challenges of mindfulness is learning to observe your thoughts without getting caught up in them. This technique involves noticing thoughts as they arise, acknowledging them without labeling them as good or bad, and allowing them to pass like clouds in the sky. It's particularly helpful for breaking free from the stories and narratives that often drive habits, like thoughts of self-doubt or the urge for instant gratification.

For Priya, a college student struggling with a habit of self-criticism, this practice was a game-changer. She had always been her own harshest critic, constantly berating herself for not studying hard enough or comparing herself to her more successful peers. These thoughts made her feel stuck, leading to a cycle of anxiety and avoidance.

When she began practicing mindfulness, Priya learned to observe her thoughts without immediately reacting to them. She would sit for a few minutes each evening, noticing the stream of thoughts that flowed through her mind. When a self-critical thought appeared - like "I'm never going to be good enough" - she would acknowledge it, label it as "thinking," and gently bring her attention back to her breath.

This practice didn't make the thoughts disappear, but it helped Priya see them for what they were - just thoughts, not truths. By observing her mind without getting swept away by negative narratives, she found a new sense of freedom. She was able to study with less pressure and approach her goals with more kindness toward herself. The habit of self-criticism began to lose its power as Priya discovered that she had the ability to choose how much attention she gave to her thoughts.

Gratitude Practice: Cultivating Positive Focus

Gratitude is another technique that can enhance mindfulness by shifting focus from what is lacking or negative to what is present and positive. A daily gratitude practice involves taking a few moments each day to reflect on things you are thankful for, helping to reframe your mindset and bring awareness to the positive aspects of life.

For David, a small business owner dealing with financial struggles, gratitude became a way to navigate challenging times. He had developed a habit of dwelling on his worries - about bills, slow sales, and the uncertainty of the market. This focus on what wasn't working made it difficult for him to see the progress he was making, leading to feelings of defeat.

A mentor suggested that David try keeping a gratitude journal. Each night before bed, he wrote down three things he was grateful for, no matter how small. Some days, it was as simple as a kind word from a customer or a beautiful sunset. Other days, it was the support of his family or the satisfaction of completing a difficult task.

Over time, David noticed that this practice helped him start each day with a more positive outlook. It didn't erase the challenges he faced, but it reminded him of the good things that existed alongside them. Gratitude helped him become more present to the moments of joy and connection in his life, creating a buffer against the anxiety that had once consumed his thoughts.

The Path of Mindfulness: A Daily Practice of Awareness

These techniques - mindful breathing, body scan meditation, mindful walking, observing thoughts, and gratitude - are all ways to deepen your mindfulness practice and build a foundation of presence. For many, like Mark, Jenna, Tom, Priya, and David, these practices became stepping stones on the path to greater self-awareness and habit transformation. They discovered that mindfulness wasn't just about sitting quietly - it was about engaging with life in a more conscious and deliberate way, creating the space needed to understand and change their habits.

Meditation and Its Role in Habit Change

Meditation emerges as a powerful ally in the process of changing habits. While often perceived as a practice of sitting quietly with a clear mind, meditation is much more dynamic and transformative. It is a tool that helps individuals develop greater awareness of their thoughts, emotions, and behaviors, offering the clarity needed to break free from automatic patterns and make more intentional choices. For those looking to change habits, meditation serves as both a mirror and a guide, revealing the underlying processes that drive behaviors and providing the mental space to reshape them.

Meditation as a Mirror for Self-Reflection

At its core, meditation is a practice of self-reflection. It creates a space where we can observe our thoughts without judgment, becoming more attuned to the patterns that govern our minds. For many, habits are like well-worn paths, ingrained over time through repetition and reinforced by unconscious thoughts. Meditation helps to bring these hidden pathways into the light, allowing us to see the impulses, cravings, and emotional triggers that fuel our behaviors.

Take the story of Mia, a marketing director who struggled with a habit of overeating whenever she felt stressed. For years, Mia believed that she simply lacked willpower, berating herself for not being able to resist late-night snacks. It wasn't until she began practicing meditation that she started to understand the deeper roots of her behavior. During her meditation sessions, she would sit quietly and focus on her breath, noticing the thoughts and feelings that surfaced.

As she continued this practice, Mia began to recognize a pattern: whenever she thought about a stressful meeting or an upcoming deadline, her mind would drift to thoughts of comfort foods - cookies, chips, anything that would offer a quick hit of pleasure. Through meditation, she saw that her habit wasn't about a lack of discipline—it was a response to her anxiety, a way of seeking comfort during moments of stress.

This insight was a turning point for Mia. By understanding the link between her emotions and her habit, she was able to approach her cravings with more compassion and curiosity. Instead of fighting the urge to snack, she learned to sit with the feeling, observing it as it rose and fell like a wave. This process of self-reflection helped her to gradually change her relationship with food, shifting from automatic reactions to more mindful choices.

Creating Space Between Impulse and Action

One of the most powerful aspects of meditation is its ability to create space between impulse and action. Habits often feel automatic, as if there's no gap between the desire to act and the action itself. Meditation helps to slow down this process, offering a moment of pause where we can choose a different path. It's like pressing the "pause" button on a mental movie, allowing us to consider our options before moving forward.

For Jack, a software engineer with a habit of smoking, meditation became a crucial part of his journey to quit. He had tried to quit smoking multiple times, but each attempt ended in frustration as he gave in to the cravings. His doctor suggested that he try meditation as a way to cope with the urges. At first, Jack was skeptical - how could sitting quietly possibly help with something as intense as nicotine cravings? But with nothing to lose, he decided to give it a try.

Jack started with short sessions, sitting for ten minutes each morning and focusing on his breath. When a craving arose, he would bring his attention to the sensation, observing how it felt in his body without immediately reaching for a cigarette. He noticed that the urge often came as a tightness in his chest or a restless feeling in his hands. Instead of reacting to it, he practiced breathing through the discomfort, watching as the craving slowly subsided.

Over time, Jack found that the space created by meditation allowed him to respond to his cravings differently. He realized that he didn't have to act on every impulse - that he could let the urge come and go like a passing cloud. This newfound awareness gave him the strength to resist smoking, not through sheer willpower, but by changing his relationship with the craving itself. Meditation became his anchor, helping him stay grounded during the most challenging moments of his habit change.

Rewiring the Brain Through Mindful Awareness

Meditation is not just about observing thoughts; it also plays a role in rewiring the brain. Neuroscience has shown that meditation can change the structure of the brain, strengthening areas associated with self-control and emotional regulation. This process, known as neuroplasticity, means that our brains are not fixed - they can adapt and grow in response to new experiences. For those looking to change habits, meditation offers a way to reshape the neural pathways that drive behavior.

For Ella, a graphic designer who struggled with a habit of negative self-talk, meditation helped her rewire the patterns that kept her stuck in a cycle of self-doubt. Every time she made a mistake or faced criticism, her mind would flood with thoughts like "I'm not good enough" or "I'll never succeed."

These thoughts fueled a habit of withdrawing from challenges, avoiding opportunities that could have advanced her career.

When she began practicing loving-kindness meditation, a form of meditation that involves silently repeating phrases of goodwill and compassion toward oneself and others, she found it incredibly difficult at first. It felt unnatural to wish herself well, to tell herself, "May I be happy. May I be healthy. May I be at peace." But as she continued the practice, she noticed a shift. Her inner critic began to soften, and she became more aware of when the negative thoughts started to creep in.

This awareness allowed Ella to catch the thoughts before they spiraled out of control. She learned to replace them with kinder, more encouraging messages, slowly building a new habit of self-compassion. The practice of meditation didn't just change her mindset - it changed her brain, helping her develop a more positive outlook and a greater sense of resilience in the face of challenges.

Meditation as a Tool for Emotional Regulation

Habits are often deeply tied to our emotional states. When we feel stressed, anxious, or overwhelmed, we turn to habits that provide temporary relief, whether it's scrolling through social media, eating comfort food, or engaging in compulsive shopping. Meditation helps us to understand and manage these emotions, offering a way to soothe ourselves without relying on external behaviors.

For Daniel, a high school teacher with a habit of emotional eating, meditation became a lifeline during difficult moments. After particularly stressful days at school, he found himself reaching for snacks as soon as he got home, using food to numb the tension and frustration that had built up throughout the day. He knew that this habit was affecting his health, but he didn't know how to cope with the emotions in a healthier way.

A friend suggested that he try a practice called RAIN, a mindfulness technique that stands for Recognize, Allow, Investigate, and Nurture. Daniel began using this meditation whenever he felt the urge to eat out of stress. He would sit quietly and recognize the emotion he was feeling - acknowledging it without trying to push it away. He would then allow the emotion to be there, giving himself permission to feel the tension and discomfort. Investigating it, he would ask himself where the feeling was coming from - was it frustration with a student, anxiety about a meeting, or simply exhaustion? Finally, he would nurture himself, offering a kind word or placing a hand on his heart.

This practice helped Daniel to see that his habit of eating wasn't really about hunger - it was about needing comfort and support after a challenging day. By turning inward and offering himself that compassion, he found that the urge to eat began to fade. Meditation taught him that he could meet his emotional needs directly, without relying on external sources of comfort.

Cultivating Patience and Persistence Through Meditation

Changing habits is not an overnight process - it requires patience, persistence, and a willingness to face setbacks with resilience. Meditation supports this process by helping us cultivate a mindset of acceptance and non-judgment, allowing us to approach habit change with a sense of curiosity rather than frustration.

For Kevin, an aspiring entrepreneur, meditation became a way to manage the impatience that had always sabotaged his efforts to develop new habits. He had tried to build a habit of daily exercise multiple times, but each time he didn't see immediate results, he would lose motivation and give up. Meditation taught him to approach his goals with a different mindset.

During his meditation sessions, Kevin practiced focusing on the present moment, letting go of his attachment to outcomes. He learned to appreciate each step of the process - the feeling of his muscles working, the rhythm of his breath, the satisfaction of showing up for himself day after day. Meditation helped him realize that the journey was just as important as the destination.

This shift in perspective allowed Kevin to persevere through the challenges of building his exercise routine. He no longer judged himself for slow progress; instead, he celebrated the small victories along the way. Meditation taught him that lasting change comes from consistency and compassion, not from harsh self-criticism. It gave him the patience he needed to stick with his new habit, ultimately leading to the results he had always hoped for.

The Transformative Power of Meditation in Habit Change

Meditation is more than just a relaxation technique - it is a path to deeper understanding and transformation. By creating a space for self-reflection, rewiring the brain, regulating emotions, and fostering patience, meditation offers the tools needed to change habits from the inside out. For many, like Mia, Jack, Ella, Daniel, and Kevin, meditation became the key that unlocked their ability to break free from old patterns and build new, healthier ones.

Chapter 8: Setting Clear Intentions and Goals

<u>Defining What You Want to Achieve</u>

The process of setting clear intentions and goals begins with a critical first step: defining what you truly want to achieve. This step is about more than just identifying a goal - it's about digging deep into your desires, understanding your motivations, and clarifying what success looks like for you. It's the foundation upon which all habit change is built, giving you a sense of direction and purpose as you navigate the challenges of breaking old patterns and building new ones. Without a clear understanding of what you want, the journey can feel aimless, like setting sail without a destination in mind.

Uncovering Your True Motivations

Defining what you want to achieve requires a level of honesty and introspection that can be both empowering and challenging. It's about looking beyond surface-level desires and asking yourself why a particular goal matters to you. This process helps you connect with the deeper reasons behind your aspirations, turning vague wishes into concrete intentions.

Take the story of Rebecca, a nurse who had struggled for years with a habit of skipping her morning exercise routine. Every New Year, she would set a resolution to work out regularly, telling herself that she wanted to "get in shape" or "be healthier." But as the weeks went by, her motivation would fizzle, and she would fall back into her old pattern of hitting the snooze button instead of getting up for a workout. It wasn't until a health scare forced her to take a closer look at her habits that Rebecca realized she needed to define her goal more clearly.

During a long conversation with her doctor, Rebecca acknowledged her fears about aging and the impact of her sedentary lifestyle on her long-term health. She realized that her true motivation wasn't just about looking a certain way it was about being able to keep up with her kids, feeling strong as she aged, and reducing her risk of chronic illness. This shift in perspective helped Rebecca see her goal in a new light. Instead of aiming to "get in shape," she redefined her intention as "building a lifestyle that supports my health and energy for the long term." This clarity gave her a sense of purpose that went far beyond aesthetics, helping her commit to the changes she needed to make.

Rebecca's story illustrates how important it is to dig deep when defining what you want to achieve. By connecting with the underlying reasons behind her goal, she turned a vague aspiration into a clear, personal mission - one that carried emotional weight and inspired her to take consistent action.

Painting a Clear Picture of Success

Once you understand your true motivations, the next step in defining what you want to achieve is to create a vivid picture of what success looks like. This process involves imagining the outcome of your efforts in as much detail as possible, giving you a mental image to strive toward. A clear vision can act as a guiding star, reminding you of where you're headed even when the path becomes difficult.

For Marcus, a sales executive who wanted to break his habit of procrastination, this exercise was a game-changer. He had spent years telling himself that he needed to "stop putting things off," but the goal felt abstract and distant. He knew he wanted to be more productive, but he had never taken the time to imagine what his life would actually look like if he succeeded. One evening, a mentor challenged him to close his eyes and visualize his ideal workday, down to the smallest detail.

Marcus pictured himself waking up early, feeling energized and ready to tackle the day. He imagined starting each morning with a clear plan, focusing on his most important tasks before checking emails or social media. He saw himself wrapping up his workday on time, feeling a sense of accomplishment as he closed his laptop and headed out for a run. In this vision, Marcus wasn't just managing his time better—he was living a life that felt balanced and fulfilling, with room for both career success and personal well-being.

This exercise helped Marcus see his goal as something tangible and achievable. He no longer focused solely on the habit he wanted to break – procrastination - but on the life he wanted to build. This vision became a source of motivation, helping him stay on track even when old habits tried to creep back in. By defining success in concrete terms, Marcus gave himself a destination to aim for, transforming his goal from a vague desire into a clear, inspiring target.

Setting the Stage for Commitment

Defining what you want to achieve also means being specific about the changes you're willing to make and the steps you're ready to take. It's about turning your vision into actionable commitments that can guide your daily choices. This level of specificity helps to bridge the gap between intention and action, making it easier to stay focused and measure progress along the way.

For Naomi, a writer with a habit of starting projects but never finishing them, this process was crucial. She had always dreamed of publishing a novel, but her goal had remained a distant fantasy for years. She would start with a burst of inspiration, only to lose momentum after a few chapters, abandoning one manuscript after another. It wasn't until she sat down with a writing coach that Naomi began to understand the importance of defining her goal in concrete terms.

Her coach asked her, "What does finishing a novel look like for you? How many words will it be? By when do you want to have the first draft completed?" At first, the questions felt daunting, but as Naomi began to think about her answers, she realized that she had been afraid to commit to a specific outcome. She decided to set a clear goal: "Finish a 70,000-word first draft by the end of the year, writing 500 words every weekday."

This level of clarity transformed Naomi's approach to her writing. Instead of feeling overwhelmed by the idea of completing an entire novel, she focused on her daily word count, knowing that each small step was bringing her closer to her goal. By defining what success looked like and breaking it down into achievable milestones, Naomi found the determination to keep going, even on days when the writing felt like a struggle.

The Power of a Well-Defined Goal

A well-defined goal is like a map that guides you through the process of change. It helps you see where you're headed and gives you a sense of direction when challenges arise. When you know what you want, it becomes easier to identify the habits that support your goal and to let go of the ones that don't.

For many, like Rebecca, Marcus, and Naomi, the journey of defining their goals was the key to unlocking their potential. They learned that setting an intention wasn't just about deciding what they didn't want - like being out of shape, procrastinating, or abandoning projects - but about envisioning a future that was worth striving for. This clarity gave them the motivation and focus they needed to stay committed, even when the process of change was difficult.

SMART Goals Framework

Setting clear intentions and goals is a cornerstone of effective habit change. One of the most practical and proven methods for doing this is the SMART Goals framework. This approach transforms vague aspirations into actionable plans, providing a roadmap for success. SMART stands for Specific, Measurable, Achievable, Relevant, and Time-bound, and each element plays a vital role in turning a desire for change into tangible progress. By breaking down goals in this way, the SMART framework helps ensure that our ambitions are not just lofty ideas but grounded in reality, guiding us steadily toward our objectives.

Making Goals Specific: From General Wishes to Clear Targets

The first component of the SMART framework is *Specificity*. A goal needs to be clearly defined so that it is easy to understand what exactly you are aiming to achieve. Specific goals provide direction, making it clear what actions are needed. Vague goals like "get healthier" or "be more organized" lack the precision necessary for sustained effort, leaving room for ambiguity and distraction.

Consider the story of Clara, a high school teacher who wanted to improve her physical fitness. For years, she had told herself that she wanted to "get in shape," but this goal never translated into consistent action. After attending a goal-setting workshop, she learned about the SMART framework and realized that her goal needed to be more concrete. Clara decided to refine her aim, setting a new goal: "Run three miles, three times a week." This new goal was specific—it left no room for interpretation and gave her a clear target to aim for.

Clara's experience illustrates the power of specificity in goal setting. Instead of feeling overwhelmed by the general idea of becoming healthier, she had a concrete plan. When she put on her running shoes, she knew exactly what she needed to accomplish that day, which kept her focused and motivated. Specific goals act like a compass, pointing directly toward the desired outcome and eliminating the confusion of where to start.

Measuring Progress: Turning Goals into Trackable Steps

The *Measurable* aspect of SMART goals is about defining how you will track progress toward your goal. This component helps ensure that you can see your progress over time, providing motivation and a sense of achievement. When a goal is measurable, it becomes easier to stay committed because you can observe your improvement and adjust your efforts as needed.

For David, an aspiring musician, the concept of measurability was a revelation. He had always dreamed of mastering the guitar but had struggled to make consistent progress. He knew he needed a more structured approach, so he turned to the SMART framework. Instead of setting a goal like "get better at playing guitar," David chose a measurable goal: "Practice guitar for 30 minutes a day, five days a week."

This shift made all the difference. Each practice session became a tangible step toward his larger goal. David kept a practice log, noting down the time spent and the specific techniques he worked on. Seeing the hours add up each week gave him a sense of accomplishment, motivating him to keep going even when progress felt slow. By making his goal measurable, David was able to track his growth, transforming his dream of playing guitar into a daily reality.

Measurable goals are crucial because they provide benchmarks along the way, turning an abstract aspiration into a series of tangible milestones. This not only helps sustain motivation but also allows for adjustments, ensuring that you remain on course.

Setting Realistic Challenges: Balancing Ambition and Achievability

The *Achievable* component of SMART goals focuses on setting goals that are challenging yet attainable. It's about finding a balance between pushing yourself and setting objectives that are realistic given your current resources, time, and abilities. Unrealistic goals can lead to frustration and burnout, while overly easy goals may fail to inspire.

For Alex, a graphic designer with a habit of overcommitting, the idea of setting achievable goals was a game-changer. He had always set lofty targets, like "double my freelance income in three months," but these ambitions often ended in disappointment when the results didn't come as quickly as he had hoped. After learning about the SMART framework, Alex decided to set a goal that was more aligned with his current circumstances: "Increase my freelance income by

10% over the next three months by adding one new client each month."

This goal was ambitious but within reach. It allowed Alex to focus on specific actions—networking, refining his portfolio, and reaching out to potential clients—without feeling overwhelmed by unrealistic expectations. The sense of accomplishment he felt when he landed his first new client boosted his confidence, reinforcing the belief that his goal was attainable.

Alex's story highlights the importance of making goals achievable. It's not about limiting yourself but about building a path that encourages steady progress. Achievable goals provide a sense of momentum, turning each small win into a stepping stone toward larger successes.

Ensuring Relevance: Aligning Goals with Your Values

The *Relevant* component of the SMART framework ensures that your goals align with your broader values and long-term vision. This step is crucial for maintaining motivation, as it helps you focus on goals that truly matter to you, rather than those imposed by external pressures or fleeting desires.

For Sophie, a nonprofit director, relevance was the missing piece in her goal-setting process. She had spent months trying to improve her public speaking skills because she believed it was expected of her in her leadership role. But despite taking classes and practicing, she felt little passion for the goal and often skipped her practice sessions. It wasn't until a colleague asked her, "Why is this important to you?" that Sophie realized her heart wasn't in it.

Reflecting on her true passions, Sophie discovered that what she really wanted was to deepen her organization's impact through strategic partnerships. She adjusted her goal to focus on networking with potential allies and creating meaningful collaborations. Her new goal - "Build five new partnerships over the next six months" - felt directly tied to her vision of expanding her nonprofit's reach.

By aligning her goal with her core values, Sophie found renewed energy and focus. She was no longer forcing herself to pursue a goal out of obligation; she was working toward something that felt deeply meaningful. Relevance ensures that your efforts are directed toward goals that resonate with your personal or professional mission, keeping you engaged and inspired along the way.

Time-Bound Goals: Creating a Sense of Urgency

The final piece of the SMART framework is making goals *Time-bound*. A deadline creates a sense of urgency, turning a distant dream into a priority. When a goal has a clear timeframe, it becomes easier to plan the necessary steps and hold yourself accountable to follow through.

For John, a recent graduate looking to transition into a new career, setting time-bound goals helped him overcome a habit of procrastination. He had been telling himself for months that he needed to "find a better job," but without a specific timeline, his job search remained half-hearted. After a career coach introduced him to the SMART framework, John set a time-bound goal: "Submit 10 job applications within the next four weeks and secure three informational interviews."

With this deadline in place, John approached his job search with new urgency. He created a weekly schedule for researching companies and tailoring his applications, and he reached out to former professors for advice. Knowing that he had a specific timeframe pushed him to take action, making the job search a priority rather than a vague intention.

John's experience shows how time-bound goals help turn plans into reality. Deadlines can provide the nudge needed to overcome inertia, helping you stay on track even when life gets busy. By breaking a large goal into smaller, time-bound steps, you create a sense of momentum, building confidence as you see progress unfold week by week.

The Transformative Power of SMART Goals

The SMART Goals framework transforms goal-setting from a wishful exercise into a practical strategy for change. It breaks down the process into clear, actionable components - Specific, Measurable, Achievable, Relevant, and Time-bound - each of which plays a crucial role in turning intentions into tangible results. For many, like Clara, David, Alex, Sophie, and John, adopting this approach provided the structure and focus they needed to overcome old habits and build new, empowering routines.

By making goals specific, you define exactly what success looks like. By making them measurable, you create a way to track your progress. By ensuring they are achievable, you set yourself up for sustainable growth. By aligning them with your values, you stay motivated through the inevitable challenges. And by setting a timeframe, you turn plans into priorities, taking consistent action toward your vision.

Aligning Habits with Personal Values

Aligning habits with personal values is a powerful strategy for creating meaningful and lasting change. It's not just about setting goals or adopting new routines; it's about ensuring that the actions we take each day reflect the deeper principles and beliefs that define who we are. When habits are in sync with our values, they become more than just tasks on a to-do list—they become expressions of our true selves, guiding us toward a life that feels authentic and fulfilling. This alignment provides a sense of purpose that can sustain motivation through even the most challenging moments of habit change.

Understanding the Connection Between Values and Habits

Aligning habits with personal values begins with understanding what truly matters to you. Values are the core principles that guide your behavior and decisions. They are the deeply held beliefs that shape your sense of identity and purpose, such as kindness, integrity, health, or creativity. When habits align with these values, they become easier to maintain because they resonate with your sense of who you want to be. This alignment helps create a natural motivation that goes beyond external rewards or pressure.

Take, for example, Rachel, a social worker who struggled with a habit of saying yes to every request that came her way. Rachel valued helping others, but she found herself constantly overwhelmed, often sacrificing her own well-being to meet the needs of her clients, friends, and family. It wasn't until a colleague introduced her to the concept of values-based habit change that Rachel realized her habit of overcommitting was out of sync with another core value she held - self-care.

Rachel spent time reflecting on her values and recognized that while helping others was important to her, so was maintaining her own mental and physical health. She realized that she wanted to be someone who could offer her support from a place of strength and balance, rather than exhaustion. With this newfound clarity, Rachel began to practice saying no more often, setting boundaries that allowed her to recharge. This shift wasn't easy - she still felt the pull to say yes - but the knowledge that she was honoring her deeper value of self-care gave her the strength to stick with her new habit.

Rachel's experience shows that when habits align with values, they become acts of self-expression. Her decision to prioritize rest wasn't just about avoiding burnout - it was about living in a way that reflected her commitment to both her clients and herself. This alignment transformed what had once felt like a burdensome change into a meaningful practice that supported her long-term goals.

Finding Your Core Values: The Key to Lasting Motivation

Before habits can align with values, it's essential to identify what those values are. This process involves asking deep questions about what you believe in, what brings you joy, and what kind of person you want to become. These reflections help to uncover the guiding principles that can make habits feel not just like duties but like extensions of your true self.

For Tom, a business consultant who struggled with a habit of neglecting his health, this introspective process was eye-opening. He had spent years focusing on his career, often working late into the night and skipping meals or exercise. His goals around health had always been framed in terms of numbers - losing weight, lowering cholesterol - but these goals never seemed to stick. It wasn't until he attended a personal development seminar that he began to explore the deeper values behind his desire for better health.

As Tom reflected, he realized that one of his core values was vitality. He wanted to feel energetic and alive, to have the stamina to travel, play with his kids, and enjoy outdoor adventures with his wife. This value of vitality went beyond simply losing weight - it was about embracing a way of living that allowed him to fully engage with the world. With this new perspective, Tom redefined his health goals, focusing not just on metrics but on habits that made him feel vibrant and strong, like daily walks, cooking nutritious meals, and spending time outdoors.

This shift in focus gave Tom a sense of purpose that had been missing before. His daily walks were no longer just exercise - they were a way to connect with the value of vitality that he held dear. On days when he felt tempted to skip his walk, he reminded himself of the bigger picture, of the energy and joy he wanted to bring into his life. This connection between his habits and his values became a powerful motivator, helping him stay committed even when challenges arose.

Transforming Everyday Actions into Meaningful Practices

When habits are aligned with values, even ordinary actions can take on new meaning. This alignment helps transform routines from chores into rituals that reflect the life you want to build. It shifts the focus from simply achieving a goal to living in a way that honors your deeper principles, creating a sense of fulfillment that extends beyond the completion of any single task.

For Maya, a creative writer who had always wanted to develop a daily journaling habit, finding this alignment was crucial. She had tried to keep a journal many times before, but it always felt like a burden - a task that she had to complete rather than an activity she truly enjoyed. But during a period of reflection, Maya identified creativity and self-expression as two of her core values. She realized that journaling wasn't just about tracking her days - it was a way to express her thoughts, capture her ideas, and engage with her inner world.

With this new understanding, Maya approached journaling differently. She began to see each entry as a chance to connect with her creativity, to explore her thoughts without judgment. Her habit became less about filling pages and more about embracing the freedom to express herself in whatever way felt right each day. This shift made it easier for her to stick with her journaling practice, turning it from a task she dreaded into a ritual she looked forward to each morning.

Maya's story demonstrates how aligning habits with values can infuse daily routines with a sense of purpose. Her journaling practice became a reflection of her desire to live creatively, helping her connect with a deeper part of herself. This alignment made her habit sustainable because it wasn't just about checking a box - it was about living out her values in a tangible way.

Overcoming Challenges Through Values Alignment

Even when habits align with values, challenges are inevitable. There will be days when motivation wanes, when the pull of old patterns feels stronger than the desire for change. During these times, reconnecting with your values can provide a source of resilience, reminding you why you started in the first place.

For James, an entrepreneur working to cut back on his habit of excessive screen time, the value of presence became his anchor during difficult moments. James valued being present with his family, but he often found himself scrolling through his phone during family dinners or checking emails during movie nights with his kids. He felt a growing sense of guilt, knowing that his habit was creating distance between him and the people he loved most.

After reflecting on his values, James made a commitment to being more present with his family, setting a goal to put his phone away during all family activities. This new habit wasn't just about reducing screen time - it was about honoring the value he placed on being truly present. On days when he felt tempted to check his phone, he reminded himself of the reason behind his decision - the desire to create meaningful memories with his kids and to model the kind of attention he wanted them to give to others.

This connection to his value of presence helped James stay committed, even when old habits tried to reassert themselves. He found that by focusing on the value behind the habit, he could push through the discomfort of change and stay true to his deeper intentions. His commitment to being present became a source of strength, helping him build a habit that brought more joy and connection into his life

Building a Life That Reflects Your Values

Aligning habits with personal values is about more than just achieving specific goals - it's about creating a life that feels authentic and true to who you are. When your daily actions are in harmony with your values, they become stepping stones toward a life that reflects your beliefs and aspirations. This alignment helps to transform the process of habit change from a struggle into a journey of self-discovery and growth.

For many, like Rachel, Tom, Maya, and James, the journey of aligning habits with values was the key to unlocking a deeper sense of purpose. They learned that change wasn't just about doing more or doing better - it was about living in a way that felt true to themselves. This shift made their habits sustainable because it connected their actions to the things that mattered most.

Chapter 9: Willpower and Discipline

Understanding Willpower as a Finite Resource

Understanding the nature of willpower is crucial for anyone looking to change their habits. Willpower is often imagined as an unyielding inner strength, a force that can push us through any challenge if only we summon enough of it. But in reality, willpower is a finite resource - one that can become depleted through use, much like a muscle that tires after a heavy workout. Recognizing this limitation is key to using willpower wisely, allowing us to conserve it for the moments that matter most and to develop strategies that don't rely solely on sheer determination.

Willpower as a Depletable Resource

The concept of willpower as a finite resource comes from the idea of "ego depletion," a psychological theory suggesting that our capacity for self-control weakens with use. Just as a runner's muscles become fatigued after a marathon, our mental reserves of willpower diminish when we constantly exert self-control throughout the day. This understanding helps explain why it can be so difficult to stick to healthy choices after a long, stressful day, or why resisting a tempting treat is harder in the evening than it is in the morning.

Consider the story of Matt, a software developer who struggled with a habit of snacking late at night. Throughout the day, he would diligently stick to his diet plan, avoiding the cookies in the break room and choosing salads over fast food for lunch. But by the time he got home in the evening, Matt often found himself reaching for a bag of chips or indulging in ice cream. He felt frustrated and confused - why was his willpower so strong in the morning but seemed to vanish by the end of the day?

It wasn't until Matt came across research on willpower depletion that he began to understand what was happening. His daily efforts to resist temptation, make decisions, and manage stress at work were all drawing from his limited reservoir of willpower. By the time he faced the temptation of snacks in the evening, his reserves were running low, making it much harder to stick to his intentions. This insight helped Matt realize that his struggle wasn't about a lack of self-discipline - it was about the natural limits of his mental energy.

The Willpower Muscle: Strengthening and Conserving Self-Control

Thinking of willpower as a muscle is a useful analogy. Like any muscle, it can be strengthened over time through regular use, but it can also become fatigued if pushed too hard without rest. This perspective suggests that while we can build up our capacity for self-control, we must also be mindful of how we use it, ensuring that we don't deplete our reserves unnecessarily.

For Sarah, a college student working to balance a demanding course load with her goal of quitting smoking, this understanding was crucial. In her first attempts to quit, she relied entirely on her willpower, telling herself that she just needed to stay strong whenever cravings hit. But as the days went on, Sarah found herself struggling more and more, especially after long study sessions or difficult exams. Each time she resisted the urge to smoke, she felt a drain on her energy, and by the evening, she often gave in, feeling defeated.

After learning about the concept of willpower as a finite resource, Sarah took a different approach. She decided to focus on strengthening her willpower gradually while also conserving it for the moments when she needed it most. She began to practice mindfulness and deep breathing exercises to manage stress, reducing the number of times she had to rely on willpower to resist cravings. She also created a structured routine, avoiding situations where she used to smoke, like taking a different route home from campus to avoid passing by the convenience store.

Sarah found that as she reduced the number of decisions she needed to make each day, she had more mental energy to handle her cravings. She realized that by conserving her willpower, she could use it more effectively when a strong urge hit. This shift in strategy allowed her to make steady progress, breaking her habit in a way that felt more sustainable.

Decision Fatigue: How Choices Drain Willpower

A key factor in the depletion of willpower is decision fatigue - the idea that the more decisions we make throughout the day, the harder each subsequent choice becomes. This phenomenon explains why we might start the morning with a clear plan to eat healthily or stick to a workout schedule, only to abandon those intentions when faced with choices later in the day.

For James, a financial analyst who was working to cut back on his habit of mindless online shopping, decision fatigue was a significant hurdle. At the beginning of the month, he would set a strict budget, determined to stick to it. But by the time he got home after a long day of analyzing data and making decisions for clients, he often found himself scrolling through shopping apps, buying things he didn't need. He would tell himself, "Just one small purchase won't hurt," and before he knew it, he had exceeded his budget.

James began to understand that his willpower wasn't failing him - his mental energy was simply running low after a day filled with decision-making. He realized that each small decision, from choosing which emails to respond to first to planning his lunch, was chipping away at his self-control. To address this, he started simplifying his daily routines, like planning his meals for the week in advance and automating bill payments. He also set a rule to only shop online during the weekends, when he felt more rested and in control.

By reducing the number of decisions he had to make during the workday, James found that he had more mental energy left for resisting impulse purchases. This strategy helped him regain control over his spending, showing that managing willpower isn't just about staying strong - it's about understanding when and how to use it.

Planning for Willpower Failures: The Role of Habits and Routines

Understanding that willpower is finite also highlights the importance of building habits and routines that reduce the need for constant self-control. When behaviors become automatic, they require less conscious effort, allowing us to preserve our willpower for situations that truly demand it. This is why habits like brushing your teeth every night or going for a morning walk can be sustained even when you're tired - these routines are ingrained, requiring minimal decision-making.

For Claire, a project manager with a habit of procrastination, this was a crucial insight. She had always relied on bursts of willpower to push through deadlines, but this approach left her feeling exhausted and stressed. After reading about the limits of willpower, she decided to focus on building routines that would make her workday smoother and less dependent on self-discipline.

Claire started by setting up a simple morning routine, beginning each day with a cup of tea and a review of her top three priorities. She also created a habit of tackling her most challenging task first thing in the morning, when her willpower was at its peak. By making these practices a part of her daily routine, she found that she no longer needed to push herself to get started - it became automatic.

This change allowed Claire to reserve her willpower for unexpected challenges that arose during the day, like handling a difficult client or managing a tight deadline. Her work became less of a constant battle with procrastination and more of a rhythm she could maintain. Building routines that aligned with her goals helped Claire move beyond the need to rely on willpower alone, making her more resilient and productive.

Embracing the Realities of Willpower

Understanding willpower as a finite resource is about embracing the reality that we all have limits, and that success in changing habits isn't about pushing past those limits indefinitely. It's about working with our minds and bodies, finding ways to use willpower wisely, and building habits that make life a little easier. For many, like Matt, Sarah, James, and Claire, this shift in perspective was the key to unlocking a more sustainable approach to self-improvement.

Recognizing the limitations of willpower doesn't mean giving up on discipline - it means using it more strategically, conserving energy for the moments that matter most, and creating systems that support long-term change.

Strategies to Strengthen Self-Control

 The journey to lasting habit change hinges on more than just understanding the limits of willpower; it also requires learning how to strengthen self-control over time. Like a muscle, self-control can be trained and developed through deliberate practice, making it easier to resist temptations and maintain focus on long-term goals. Strengthening self-control is not about forcing yourself to endure every challenge through sheer determination - it's about adopting strategies that make self-discipline a natural and sustainable part of your daily life.

Building Self-Control Through Small Wins

One of the most effective strategies for strengthening self-control is to start small and build momentum through manageable challenges. Just as a runner doesn't begin training by running a marathon, those looking to improve self-discipline should begin with small, achievable tasks that gradually build their capacity for self-control. This approach allows you to experience success early on, creating a positive feedback loop that encourages you to keep going.

Take the story of Jessica, a student who struggled with a habit of procrastination. She often found herself overwhelmed by large assignments, pushing deadlines until the last minute and then cramming through stressful all-nighters. After reading about the benefits of starting small, she decided to try a different approach. Instead of forcing herself to work on an entire essay at once, she set a goal to write just one paragraph each day. It seemed like a tiny change, but it was one she felt she could stick to consistently.

This small win had a surprising effect. Each time Jessica sat down to write her paragraph, she often found herself writing more than she had planned. The act of getting started became less intimidating, and she built a sense of accomplishment that fueled her motivation. Over time, Jessica increased her goal to two paragraphs, then a page. The habit of regular writing became ingrained, and she found herself finishing assignments well before the deadline, with less stress and better results.

Jessica's story illustrates how small wins can be a powerful way to build self-control. By focusing on manageable goals, she gradually strengthened her capacity for discipline, turning a habit that once felt like a burden into a source of pride. This approach not only made the process of change more enjoyable but also prepared her to tackle larger challenges with greater confidence.

Practicing Delayed Gratification: The Art of Patience

Delayed gratification is a classic method for strengthening self-control. It involves resisting the temptation of immediate rewards in favor of more significant benefits that come with patience. Learning to delay gratification is like training a muscle that helps you endure short-term discomfort for long-term gains, making it easier to stick to habits that support your larger goals.

For Daniel, a software engineer who wanted to save money for a down payment on a house, this concept was transformative. He had a habit of buying the latest gadgets as soon as they were released, a tendency that kept his savings account from growing. After a conversation with a financial advisor, Daniel decided to challenge himself to delay gratification by waiting 30 days before making any major purchases. If he still wanted the item after the waiting period, he would allow himself to buy it.

At first, the waiting felt excruciating. He found himself checking tech blogs and reading reviews, convincing himself that he needed the latest smartphone or tablet. But as the days passed, the initial excitement began to fade, and he realized that many of the purchases he had once seen as essential weren't as important as he had thought. Daniel discovered that by waiting, he could distinguish between impulses and genuine desires. The habit of delaying gratification helped him save more money than he had thought possible, bringing him closer to his goal of homeownership.

This practice taught Daniel an important lesson: self-control isn't just about saying no - it's about giving yourself time to make thoughtful decisions. By learning to wait, he gained greater control over his spending, making choices that aligned with his long-term vision rather than his immediate desires.

Reframing Temptation: Changing the Way You See Challenges

Another strategy for strengthening self-control is to reframe how you view temptations and challenges. This approach involves changing the narrative around difficult moments, seeing them not as threats to your willpower but as opportunities to grow stronger. Reframing helps shift your mindset from one of deprivation to one of empowerment, making it easier to stick to your goals even when faced with temptation.

For Maya, a graphic designer who wanted to cut back on her habit of eating sweets, reframing temptation became a game-changer. She loved desserts and often found herself indulging in treats after dinner, despite her efforts to stick to a healthier diet. Instead of viewing her cravings as a sign of weakness, Maya decided to see them as opportunities to practice self-control.

Each time she felt the urge to eat a piece of cake or reach for a chocolate bar, Maya reminded herself, "This is my chance to get stronger." She began to treat each moment of temptation as a mini-challenge, a chance to prove to herself that she could resist. This shift in perspective helped her feel more in control, transforming what had once felt like a battle into a source of pride.

Reframing temptation doesn't eliminate cravings or make challenges disappear, but it changes how you respond to them. For Maya, it turned a difficult experience into an opportunity for growth, helping her build a sense of accomplishment with each choice she made. This strategy made her feel empowered rather than deprived, allowing her to build a healthier relationship with food.

Using Visualization Techniques to Strengthen Resolve

Visualization is another powerful tool for building self-control. By imagining yourself succeeding in difficult situations, you can mentally rehearse the actions you want to take, making it easier to follow through when the moment arrives. Visualization can help strengthen the neural pathways associated with positive behaviors, making them more automatic over time.

For Kevin, a professional athlete working to improve his focus during training, visualization was an essential part of his routine. He had a habit of losing concentration during long practice sessions, often becoming frustrated when he couldn't master a new technique right away. His coach suggested that

172

he try visualizing himself performing each move perfectly before stepping onto the field.

At first, Kevin found the practice of visualization strange. Sitting quietly and imagining himself succeeding felt like a waste of time. But as he continued, he began to notice a difference. When he visualized himself maintaining focus, handling frustration calmly, and executing each technique with precision, he found it easier to translate those mental images into real actions. His focus improved, and he felt more in control during practice, even when faced with challenging drills.

Visualization helped Kevin strengthen his self-control by allowing him to mentally prepare for difficult moments. It made the desired behavior feel more familiar, reducing the effort required to maintain focus when it counted. For Kevin, the practice became a secret weapon, helping him stay disciplined even in high-pressure situations.

Creating Self-Control Rituals: Anchoring Positive Behaviors

Establishing rituals around moments of potential weakness can also help strengthen self-control. These rituals act as cues that remind you of your commitment to a goal, creating a structured response to situations where your willpower might otherwise waver.

For Carla, a writer with a habit of checking social media during work hours, creating a ritual helped her stay focused. She found that each time she faced a challenging paragraph or hit a creative block, she would instinctively reach for her phone, losing valuable time to scrolling through posts. To address this, she created a simple ritual: whenever she felt the urge to check her phone, she would take three deep breaths, stand up, and stretch for a minute.

This ritual gave Carla a new way to manage her impulses. The deep breaths and stretch served as a reset button, helping her refocus before returning to her writing. It wasn't about eliminating the desire to check her phone - it was about creating a structured response that allowed her to pause and choose a more productive action. Over time, this ritual became second nature, making it easier for Carla to maintain her concentration and get her work done without the distraction of social media.

Carla's experience shows how creating rituals can anchor positive behaviors, providing a reliable way to manage moments of temptation. These rituals don't require extreme effort - they simply create a habit of responding thoughtfully rather than automatically, helping you stay aligned with your goals.

Strengthening Self-Control Through Reflection and Growth

Strengthening self-control is ultimately about developing a mindset of continuous improvement. It involves recognizing that setbacks are part of the process and using each challenge as an opportunity to learn and grow. By approaching self-discipline as a skill that can be refined over time, rather than an innate trait, you can cultivate a more resilient attitude toward your goals.

For many, like Jessica, Daniel, Maya, Kevin, and Carla, the journey to greater self-control was not about achieving perfection but about finding strategies that made discipline sustainable. They learned that self-control isn't a battle of will - it's a process of building habits, adopting new perspectives, and creating a life that supports their best selves. Through small wins, delayed gratification, reframing, visualization, and rituals, they found ways to make self-discipline a natural part of their daily lives.

Overcoming Temptations and Urges

Overcoming temptations and urges is a crucial part of mastering willpower and discipline. Temptations often arise when we least expect them - during moments of fatigue, stress, or boredom - testing our resolve and pulling us toward behaviors we're trying to change. Whether it's the craving for a late-night snack, the urge to skip a workout, or the impulse to buy something unnecessary, these moments can feel like powerful forces, demanding immediate satisfaction. But learning to navigate these urges is not about eliminating them; it's about developing strategies that help you recognize, manage, and move beyond them with greater ease.

Understanding the Nature of Temptations

Temptations and urges are a natural part of being human. They are not signs of weakness but rather signals from the brain, often linked to the desire for pleasure or the avoidance of discomfort. Understanding this helps to shift the perspective on temptations - they are not obstacles to fight but experiences to understand. This shift is crucial because it allows us to approach urges with curiosity rather than frustration, turning moments of temptation into opportunities for growth.

Take the story of Emily, a graphic designer who struggled with a habit of eating sweets whenever she felt stressed. For years, she believed that she just needed more willpower to resist the cookies and chocolates in her pantry. But the more she tried to suppress her cravings, the stronger they seemed to become. It wasn't until she read about the brain's response to stress and reward that she realized her cravings were not about the sweets themselves - they were about seeking comfort during tough moments.

This realization changed how Emily approached her temptations. Instead of berating herself for wanting a cookie, she began to pause and ask herself, "What am I really feeling right now? And what do I actually need?" Sometimes, the answer was that she needed a break from her work, or a few minutes to unwind. Other times, she realized she just needed a moment of self-compassion. By acknowledging her underlying feelings, Emily found that the urge to reach for sweets often subsided on its own.

Emily's experience illustrates that understanding the nature of temptations is the first step in overcoming them. By recognizing that urges are signals rather than commands, she was able to break the automatic link between feeling stressed and reaching for a treat, giving herself the space to choose a different response.

The Power of the Pause: Creating Space Between Impulse and Action

One of the most effective techniques for overcoming temptations is to create a pause between the moment when an urge arises and the action you take. This pause is like a buffer that allows you to regain control and think more clearly about your next step. It gives you the chance to evaluate the situation, ask yourself what you truly want, and decide whether acting on the impulse aligns with your long-term goals.

For Tom, a busy entrepreneur trying to cut back on his habit of smoking, the power of the pause became a key strategy. He had tried to quit smoking multiple times, but each time he felt a craving, he found himself reaching for a cigarette before he even realized what he was doing. A therapist suggested that he try a simple technique: whenever he felt the urge to smoke, he would take five deep breaths before deciding what to do next.

At first, the practice felt awkward and frustrating. Tom still wanted to smoke, and taking deep breaths seemed like a poor substitute. But as he persisted, he began to notice something interesting: the urge to smoke wasn't as overpowering as he had thought. By pausing for just a minute, he found that the craving would peak and then gradually diminish. Sometimes, after taking his deep breaths, he still chose to smoke—but other times, he decided to distract himself with a walk or a phone call instead.

Over time, the pause became a powerful tool in Tom's journey to quit. It helped him see that the urge to smoke was just that—an urge, not a command. By giving himself a moment to pause, he was able to separate himself from the craving, making it easier to resist. The pause didn't eliminate the temptation, but it gave him back the power to choose how he responded.

Replacing the Urge with a Positive Action

Another effective way to manage temptations is to replace the urge with a positive action. This strategy involves redirecting your energy away from the tempting behavior and channeling it into something that aligns with your goals. By creating a new association in your mind, you can gradually weaken the old habit loop and strengthen a healthier alternative.

For Clara, a stay-at-home mom trying to break her habit of scrolling through social media late into the night, replacing the urge with a new activity made all the difference. She found that as soon as her kids went to bed, she would sit down on the couch with her phone, intending to browse for just a few minutes. But those few minutes often turned into hours, leaving her feeling tired and unproductive the next day.

Determined to change, Clara decided to replace her evening scrolling with a new ritual - reading a book. She kept a novel on her coffee table as a reminder, and whenever she felt the urge to pick up her phone, she would reach for the book instead. At first, it felt like a struggle; she still wanted to see what was happening online. But as the weeks passed, Clara began to look forward to her reading time, enjoying the escape that a good story provided.

This replacement strategy helped Clara break the cycle of mindless scrolling. By shifting her focus to something that aligned with her desire for relaxation and mental stimulation, she found that the urge to check her phone gradually lost its power. Replacing an old habit with a new, more fulfilling one allowed her to satisfy her needs without giving in to temptation.

Surfing the Urge: Riding Out the Waves of Craving

One powerful technique for managing urges is known as "urge surfing," a mindfulness-based approach that teaches you to observe your cravings without acting on them. The idea is to imagine the urge as a wave, rising in intensity and then gradually subsiding. Instead of fighting the wave, you ride it out, knowing that it will eventually pass.

For James, a college student who struggled with a habit of binge eating, urge surfing became a lifeline. He had tried to control his eating through strict diets, but every time he faced a stressful exam or a rough day, he found himself eating until he felt sick. A counselor introduced him to the concept of urge surfing, and at first, James was skeptical. How could sitting with his cravings help him when they felt so overwhelming?

But as he practiced, James discovered that the technique was more powerful than he had expected. When he felt the urge to binge, he would close his eyes, take a few deep breaths, and focus on the sensations of the craving—where he felt it in his body, how it changed over time. He noticed that the urge would peak, feeling almost unbearable, but then it would begin to fade, like a wave rolling back into the ocean.

This practice helped James realize that his cravings weren't as permanent as they seemed. By learning to ride the wave of the urge, he found that he could endure the discomfort without giving in to it. Urge surfing became a way for him to face his cravings with courage and patience, allowing him to make choices that supported his well-being.

Changing the Environment: Reducing Exposure to Temptation

Sometimes, the best way to overcome temptations is to change the environment that triggers them. By reducing your exposure to the cues that prompt unwanted behaviors, you make it easier to stay on track. This strategy isn't about avoiding challenges forever—it's about giving yourself the space to build up your strength before facing them.

For David, a young professional working to cut back on his habit of drinking soda, changing his environment was a game-changer. He knew that he couldn't resist a cold soda when he saw one in the fridge, so he decided to stop buying soda altogether. Instead, he stocked his fridge with flavored sparkling water and kept a pitcher of lemon-infused water on his kitchen counter.

This small change made a big difference. Without soda readily available, David found that the urge to drink it occurred less frequently. When he felt a craving, he reached for the sparkling water instead, and over time, he began to enjoy it just as much as he had once enjoyed soda. By changing his environment, he reduced the number of times he needed to rely on willpower, making it easier to stick to his goal.

David's story shows that sometimes, the best way to resist temptation is to remove the source of temptation. It's not about avoiding challenges forever, but about creating an environment that supports your success while you build new habits.

Turning Temptations into Opportunities for Growth

Overcoming temptations and urges is not about eliminating the desire for instant gratification - it's about learning to navigate those moments with greater awareness and intention. For many, like Emily, Tom, Clara, James, and David, the journey of managing urges was filled with challenges, but it was also filled with moments of insight and self-discovery. They learned that temptations don't have to derail progress - they can be opportunities to practice self-control, build resilience, and deepen their understanding of themselves.

Part IV: Transforming Bad Habits into Positive Ones
Chapter 10: Breaking the Cycle

Interrupting the Cue-Routine-Reward Loop

Breaking the cycle of a bad habit requires understanding and interrupting the cue-routine-reward loop - a powerful framework that explains how habits form and become entrenched in our daily lives. This loop, which consists of a cue that triggers a routine followed by a reward, creates a self-reinforcing cycle that is difficult to break without conscious intervention. However, by learning to identify and disrupt each part of this loop, it's possible to transform negative behaviors into positive ones, paving the way for lasting change.

Understanding the Cue-Routine-Reward Loop

At the heart of every habit lies a simple but potent sequence: a cue, which triggers a specific behavior (the routine), followed by a reward that reinforces the behavior, making it more likely to occur again in the future. This cycle operates largely on autopilot, allowing our brains to conserve energy by automating repetitive actions. It's why habits, both good and bad, can become so deeply ingrained.

For instance, imagine Lucas, a busy accountant who has developed a habit of checking his phone for social media updates whenever he feels stressed at work. The cue in Lucas's habit loop is the feeling of stress - perhaps triggered by a difficult email or a tight deadline. His routine is to reach for his phone and scroll through social media, seeking a distraction from the stress. The reward comes in the form of a brief sense of relief or pleasure, as the amusing posts or notifications temporarily take his mind off his worries.

Over time, this cycle becomes automatic. Each time Lucas feels stressed, his brain knows that checking his phone will provide a quick reward, reinforcing the habit. To Lucas, it may feel as though he's barely making a choice at all - the action is so ingrained that it seems to happen without thought. But by learning to dissect this loop, he can begin to regain control over his behavior.

Identifying the Cue: Recognizing the Triggers

The first step in interrupting the cue-routine-reward loop is to identify the cue—the trigger that sets the habit into motion. Cues can come in many forms: emotions like stress or boredom, specific times of day, places, or even the presence of certain people. Recognizing these triggers is essential because it allows you to understand why and when a habit is activated, giving you the opportunity to address it before the routine takes over.

Lucas decided to keep a journal for a week, noting down every time he felt the urge to check his phone at work. He paid attention to what he was feeling, what time it was, and what was happening around him when the urge struck. After a few days, a pattern emerged: most of his urges occurred after receiving particularly stressful emails or when he was working on a complex task.

This awareness was a revelation for Lucas. He realized that his habit wasn't just about boredom - it was a way of coping with stress. By pinpointing the exact moments when the habit was triggered, Lucas took the first step toward breaking the cycle. He now had a clearer sense of when to expect the urge and could begin to plan how to respond differently.

Changing the Routine: Finding Healthier Alternatives

Once the cue has been identified, the next step is to change the routine - the behavior that follows the trigger. The goal is not necessarily to eliminate the cue but to replace the automatic response with a new, healthier routine that still satisfies the underlying need or desire.

Lucas knew that he couldn't eliminate stress from his job, but he could change how he responded to it. Instead of reaching for his phone every time he felt overwhelmed, he decided to experiment with new routines that could offer a similar sense of relief without the distraction of social media. He tried different options, like taking a short walk around the office, doing a few deep breathing exercises, or even jotting down a quick note about what was bothering him.

At first, the new routines felt awkward and less satisfying than scrolling through his phone. But as he persisted, Lucas found that the short walks helped clear his mind, and the deep breaths calmed his racing thoughts. Over time, these new routines began to feel more natural, providing a sense of relief without the guilt or distraction that came with his old habit. By finding healthier alternatives, Lucas managed to change the middle part of his habit loop, making it easier to resist the urge to check his phone when stress hit.

Reassessing the Reward: Understanding What You Truly Need

The final part of the cue-routine-reward loop is the reward - the positive outcome that reinforces the behavior. To fully break a habit, it's crucial to understand what the reward is really providing and to find new ways to meet that need. Often, the reward is not as straightforward as it seems; it might be offering comfort, a sense of accomplishment, or a temporary escape from discomfort.

For Lucas, the reward of checking his phone was more than just the distraction - it was the brief relief from the pressure of his workload. Understanding this allowed him to experiment with new rewards that could meet the same need. After a particularly stressful meeting, he would give himself a five-minute break to step outside and enjoy the fresh air. He also started keeping a small notebook where he could write down three things he had accomplished that day, giving him a sense of progress even amidst a busy schedule.

These new rewards helped Lucas feel more in control of his time and stress levels, gradually replacing the pleasure he used to get from social media. By addressing the real need behind the habit - the desire for a moment of respite - he was able to create a new loop that was both more satisfying and more aligned with his long-term goals.

Creating Disruptions: Breaking the Cycle Through Conscious Intervention

Breaking the cue-routine-reward loop doesn't happen overnight. It requires patience, self-reflection, and a willingness to experiment with different strategies. But each time you interrupt the loop, you weaken the automatic connection between the cue and the old routine, making it easier to adopt new behaviors.

For Maya, an artist who wanted to reduce her habit of mindless snacking in the evenings, breaking the loop involved a series of small but deliberate changes. She realized that her cue was the feeling of boredom that crept in after dinner, when she had free time before bed. Her routine was to head to the kitchen and snack while watching TV, and the reward was the comfort and satisfaction of eating.

To disrupt the loop, Maya decided to place a bowl of fruit on the counter instead of her usual snacks. She also experimented with different evening activities, like sketching or reading, that could fill the time when she usually snacked. When the urge to snack hit, she would take a piece of fruit instead and settle into a new activity. At first, the urge for her usual treats was strong, but over time, the new behaviors began to feel more satisfying.

Maya's story shows that breaking the cycle isn't about depriving yourself of pleasure - it's about finding new ways to meet your needs that align with your goals. By consciously disrupting the old loop, she was able to create a new habit that still provided relaxation but without the downsides of mindless eating.

The Path to Lasting Change: Reinforcing the New Loop

Interrupting the cue-routine-reward loop is not a one-time event; it's a process of gradually rewiring your brain to associate new behaviors with familiar triggers. As Lucas, Maya, and many others discovered, the key to lasting change is to stay patient and celebrate small victories along the way. Each time you choose a new routine over an old one, you strengthen the neural pathways associated with the new behavior, making it easier to repeat in the future.

By understanding the mechanics of the habit loop, you can regain control over behaviors that once felt automatic, transforming bad habits into positive routines that support your growth. It's a process that requires awareness, experimentation, and resilience, but with each effort, you come closer to breaking free from the patterns that no longer serve you.

Substitution: Replacing Bad Habits with Good Ones

one of the most effective strategies for breaking the cycle of negative behaviors is substitution - replacing bad habits with positive ones. This approach recognizes that habits don't simply disappear; they need to be replaced with new behaviors that satisfy the same needs or desires in a healthier way. Substitution is about creating a new pathway for your brain to follow, redirecting the energy that once fueled a negative habit into an action that supports your well-being and goals. It's a process of transformation that turns moments of temptation into opportunities for growth.

Understanding the Principle of Substitution

At its core, substitution involves identifying the underlying need that a bad habit fulfills and finding a new behavior that can meet that need in a more constructive way. This process is grounded in the understanding that habits are not just about the actions themselves - they're about the rewards we seek, whether it's comfort, distraction, or a sense of achievement. By offering your brain an alternative route to the same reward, you can gradually weaken the pull of the old habit and build a new one in its place.

Take the story of Anna, a marketing manager who struggled with a habit of smoking whenever she felt anxious. She knew that smoking was harmful to her health and had tried quitting several times, but each attempt ended in frustration. The cravings would become unbearable, especially during stressful moments at work. It wasn't until she spoke with a counselor that Anna began to understand that her smoking habit wasn't just about nicotine - it was about the relief and calm it provided during anxious times.

With this new perspective, Anna decided to try substituting her smoking habit with deep breathing exercises. Each time she felt the urge to smoke, she would step outside as she normally did, but instead of lighting a cigarette, she would take five slow, deep breaths, focusing on the sensation of the air filling her lungs. At first, the craving for a cigarette remained strong, and the deep breathing felt like a poor substitute. But as she persisted, Anna noticed that the breathing exercises began to have a calming effect, similar to what she experienced with smoking.

Over time, this new routine became more familiar, and the urge to smoke gradually diminished. By substituting her old habit with a healthier alternative, Anna found a way to meet her need for calm without relying on cigarettes. Her story illustrates that substitution is not about denying yourself the comfort or reward you're seeking - it's about finding a better way to achieve it.

Replacing the Routine, Not the Reward

Successful substitution hinges on understanding that while the behavior must change, the reward often stays the same. This approach allows you to preserve the positive aspect of the habit - the feeling of satisfaction or relief - while changing the action that leads to it. This makes the transition from a bad habit to a good one smoother and more sustainable.

For Mark, a software engineer with a habit of snacking late at night, this principle was key. He realized that his late-night eating wasn't driven by hunger - it was a way to unwind after long hours in front of his computer. The reward he sought was relaxation, not necessarily the taste of the snacks. Mark decided to replace his nightly snack with a different ritual: making himself a cup of herbal tea and reading a few pages of a novel before bed.

At first, the routine felt unnatural. He missed the crunch of chips and the familiar comfort of ice cream. But as he continued the new habit, Mark found that the ritual of preparing tea and reading a book provided the same sense of relaxation he had been seeking. He began to look forward to this new bedtime routine, which helped him wind down without the extra calories.

Mark's experience shows that effective substitution doesn't require giving up the reward you crave - it's about changing the behavior that leads to it. By shifting his focus from food to a different form of relaxation, he was able to break the cycle of his late-night snacking habit, creating a routine that supported his health and well-being.

Experimenting with Different Substitutes: Finding What Works

Finding the right substitute is often a process of trial and error. It's important to be patient and willing to experiment with different alternatives until you discover what feels right for you. The goal is to find a replacement behavior that satisfies the same underlying need in a way that is both enjoyable and sustainable.

For James, a sales representative with a habit of reaching for a drink after stressful meetings, finding the right substitute took time. He knew that his evening drinks were a way to unwind, but he also recognized that the habit was affecting his sleep and overall health. He tried replacing his drinks with soda, but the sugar left him feeling jittery and unsatisfied. Next, he tried exercising after work, but he found that on particularly stressful days, he lacked the motivation to hit the gym.

Eventually, James discovered that going for a walk in the park provided the right balance. The fresh air and change of scenery helped him decompress, and the act of walking gave him a sense of calm that mirrored the relaxation he had once found in his evening drink. It wasn't an immediate fix - there were days when he still craved the familiar comfort of a cold beer. But over time, the walks became a new source of pleasure, helping him to let go of the old habit.

James's story highlights that substitution is a personal journey. What works for one person may not work for another, and it's important to approach the process with a spirit of curiosity. By experimenting with different activities, you can find the substitute that resonates with you, making it easier to transition from an old habit to a new one.

Strengthening the New Habit: Reinforcing Positive Change

Once you've identified a suitable substitute, the next challenge is to reinforce the new behavior until it becomes automatic. This involves creating conditions that make it easy to repeat the new routine and rewarding yourself for sticking with it. The more you repeat the new behavior, the more ingrained it becomes, eventually replacing the old habit altogether.

For Clara, a teacher who wanted to reduce her habit of mindless TV watching after work, reinforcing her new habit was crucial. She decided to replace her TV time with a new routine: taking a yoga class at her local studio. At first, it was difficult to get up off the couch and drive to the studio, especially after a tiring day. To make the new habit easier,

Clara put her yoga mat and workout clothes by the door each morning as a reminder. She also treated herself to a small reward - like a hot bath - after each class, giving herself an extra incentive to stick with the change.

As the weeks went by, Clara noticed that the urge to watch TV after work began to fade. The yoga classes became a habit, providing the relaxation and stress relief she had once sought from her favorite shows. By making the new behavior easy and rewarding, Clara was able to replace her old habit with a positive routine that enriched her life.

Clara's experience shows that substitution is not just about finding a new activity - it's about creating an environment that supports the change. By making the new habit convenient and rewarding, you can strengthen it over time, allowing it to take the place of the behavior you're trying to change.

Embracing the Journey of Transformation

Transforming bad habits into positive ones through substitution is a process of self-discovery and growth. It requires patience, experimentation, and a willingness to look beyond the surface of your habits to understand the deeper needs they fulfill. For many, like Anna, Mark, James, and Clara, the journey of substitution was filled with ups and downs, but it ultimately led to a more fulfilling and balanced way of living.

By focusing on the rewards you truly seek and finding healthier ways to achieve them, you can break free from the habits that hold you back and build new routines that support your goals. The process of substitution allows you to create a life that aligns with your values and aspirations, transforming moments of temptation into opportunities for positive change.

Gradual vs. Immediate Change Strategies

The journey of breaking bad habits and cultivating positive ones often involves deciding between two fundamental approaches: gradual change and immediate change. Each strategy offers unique benefits and challenges, and the choice between them can greatly influence your experience of transformation. Understanding these approaches helps you select the one that aligns best with your needs, lifestyle, and the nature of the habit you wish to change. This narrative explores the nuances of both gradual and immediate change strategies, shedding light on how each can lead to success.

The Power of Gradual Change: Building Momentum Step by Step

Gradual change is a process of transforming habits in small, manageable increments over time. This approach focuses on making consistent, incremental improvements, allowing you to adjust to each change without overwhelming yourself. The philosophy behind gradual change is that small steps, when repeated consistently, add up to significant progress. It's like planting a seed and nurturing it daily until it grows into a thriving tree.

Consider the story of Sarah, a project manager who wanted to break her habit of staying up late watching TV and replace it with a healthier bedtime routine. For years, she struggled with insomnia, knowing that her late-night screen time was a major contributor. But every time she tried to quit cold turkey, she found herself relapsing within a few days, feeling frustrated and deprived.

After reading about gradual change, Sarah decided to take a different approach. Instead of banning TV altogether, she set a goal to turn off her screens just 10 minutes earlier each night. It was such a small adjustment that it felt almost effortless. Over the course of a few weeks, she gradually extended her screen-free time by another 10 minutes, then another, until she was consistently turning off the TV an hour before bed. During this time, she introduced new relaxing activities, like reading or taking a warm shower, to ease her transition into sleep.

Sarah's story demonstrates the power of gradual change. By breaking her goal into tiny, achievable steps, she avoided the shock of drastic change and allowed herself to adapt slowly. This approach made the habit change feel less intimidating and more sustainable, giving her time to adjust to each new stage. Over time, Sarah's small adjustments led to a significant transformation in her bedtime routine, helping her sleep better and wake up feeling more refreshed.

Gradual change is particularly effective for habits that are deeply ingrained or tied to daily routines. It's like learning to swim in the shallow end of the pool before venturing into deeper waters - it allows you to build confidence and adjust to the changes without feeling overwhelmed. This approach is often recommended for people who are wary of change or who have experienced setbacks with more abrupt methods in the past.

The Allure of Immediate Change: Embracing a Fresh Start

Immediate change, on the other hand, is about making a decisive, often dramatic shift in behavior. This approach is sometimes referred to as the "all-or-nothing" strategy or the "cold turkey" method. It involves drawing a clear line in the sand and committing to a new way of living without easing into it. The idea is that by making a bold change, you can break free from old patterns and jumpstart a new habit with a sense of urgency and determination.

For Michael, a sales executive with a habit of drinking several sodas a day, the idea of gradual change felt too slow. He had tried cutting back before, telling himself he would limit his soda intake to one can a day, but he always found reasons to have just one more. Frustrated with his lack of progress, Michael decided to try a different tactic: he quit drinking soda altogether, replacing it with water and herbal tea.

The first few days were difficult. He experienced headaches and intense cravings, and he often found himself staring at the soda aisle during his grocery runs. But Michael was determined. He kept a large water bottle at his desk and reminded himself daily of why he had made the change - to improve his energy levels and support his health. After about a week, the cravings began to fade, and he started to notice small improvements, like feeling less sluggish in the afternoon.

Michael's experience with immediate change highlights its potential power. By cutting ties with his old habit all at once, he was able to create a sense of momentum that kept him focused on his goal. The discomfort of the initial adjustment was intense, but it was short-lived, and he emerged on the other side with a renewed sense of confidence in his ability to stick to his commitments. For Michael, the clarity and decisiveness of immediate change provided a sense of freedom, helping him to fully embrace a new, healthier routine.

Immediate change is often ideal for those who thrive on clear boundaries and decisive action. It works well for habits that need a complete reset, especially when the old behavior is causing significant harm or distress. However, it requires a strong commitment and the ability to push through the initial discomfort, making it more challenging to sustain without a clear support system or a deeply motivating reason for change.

Choosing the Right Approach: Matching Strategy to Situation

The decision between gradual and immediate change depends on a variety of factors, including the nature of the habit, your personality, and the circumstances of your life. For some, like Sarah, gradual change provides a gentler path that allows them to adjust slowly, making it easier to stick with the new behavior in the long run. For others, like Michael, immediate change offers a fresh start, allowing them to break free from old patterns with a clean slate.

One important consideration is the level of attachment to the habit. Gradual change can be especially helpful for behaviors that are deeply embedded in daily routines or tied to emotional needs. It allows you to make adjustments without feeling deprived, making it easier to maintain motivation. This approach also gives you time to build new skills or coping mechanisms, making the transition smoother.

For example, when Emma, a college student, wanted to cut back on her social media use, she realized that the habit was closely tied to her feelings of loneliness and boredom. Instead of deleting her accounts entirely, she decided to start by reducing her screen time by 15 minutes each week. During the extra time, she focused on activities like journaling and calling friends. Over the course of two months, Emma reduced her daily social media time by over an hour without feeling like she was missing out. The gradual shift allowed her to find new ways to connect with others and to fill her time with more meaningful activities.

On the other hand, immediate change can be powerful when a habit has clear negative consequences or when a person feels ready to make a drastic shift. It creates a sense of urgency that can inspire action and help you break free from the comfort zone that has allowed the habit to persist. This approach can be particularly effective when combined with a strong support network, like a friend, coach, or community group, to help maintain accountability during the initial adjustment period.

When David, a graphic designer, decided to quit smoking, he knew that his health depended on making a drastic change. He chose a specific date to quit and made a plan to avoid situations where he would be tempted to smoke. He also reached out to a support group, finding encouragement from others who were on the same journey. The initial weeks were challenging, but the clear sense of purpose and support helped him push through the cravings. For David, immediate change was the right choice because it allowed him to fully commit to a healthier lifestyle without looking back.

Blending the Approaches: Combining Gradual and Immediate Strategies

In some cases, the most effective strategy might be a blend of both gradual and immediate change. This hybrid approach allows you to make a bold shift in one area while taking smaller steps in others, creating a balanced path that supports sustainable growth.

For instance, when Carla, a writer, decided to overhaul her diet, she took an immediate approach to cutting out sugary drinks, switching entirely to water and herbal teas. But when it came to other dietary changes, like reducing processed foods, she chose a more gradual path. She started by swapping out one unhealthy snack for a healthier option each week, giving herself time to adjust to each new change. This blended approach allowed Carla to see quick progress in some areas while building new habits more slowly in others, making the overall transition feel more manageable.

Carla's story shows that it's possible to tailor your strategy to fit different aspects of your habit change journey. This flexibility can be especially helpful when working toward complex goals that involve multiple behaviors, like improving overall health or building a more balanced lifestyle.

Embracing the Journey of Change

Whether you choose gradual change, immediate change, or a combination of the two, the key to success lies in understanding yourself and being patient with the process. For many, like Sarah, Michael, Emma, and David, finding the right approach was a journey of self-discovery -learning what worked best for their unique needs and situations. By respecting the time and effort it takes to transform habits, they found a path to change that felt both empowering and sustainable.

Chapter 11: Building Positive Habits

Habit Stacking: Leveraging Existing Routines

One of the most effective strategies for building new, positive habits is habit stacking—a method that leverages existing routines to make it easier to adopt new behaviors. Habit stacking is based on the idea that our brains are already accustomed to certain actions we perform regularly, making these established routines fertile ground for integrating new habits. By linking a new behavior to a habit that's already automatic, you can create a smooth transition, making the new habit feel like a natural extension of what you're already doing.

The Concept of Habit Stacking: Making New Habits Feel Effortless

Habit stacking works by using an existing habit as a trigger for a new one. Instead of trying to build a new routine from scratch, you "stack" the desired behavior onto a habit that is already firmly in place. This approach is powerful because it taps into the brain's preference for familiarity, making it easier to remember and stick to new habits. The existing habit acts as a cue, reminding you to carry out the new action until it, too, becomes second nature.

Consider the story of Laura, a busy mother of two who wanted to incorporate meditation into her daily routine to reduce stress. Laura had tried to establish a meditation practice before, but she often forgot or felt too overwhelmed to make time for it. It wasn't until she learned about habit stacking that she found a way to make it work. She decided to pair her new meditation habit with an existing routine that was already automatic: brushing her teeth in the morning.

Each morning, after brushing her teeth, Laura would sit down for five minutes of meditation. The act of brushing her teeth served as a reminder, a signal that it was time to take a few moments for herself. At first, it felt a bit unusual, but after a few weeks, it became a seamless part of her morning routine. Brushing her teeth and meditating became a single, connected ritual, helping her start the day with a clear mind.

Laura's experience demonstrates how habit stacking can make new habits feel less like an added burden and more like a natural extension of existing routines. By building on a behavior that was already automatic, she was able to integrate meditation into her life without feeling like she had to carve out extra time or energy.

Choosing the Right Anchor Habits: Finding Natural Pairings

The key to successful habit stacking is choosing the right anchor habit - an established routine that naturally pairs with the new behavior you want to adopt. An anchor habit should be something you do consistently, without much thought, like making coffee in the morning, taking a shower, or locking the front door before leaving the house. By attaching a new habit to a well-established anchor, you increase the likelihood of remembering to perform the new action.

For Daniel, a software developer who wanted to start journaling each day, finding the right anchor habit was essential. He knew that he was more likely to stick with journaling if he could fit it into his morning routine. After some thought, he realized that he already had a consistent habit of making coffee each morning. He decided to place his journal and a pen next to the coffee maker, so every time he poured his first cup, he would see the journal and write a few lines about his thoughts for the day.

At first, Daniel struggled with what to write, but the presence of the journal beside his coffee cup became a visual cue that prompted him to give it a try each morning. As the weeks passed, the act of journaling began to feel as natural as brewing coffee. Daniel found that the few minutes he spent writing helped him organize his thoughts and set a positive tone for the day. By pairing journaling with his coffee-making routine, he created a new habit that felt effortless, supported by the rhythm of his existing morning ritual.

Daniel's story highlights the importance of choosing an anchor habit that fits naturally with the new behavior. When the two actions are compatible, it's easier for the brain to accept the new routine as a part of the established sequence, making the transition smoother and more intuitive.

Stacking Habits Throughout the Day: Building a Chain of Positive Actions

One of the strengths of habit stacking is that it can be applied to different parts of your day, creating a chain of positive actions that support your goals. By adding small, positive habits to routines that are already in place, you can gradually build a daily rhythm that aligns with your aspirations, without feeling like you're making drastic changes all at once.

For Sam, a graphic designer working to improve his physical fitness, habit stacking became a key part of his journey. He had always struggled to find time for exercise, feeling overwhelmed by the idea of long workouts. But he noticed that he had a consistent habit of taking a break each afternoon to stretch his legs. He decided to build on this habit by adding a few minutes of push-ups and squats after each stretch break.

By stacking a short burst of exercise onto his existing stretch routine, Sam made physical activity a regular part of his day. He didn't have to remember to schedule workouts or feel guilty about skipping the gym; instead, he simply extended a habit he was already doing. Over time, he added more exercises to his routine, gradually increasing the intensity as his fitness improved. This approach helped Sam build a healthier lifestyle without feeling like he had to overhaul his schedule.

Sam's experience illustrates how habit stacking can help integrate new behaviors into your life in a gradual yet powerful way. By creating a series of small, positive actions throughout the day, he transformed his routine into a chain of habits that supported his health and well-being.

Overcoming Challenges with Habit Stacking: Consistency and Patience

While habit stacking is a powerful strategy, it's not without its challenges. The key to success is consistency - making sure that the new habit is practiced alongside the anchor habit every time. It can be easy to forget or to skip the new behavior, especially in the early stages, when it hasn't yet become automatic. However, with patience and persistence, the new habit can become just as natural as the original routine.

For Maya, a schoolteacher who wanted to drink more water throughout the day, habit stacking helped her reach her goal, but it required some adjustments along the way. Maya decided to stack her new habit of drinking a glass of water with each meal, using the act of sitting down to eat as her reminder. At first, she often forgot to reach for her water during lunch, distracted by conversations with colleagues or thoughts about her next class.

To reinforce the habit, Maya placed a water bottle on her desk and set a reminder on her phone to drink water at mealtimes. She also made a point of taking a sip before each bite of food, turning it into a small ritual that was easy to remember. As the weeks went by, she found that she no longer needed the reminders - drinking water with her meals had become automatic, a seamless part of her daily routine.

Maya's story shows that habit stacking can require some fine-tuning, especially in the beginning. It's important to be patient with yourself and to find ways to reinforce the new behavior until it becomes second nature. By being consistent and making small adjustments as needed, you can strengthen the connection between the old and new habits, making it easier to sustain the change.

The Long-Term Benefits of Habit Stacking: Creating Lasting Change

The beauty of habit stacking lies in its simplicity. By building on routines that are already familiar, you can make positive changes without feeling like you're starting from scratch. This approach allows you to create new habits with less mental effort, making it easier to stay committed over the long term. The result is a life where positive behaviors are woven into the fabric of your daily routines, supporting your goals in a way that feels natural and sustainable.

For many, like Laura, Daniel, Sam, and Maya, habit stacking was the key to transforming their lives one small step at a time. They discovered that change doesn't always have to be drastic - it can be as simple as adding a few minutes of meditation after brushing your teeth or doing push-ups after a stretch break. By leveraging the power of existing routines, they created a path to growth that felt both achievable and rewarding.

The 21/66/90-Day Rule: Myth vs. Reality

the 21/66/90-day rule is a popular concept that many people turn to when trying to build new habits or break old ones. This idea suggests that habits can be formed or changed within a fixed period - 21 days, 66 days, or 90 days - each number carrying its own promise of transformation. But as appealing as the simplicity of these timelines might seem, the reality of habit change is far more nuanced. Understanding the origins of these timeframes, their myths, and their truths can help set more realistic expectations, guiding you toward lasting change.

The Origin of the 21-Day Rule: A Misinterpreted Insight

The idea that it takes 21 days to form a new habit traces back to the work of Dr. Maxwell Maltz, a plastic surgeon in the 1950s. In his book *Psycho-Cybernetics*, Maltz observed that his patients took about 21 days to adjust to changes in their physical appearance, such as getting used to their new nose after rhinoplasty. He noticed a similar adjustment period for himself when adopting new behaviors. He wrote that "it requires a minimum of about 21 days for an old mental image to dissolve and a new one to gel."

While Maltz's observation was insightful, it was never intended to be a definitive rule for habit formation. Yet, over time, the idea of 21 days as the magic number for building habits spread, gaining traction in self-help literature and popular culture. It became a widely accepted belief, promising a quick path to change - just stick with a new habit for three weeks, and it would become automatic.

However, the reality is more complex. While 21 days might be enough for some simple behaviors - like drinking a glass of water each morning or saying affirmations - it is rarely sufficient for more challenging habits, such as adopting a regular exercise routine or quitting smoking. The simplicity of the 21-day rule can lead to frustration when change doesn't happen as quickly as expected, causing many to give up before a new habit has a chance to take root.

The 66-Day Rule: A More Research-Based Approach

The concept of the 66-day rule is rooted in more recent research, specifically a study conducted by Dr. Phillippa Lally, a health psychology researcher at University College London, in 2009. Lally's study sought to determine how long it actually takes for a behavior to become automatic. She and her team followed 96 participants as they attempted to adopt new habits, such as eating a piece of fruit with lunch or doing 50 sit-ups every morning.

The study revealed that, on average, it took participants 66 days for a new habit to become automatic. But the results also showed a wide range of individual variation. Some participants formed habits in as little as 18 days, while others took as long as 254 days. The 66-day average became a popular benchmark, offering a more grounded estimate than the overly simplistic 21-day rule. It acknowledged that habit formation is a gradual process that requires patience and consistency.

For many, the 66-day rule serves as a reminder that habits take time to solidify and that the journey may be longer than expected. For instance, take Jack, a fitness enthusiast who wanted to build a daily running habit. When he first read about the 66-day rule, he felt more prepared for the ups and downs of his commitment. He knew that if he stayed consistent for a little over two months, the routine would eventually become easier. On days when he struggled to lace up his shoes, Jack reminded himself that he was still building the neural pathways for his new habit. By day 70, he found that running felt like a natural part of his day, something he did without much thought or resistance.

Jack's experience illustrates the value of the 66-day rule as a guideline rather than a strict deadline. It encourages people to commit to their goals with the understanding that while progress may be slow at first, it will eventually lead to lasting change. However, it also recognizes that the timeline for habit formation is not the same for everyone, and flexibility is key.

The 90-Day Rule: Building a Lifestyle, Not Just a Habit

The 90-day rule extends the timeline further, suggesting that it takes about three months to make a habit truly ingrained as part of a lifestyle. This idea is often embraced in fitness challenges, productivity programs, and lifestyle changes where the goal is not just to adopt a single habit but to create a new way of living.

The appeal of the 90-day rule lies in its emphasis on building a sustainable routine rather than focusing solely on the habit itself. It suggests that after three months of consistent effort, the new behavior becomes deeply integrated into daily life, making it harder to revert to old patterns. This longer timeframe allows for the ebb and flow of motivation, recognizing that some days will be harder than others but that overall, the new behavior becomes a part of your identity.

For Chloe, a marketing executive who wanted to shift to a plant-based diet, the 90-day rule provided a realistic framework for her transition. She knew that making such a significant dietary change wouldn't happen overnight, and she didn't expect it to. Instead, she approached it as a three-month journey, gradually learning new recipes, adjusting to different flavors, and understanding how to meet her nutritional needs. There were moments of frustration - days when she missed her favorite foods or struggled to find suitable options while eating out. But by thinking of her change as a 90-day experiment, Chloe gave herself permission to make mistakes and keep moving forward.

By the end of the 90 days, Chloe found that her plant-based eating habits had become second nature. She no longer needed to remind herself to reach for vegetables or to check ingredient labels - it was simply the way she lived. The longer timeframe allowed her to build confidence and knowledge, transforming her diet into a lifestyle change that felt sustainable.

Myth vs. Reality: The Truth About Time and Habit Formation

The 21/66/90-day rules each offer a different perspective on the process of building habits, but they share a common myth: the idea that a specific number of days can guarantee transformation. The reality is that habit formation is highly individualized, depending on factors like the complexity of the behavior, the level of motivation, the consistency of practice, and the emotional and psychological ties to the old habit.

For example, a simple habit like drinking a glass of water before breakfast may become automatic within a few weeks, while a more complex habit like quitting a long-standing smoking addiction can take many months, or even years, to fully replace with a new routine. The time it takes to build a habit is not just about the number of days - it's about the quality of effort, the strategies used to overcome setbacks, and the alignment of the habit with one's values and goals.

The rigidity of these time-based rules can lead to unrealistic expectations, making people feel like failures if they don't see results within the prescribed timeframe. However, they also serve as helpful benchmarks, offering a structure for tracking progress and a reminder that change requires time. The true value of the 21/66/90-day concepts lies not in their exact timelines but in their encouragement to stay committed through the ups and downs of the habit-building journey.

Embracing a Flexible Approach to Habit Formation

For many, like Jack and Chloe, the realization that there is no one-size-fits-all timeline for habit formation is freeing. It allows them to focus less on the countdown and more on the process of change, understanding that habits are built through consistency and resilience rather than through arbitrary deadlines. This perspective encourages a mindset of patience and self-compassion, making it easier to stay on track even when progress feels slow.

The Role of Consistency and Repetition

One of the most crucial elements in building positive habits is the power of consistency and repetition. While motivation may inspire the initial decision to change, it is consistency - showing up day after day - that transforms intention into habit. Repetition, on the other hand, solidifies these actions, turning what was once a conscious effort into an automatic behavior. Together, consistency and repetition form the backbone of habit formation, guiding the process from a conscious practice to an ingrained part of daily life.

The Power of Consistency: Small Efforts, Big Changes

Consistency is the foundation upon which habits are built. It involves making the same effort repeatedly, even when it feels challenging or monotonous, trusting that each small action contributes to a larger outcome. While motivation can fluctuate, consistency ensures that progress continues, providing a steady rhythm that keeps you moving forward, even when the excitement of starting something new has faded.

Consider the story of Alex, a high school teacher who wanted to develop the habit of writing every day. Alex had always dreamed of finishing a novel, but his attempts to write were sporadic - he would write feverishly for a few days, then go weeks without putting pen to paper. He realized that his lack of consistency was preventing him from making real progress, so he decided to adopt a new approach: writing for just 15 minutes every morning before work, no matter what.

At first, 15 minutes didn't seem like much. Some days, he barely managed a few sentences, while on others, he wrote entire pages. But Alex committed to the process, knowing that the key was not how much he wrote each day, but that he wrote every day. As the weeks passed, the habit began to feel more natural. He no longer had to convince himself to write each morning - it became a part of his routine, as automatic as brushing his teeth.

Over the course of several months, Alex completed the first draft of his novel. He realized that the power of consistency had transformed what once seemed like an impossible goal into a series of manageable daily actions. By focusing on small, regular efforts, he made steady progress, proving that consistency can bridge the gap between dreams and reality.

Alex's experience illustrates that consistency is about showing up, even on the days when progress feels slow or unremarkable. It's about understanding that each small effort contributes to a larger whole, building momentum over time. Through consistent action, the brain begins to recognize the behavior as a regular part of life, making it easier to maintain the habit even when motivation wanes.

Repetition: Reinforcing Neural Pathways and Building Automaticity

While consistency keeps you on track, repetition is what solidifies a habit in the brain. Each time a behavior is repeated, the brain strengthens the neural pathways associated with that action, making it easier to perform without conscious thought. This process, known as "automaticity," is what turns a new behavior into something you do naturally, without needing to remind yourself or muster up willpower.

For Maria, a nurse who wanted to build a habit of exercising, repetition was key to her success. She had tried to start a workout routine many times before but always found herself quitting after a few weeks. This time, she decided to focus on repeating the same simple exercise - a 20-minute walk - every day after work. By keeping the exercise manageable and doing it at the same time each day, she aimed to make it a regular part of her evening routine.

At first, Maria had to push herself to go on the walks, especially on days when she felt tired after a long shift. But as she repeated the action day after day, something changed. She found that she no longer had to think about whether or not she would go for her walk - it became a part of her transition from work to home, a way to unwind and clear her mind.

After a few months, Maria decided to add more variety to her workouts, but the habit of exercising each evening remained. The daily repetition had laid a solid foundation, making it easier to expand her routine without losing momentum. For Maria, repetition wasn't just about building physical fitness - it was about training her brain to recognize exercise as a natural part of her day.

Maria's journey highlights how repetition can turn conscious effort into automatic behavior. Each time she laced up her shoes and headed out the door, she reinforced the neural pathways that made her evening walk feel more effortless over time. Repetition transforms the unfamiliar into the familiar, making it easier to sustain a habit for the long term.

The Challenges of Consistency and Repetition: Navigating the Plateau

Despite the importance of consistency and repetition, many people find themselves struggling during a phase known as "the plateau of latent potential." This plateau is a period where progress feels slow or nonexistent, even though you are consistently putting in the effort. It's a common challenge in habit formation, where it seems like nothing is changing despite your best efforts.

For Jacob, a young professional learning to play the guitar, the plateau became a significant hurdle. He had committed to practicing for 20 minutes each day, and at first, he saw rapid improvement. He learned a few chords, began to play simple songs, and felt excited about his progress. But after a few weeks, his improvement seemed to stall. The new chords and techniques felt difficult, and he wasn't seeing the same leaps in skill that he had experienced earlier.

Frustrated, Jacob considered giving up, wondering if he simply didn't have the talent for music. But his guitar teacher encouraged him to keep practicing, explaining that the plateau was a normal part of the learning process. The teacher reminded Jacob that every time he practiced, he was building muscle memory and reinforcing his knowledge, even if the results weren't immediately visible.

With renewed determination, Jacob kept up his daily practice, and slowly, he began to see improvement again. He realized that the plateau was not a sign of failure - it was a sign that he was laying the groundwork for future growth. By staying consistent and repeating his practice even when it felt like he wasn't making progress, Jacob eventually reached a new level of skill, finding joy in his music once more.

Jacob's story shows that consistency and repetition are not always easy, but they are essential for breaking through the tough moments of habit change. The plateau is a natural part of the process, where the efforts you make today may not pay off until weeks or months down the line. But by trusting in the power of repetition, you can push through the difficult periods and build habits that stand the test of time.

Consistency, Repetition, and the Path to Mastery

Consistency and repetition do more than help you form new habits - they are the keys to mastery. While anyone can start a new habit, it is the consistent, repeated effort that leads to true growth and transformation. This process is not just about building habits but about creating a life where positive behaviors are seamlessly woven into the fabric of each day.

For Emma, a graphic designer working on her mindfulness practice, this lesson was particularly meaningful. She had always been drawn to meditation but found it difficult to stick with it for more than a few days at a time. Inspired by the idea that consistency and repetition could make meditation a more natural part of her life, she committed to a daily practice of just five minutes. She set a timer each morning and focused on her breath, repeating the practice even on days when her mind wandered or when she felt too busy.

At first, Emma's progress was slow, and she often felt like she wasn't getting better at staying focused. But as she continued, she began to notice subtle changes - moments of calm during stressful days, a greater awareness of her thoughts, and a sense of patience that she hadn't felt before. By showing up every day, she reinforced the habit, and meditation became a source of balance in her life.

After a year, Emma reflected on how far she had come. The habit of meditation was no longer something she had to remind herself to do - it had become a natural part of her morning routine, something she looked forward to each day. Consistency and repetition had taken a simple five-minute practice and turned it into a transformative part of her life, helping her find greater peace and clarity.

Emma's journey shows that the path to building positive habits is not about perfection - it's about persistence. Consistency and repetition are the quiet forces that shape our behavior, turning small actions into enduring habits.

Chapter 12: Practical Techniques for Habit Change

Cognitive Behavioral Strategies

Cognitive behavioral strategies play a pivotal role in the process of changing habits. Cognitive Behavioral Therapy (CBT) is widely known for its effectiveness in addressing negative thought patterns and behaviors, making it an invaluable tool for those looking to transform their habits. By using techniques from CBT, individuals can better understand the thoughts and emotions driving their habits, learn to challenge unhelpful beliefs, and develop healthier ways to respond to their triggers. This approach goes beyond surface-level changes, targeting the underlying mental processes that keep habits in place.

Understanding the Connection Between Thoughts, Emotions, and Habits

At the core of CBT is the idea that our thoughts, emotions, and behaviors are interconnected. The way we think about a situation influences how we feel, which in turn shapes how we act. This framework is particularly useful in habit change because it helps people see how negative thinking patterns can reinforce unhelpful behaviors.

Take the story of Caroline, a software engineer who struggled with procrastination. She often found herself delaying important tasks, only to feel overwhelmed as deadlines approached. Through CBT techniques, Caroline began to explore the thoughts that surfaced whenever she faced a challenging project. She realized that her procrastination was driven by a fear of failure; she believed that if she started the task and didn't do it perfectly, it would confirm her doubts about her abilities.

By identifying this thought pattern, Caroline took the first step toward change. She began using a CBT technique called "cognitive restructuring," which involves challenging negative beliefs and replacing them with more balanced thoughts. Instead of telling herself, "If I don't get this right, I'm a failure," she practiced thinking, "This project is difficult, but I can make progress if I break it into smaller steps." Over time, she noticed that these new thoughts reduced her anxiety, making it easier to start tasks without the fear of imperfection holding her back.

Caroline's story illustrates how cognitive behavioral strategies can address the mental barriers that fuel bad habits. By changing the way she thought about her work, she was able to change her emotional response, which made it easier to adopt new, more productive behaviors. This approach helped Caroline understand that her procrastination wasn't just a matter of poor time management - it was a pattern of thinking that she had the power to change.

Identifying Cognitive Distortions: The Key to Changing Unhelpful Thoughts

One of the most powerful aspects of CBT is its focus on identifying cognitive distortions - biased or irrational ways of thinking that can trap us in negative behavior patterns. Common distortions include black-and-white thinking (seeing things in extremes), catastrophizing (expecting the worst possible outcome), and overgeneralization (believing that one negative experience applies to all situations). Recognizing these patterns is an essential step in breaking free from habits that don't serve us.

For example, when David, a college student, wanted to break his habit of overeating, he discovered that his thoughts often fell into the trap of "all-or-nothing" thinking. If he ate one unhealthy snack, he would think, "I've already blown my diet today, so I might as well keep eating." This mindset led him to spiral into binge eating, followed by feelings of guilt and frustration.

Through CBT exercises, David learned to catch these distorted thoughts and challenge them. He began practicing a technique called "thought-stopping," where he would pause and question his thoughts before acting on them. When he noticed himself thinking, "I've blown it," he replaced that thought with, "One snack doesn't ruin my progress - I can make a healthier choice for my next meal."

This shift in thinking helped David break the cycle of overeating. By challenging the cognitive distortion that had kept him trapped, he was able to adopt a more balanced perspective, which made it easier to get back on track after a slip-up. Over time, this change in mindset became a natural part of how he responded to cravings, helping him build a healthier relationship with food.

David's experience shows that cognitive distortions can have a powerful influence on behavior, but they can be changed through conscious effort. By learning to recognize and challenge these patterns, individuals can create new ways of thinking that support positive habit change.

Behavioral Experiments: Testing New Ways of Thinking

CBT also emphasizes the use of behavioral experiments—practical tests that challenge unhelpful beliefs by encouraging individuals to try new behaviors and observe the results.

These experiments help people see that their negative predictions are often unfounded, allowing them to build confidence in their ability to change.

For Julia, a manager who struggled with a habit of avoiding difficult conversations, behavioral experiments were a turning point. She believed that if she confronted a colleague about an issue, it would lead to conflict and make her work environment uncomfortable. This belief kept her from addressing problems directly, which led to ongoing frustrations and misunderstandings with her team.

With the guidance of a therapist, Julia designed a behavioral experiment. She chose a minor issue that she needed to address with a coworker and prepared herself to have a calm, respectful conversation about it. After the discussion, she took note of what actually happened: her colleague listened, the issue was resolved, and there was no fallout.

This experience helped Julia see that her fears were based on assumptions rather than reality. Each time she repeated the experiment with other conversations, her confidence grew, and her habit of avoidance diminished. She realized that she had been underestimating her ability to handle difficult situations and that by facing them head-on, she could improve her relationships at work.

Julia's story highlights how behavioral experiments can be a powerful way to break the hold of fear-based habits. By testing new behaviors and observing the results, she was able to gather evidence that countered her old beliefs, making it easier to adopt more effective ways of interacting with her colleagues.

Reframing Triggers: Turning Obstacles into Opportunities

CBT also offers strategies for reframing the triggers that often lead to unwanted habits. Reframing involves changing the way you interpret a situation, allowing you to see triggers as opportunities for growth rather than obstacles to avoid. This shift in perspective can make it easier to respond to challenging situations in a way that aligns with your goals.

For Sophie, a recent graduate working to build a habit of regular exercise, the trigger of rainy weather often derailed her progress. Whenever she saw clouds in the sky, she would think, "It's too wet to go for a run - I'll skip today." This thought pattern kept her from building consistency, making it difficult for her to reach her fitness goals.

With the help of CBT techniques, Sophie began to reframe her reaction to rainy days. Instead of seeing the weather as a barrier, she told herself, "This is a chance to build resilience and prove to myself that I can stick to my goals no matter what." She also planned indoor workouts for rainy days, giving herself a flexible way to maintain her routine.

By reframing her trigger, Sophie transformed a challenge into a motivation boost. She found that sticking to her exercise routine on rainy days gave her a sense of accomplishment that made her more confident in her ability to stay committed. Over time, this new mindset became her default response, helping her stay active regardless of the weather.

Sophie's experience shows that reframing is a powerful way to change how you respond to triggers. By shifting your perspective, you can turn moments that used to lead to setbacks into opportunities for growth, making it easier to maintain positive habits.

The Long-Term Impact of Cognitive Behavioral Strategies

The power of cognitive behavioral strategies lies in their ability to address the deeper thoughts and beliefs that drive our habits. Unlike approaches that focus solely on changing behaviors, CBT helps individuals understand the "why" behind their actions, providing tools to reshape their thinking patterns and emotional responses. This deeper understanding makes habit change more sustainable, as it targets the root causes of behaviors rather than just the symptoms.

For many, like Caroline, David, Julia, and Sophie, CBT techniques offered a new way of approaching the challenges of habit change. They learned that their habits were not fixed or unchangeable - they were the result of thoughts and beliefs that could be questioned, challenged, and transformed. Through cognitive restructuring, thought-stopping, behavioral experiments, and reframing, they found new ways to think about themselves and their actions, making it possible to build habits that aligned with their values and aspirations.

Positive Reinforcement and Rewards

Positive reinforcement and rewards play a crucial role in the process of transforming negative behaviors into positive habits. The concept of positive reinforcement, rooted in behavioral psychology, focuses on the idea that behaviors followed by a rewarding experience are more likely to be repeated. When we use rewards effectively, we can shape our habits in a way that aligns with our goals, turning the hard work of change into a process that feels rewarding and sustainable. This approach shifts the focus from deprivation and discipline to encouragement and growth, making habit change a more enjoyable and motivating journey.

The Science Behind Positive Reinforcement: Building Habits Through Rewards

Positive reinforcement operates on a simple yet powerful principle: when a behavior is followed by a positive outcome, the brain learns to associate that behavior with pleasure, making it more likely to repeat. This process is guided by the release of dopamine -a neurotransmitter that plays a key role in how we experience motivation and reward. Each time we receive a reward, our brain releases a surge of dopamine, creating a sense of satisfaction that encourages us to seek out that experience again.

Consider the story of Jordan, a marketing consultant who wanted to build a habit of exercising regularly. For years, he had struggled with staying consistent in his workouts, finding it hard to motivate himself after a long day at work. He often started new exercise routines with enthusiasm, but after a few weeks, his commitment would wane, and he'd find himself slipping back into old patterns.

Jordan's perspective changed when he learned about positive reinforcement. He realized that he had been focusing too much on the difficulty of exercise and not enough on the rewards that could follow. He decided to try a new approach: each time he completed a workout, he allowed himself to watch an episode of his favorite TV show as a reward. This simple shift made a huge difference. Instead of dreading his workouts, he found himself looking forward to the reward that came afterward. The promise of enjoying his favorite show helped him power through the tough moments of his routine.

As the weeks went by, Jordan noticed that his workouts began to feel less like a chore and more like a part of his day that he actually looked forward to. The reward didn't just make the exercise itself more appealing - it also helped him associate his workouts with a sense of satisfaction and pleasure. Over time, the habit of exercising became more ingrained, and he even found himself starting to enjoy the physical benefits of his routine, like increased energy and improved mood.

Jordan's story illustrates how positive reinforcement can transform the experience of habit change. By pairing his workouts with a reward, he was able to shift his focus from the immediate effort to the satisfaction that followed, making it easier to stay consistent. The reward served as a bridge between the effort and the long-term benefits, helping him maintain motivation even when the initial excitement wore off.

Choosing the Right Rewards: Aligning Incentives with Your Goals

The key to effective positive reinforcement is choosing rewards that align with your goals and enhance the habit you're trying to build. A well-chosen reward should feel meaningful and enjoyable, but it should also support the overall direction of your habit change. When rewards are carefully selected, they can amplify the positive emotions associated with the new behavior, reinforcing the habit in a way that feels both rewarding and sustainable.

For Mia, a graphic designer who wanted to reduce her habit of ordering takeout and start cooking more at home, finding the right reward was essential. She had tried to make the shift before, but each time she fell back into the convenience of delivery apps. This time, she decided to reward herself with a small treat after each home-cooked meal - something she wouldn't normally indulge in, like a piece of dark chocolate or a relaxing bath with her favorite essential oils.

At first, the rewards felt like a small incentive, but as she continued, Mia found that they made a big difference in her motivation. The thought of enjoying a treat at the end of a meal made the effort of cooking feel more worthwhile, and over time, the act of cooking itself became more enjoyable. The reward shifted her mindset from focusing on what she was giving up - convenience and time - to what she was gaining - a sense of accomplishment and self-care.

Mia's experience shows that choosing the right rewards is about more than just finding something pleasurable - it's about finding a way to celebrate progress and make the new habit feel meaningful. By aligning her rewards with her values, Mia turned the process of cooking into a positive experience, helping her stay committed to her goal of eating healthier and saving money.

Using Rewards to Break Free from Negative Habits

Positive reinforcement can also be a powerful tool for breaking free from negative habits by creating new associations and encouraging alternative behaviors. When we focus on rewarding ourselves for avoiding a bad habit or choosing a healthier alternative, we can retrain our brains to find satisfaction in the change, reducing the pull of the old behavior.

For Sam, a project manager who wanted to cut back on his habit of scrolling through social media during work hours, this approach made a significant impact. He realized that his scrolling habit was driven by a desire for a mental break, but it often left him feeling more distracted and unproductive. To change this, he set up a simple reward system: every time he avoided checking his phone during a work session, he allowed himself to take a 10-minute walk outside or treat himself to a coffee from his favorite café.

The reward of a walk or a coffee break gave Sam a positive alternative to the mindless scrolling that had once dominated his afternoons. The more he practiced this new routine, the less appealing social media became as a way to unwind. He found that the rewards not only provided a break from work but also helped him feel more refreshed and focused when he returned to his desk.

Sam's story highlights how positive reinforcement can help replace negative habits with healthier ones by creating new pathways for satisfaction. Instead of relying on willpower alone, he used rewards to shift his focus, making the new behavior feel more rewarding than the old one. This approach allowed him to transform a habit that had once been a source of frustration into an opportunity for relaxation and renewal.

Balancing Immediate Rewards with Long-Term Benefits

While rewards can be powerful motivators, it's also important to balance immediate rewards with an appreciation for the long-term benefits of habit change. Short-term incentives can help sustain motivation during the early stages, but over time, it's crucial to shift focus to the intrinsic rewards that come from achieving your goals - like the sense of pride, well-being, or accomplishment that comes from sticking with a positive habit.

For Raj, a small business owner working to build a habit of daily meditation, this balance was key. At first, he rewarded himself with a small treat - a special cup of tea - after each meditation session. The tea became a comforting ritual that made it easier for him to stick with his practice, even when his mind felt restless.

As the weeks passed, however, Raj began to notice that the meditation itself started to feel like a reward. He realized that the sense of calm and focus he experienced after each session was more valuable than the external treat he had originally used as an incentive. Gradually, he found that he no longer needed the tea to motivate him - he meditated each day because he enjoyed the benefits it brought to his life.

Raj's experience shows that while positive reinforcement can help kickstart a new habit, it's also important to recognize when the habit itself becomes rewarding. By balancing short-term incentives with an appreciation for long-term benefits, you can ensure that your habit change is not just about chasing rewards but about creating a life that feels fulfilling and aligned with your values.

Embracing the Power of Positive Reinforcement

Positive reinforcement and rewards offer a way to make habit change a more joyful and engaging process. For many, like Jordan, Mia, Sam, and Raj, the use of rewards transformed their relationship with habit change, turning challenging moments into opportunities for celebration and growth. By focusing on the pleasure that follows each small success, they found that change no longer felt like a struggle - it became a journey of discovery and self-care.

Accountability Partners and Support Systems

The role of accountability partners and support systems is emphasized as a powerful technique for achieving lasting habit change. While building new habits can often feel like a solitary journey, the presence of others - whether friends, family, mentors, or support groups - can make a significant difference in maintaining consistency, overcoming setbacks, and celebrating progress. Accountability and support systems provide encouragement, motivation, and a sense of connection that help turn personal goals into shared experiences, making the path to change more manageable and rewarding.

The Power of Accountability: Turning Goals into Commitments

Accountability partners play a vital role in turning abstract intentions into concrete commitments. When you share your goals with someone else, you create a social contract - an agreement that you will not only strive to achieve your goals but that you will keep someone else informed of your progress. This added layer of responsibility can be a powerful motivator, as it shifts the focus from internal promises to external commitments.

Consider the story of Alex, a graphic designer who wanted to build a habit of waking up early to exercise. For years, he struggled with hitting the snooze button and skipping his morning workout, despite his best intentions. But when Alex invited his friend Mark to join him for morning runs, everything changed. Each night, they texted each other their plan for the next morning, and every day they met at the park at 6:30 a.m. to run together.

The presence of an accountability partner made a huge difference for Alex. He found that it was much harder to stay in bed when he knew Mark was waiting for him at the park. On the days when he felt tired or unmotivated, the thought of letting his friend down pushed him to get out of bed and show up. Over time, the morning runs became a routine, something he looked forward to rather than something he had to force himself to do.

Alex's experience shows that accountability partners can provide the extra push needed to turn a desire for change into consistent action. By creating a sense of shared responsibility, accountability partners make it more difficult to abandon new habits, reinforcing the commitment to change even on challenging days. This dynamic turns what could be a solitary struggle into a collaborative effort, where both partners encourage each other to stay on track.

Support Systems: Finding Strength in Community

While accountability partners offer one-on-one support, broader support systems provide a sense of community that can be equally transformative in the journey of habit change. Support systems can include friends, family, colleagues, or online communities where individuals with similar goals come together to share their experiences, challenges, and victories. The sense of belonging that comes from being part of a supportive group can provide comfort during setbacks and amplify the joy of progress.

For Mia, a recent college graduate trying to build a habit of healthy eating, her support system made all the difference. She joined an online community focused on plant-based living, where members shared recipes, posted about their struggles, and celebrated their successes. At first, Mia was hesitant to share her own story, feeling unsure about whether she could stick to her new diet. But as she read the posts from others and saw how they supported each other, she felt encouraged to participate.

Each time she tried a new recipe or made it through a week without turning to junk food, Mia posted an update to the group. The positive feedback she received made her feel like she was part of something larger than herself, turning her individual goal into a collective journey. Even when she faced moments of doubt or cravings, the encouragement from her online friends kept her motivated. She knew she wasn't alone in her struggles, and that knowledge helped her push through the difficult times.

Mia's story demonstrates how support systems can create a sense of connection and accountability that extends beyond individual effort. Being part of a group with shared goals makes the process of change feel less isolating, providing a space where successes are celebrated and setbacks are met with empathy rather than judgment. This communal aspect can be a crucial source of motivation, helping individuals feel seen and understood in their pursuit of new habits.

Overcoming Setbacks with the Help of Accountability and Support

One of the greatest benefits of accountability partners and support systems is their ability to provide perspective and encouragement during setbacks. Everyone encounters challenges on the path to change, whether it's a missed workout, a slip-up in a diet, or a return to an old habit. Having someone to turn to during these moments can be the difference between giving up and finding the strength to try again.

For David, a sales manager working to quit smoking, setbacks were a constant source of frustration. He had tried to quit multiple times before, but each attempt ended in relapse, leaving him feeling defeated. This time, he joined a support group for people trying to quit smoking. He also asked his brother, who had successfully quit smoking a year earlier, to be his accountability partner.

When David experienced cravings or slipped up and smoked a cigarette, he reached out to his brother or the group instead of keeping it to himself. Instead of facing his struggles alone, he found encouragement and practical advice from others who had been through the same challenges. His brother reminded him of how far he had come, while members of the support group shared tips for dealing with cravings and reassured him that setbacks were a normal part of the process.

Over time, David began to see setbacks not as failures but as opportunities to learn and adjust his approach. The support he received helped him shift his mindset from one of self-criticism to one of resilience, making it easier to get back on track each time he stumbled. This shift in perspective was a turning point, allowing him to make steady progress toward his goal of quitting smoking for good.

David's experience highlights how accountability and support can turn moments of discouragement into stepping stones for growth. By sharing his struggles and receiving encouragement, he was able to maintain his commitment to change, even when the journey was difficult. This support helped him develop the resilience needed to face challenges with a sense of hope rather than despair.

Celebrating Success Together: Amplifying the Joy of Progress

Accountability partners and support systems don't just help during difficult times - they also amplify the joy of progress. When you achieve a milestone or reach a goal, sharing that success with others can make it feel even more meaningful. The act of celebrating together reinforces the positive emotions associated with the new habit, making it more likely that you will continue to pursue your goals.

For Leah, an artist who wanted to build a habit of daily sketching, celebrating her progress with her friends was a source of motivation. She started a group chat with two friends who were also working on creative projects, where they each shared a photo of their work every day. Each time she completed a sketch, she posted it to the chat, and her friends responded with encouragement and feedback.

The act of sharing her work made Leah feel more accountable to her goal, but it also turned her progress into a shared celebration. When she reached a milestone, like filling up an entire sketchbook, her friends cheered her on, making the achievement feel even more rewarding. Knowing that she had a community that appreciated her efforts made it easier for her to stay committed, even on the days when her creative energy felt low.

Leah's experience shows how accountability and support can transform habit change into a more joyful experience. By celebrating progress together, individuals can deepen their sense of connection and reinforce their commitment to their goals. The act of sharing success becomes a reminder of the progress made, helping to build momentum and maintain motivation over time.

Building a Network of Support: Finding the Right People for Your Journey

The effectiveness of accountability partners and support systems depends on finding the right people - those who understand your goals, respect your journey, and are willing to provide support without judgment. It's important to choose partners who are reliable and who share a similar level of commitment, as this ensures that the relationship remains mutually supportive and motivating.

For Ethan, a young professional working to build better study habits while pursuing a part-time degree, finding the right accountability partner was key. He connected with a classmate who had a similar goal, and they agreed to check in with each other every week to discuss their progress and challenges. The partnership kept both of them focused and helped them develop a routine that made studying a regular part of their schedules.

Ethan's choice of accountability partner worked well because they were both equally invested in their academic success, making their check-ins a positive and motivating experience. They pushed each other to stay on track, but they also understood the pressures of balancing work and study, offering empathy and encouragement when one of them had a particularly tough week. This balance of challenge and support made their partnership effective, turning what could have been a stressful goal into a shared adventure.

Ethan's story emphasizes the importance of choosing the right people to support you on your habit change journey. Whether it's a friend, family member, or online community, the right support can make all the difference, helping you stay focused, overcome setbacks, and celebrate your progress along the way.

The Transformative Power of Accountability and Support

Accountability partners and support systems are more than just a safety net - they are a source of strength, motivation, and connection that can turn the often difficult process of habit change into a shared journey. For many, like Alex, Mia, David, Leah, and Ethan, the presence of others made the difference between giving up and persevering, helping them to achieve goals they had once thought were out of reach.

Part V: Sustaining Long-Term Habit Change
Chapter 13: Overcoming Obstacles and Setbacks

Dealing with Relapses and Slip-Ups

The journey toward sustaining long-term habit change often involves confronting the reality of relapses and slip-ups. These moments, where old habits resurface or new routines falter, can feel discouraging and even lead to a sense of failure. However, dealing with these setbacks effectively is a critical part of the habit-building process. Relapses are not signs of defeat but opportunities to learn, adapt, and strengthen your commitment to change. By understanding why slip-ups happen and developing strategies to recover from them, you can maintain momentum on your path to positive transformation.

The Reality of Relapses: Understanding Why They Happen

Relapses and slip-ups are a natural part of the process of changing deeply ingrained habits. When trying to replace long-standing behaviors with new ones, the brain doesn't instantly forget old patterns. Instead, it learns to create new pathways, gradually weakening the hold of the old habit while strengthening the new one. During this transition, it's common to encounter moments where the old habit resurfaces - especially in times of stress, fatigue, or emotional upheaval.

Take the story of Sarah, a busy mother of two who worked hard to reduce her habit of stress eating. For months, she made excellent progress, replacing her nightly snack with a cup of herbal tea and a few minutes of journaling. But one particularly challenging day, after dealing with a difficult meeting at work and a tense evening with her kids, she found herself standing in the kitchen, reaching for a bag of chips. It wasn't until the bag was nearly empty that she realized what had happened.

In that moment, Sarah felt a wave of guilt and frustration wash over her. It seemed as if all her hard work had been undone in a single evening. But with time, she learned to see this relapse not as a failure, but as a reminder of the underlying stress she hadn't fully addressed. She realized that her old habit of stress eating was her brain's way of seeking comfort during difficult moments, and that by understanding this pattern, she could make adjustments to prevent it from taking over again.

Sarah's experience illustrates that relapses don't happen in a vacuum - they are often triggered by specific emotions, circumstances, or stressors that make it harder to stick to new behaviors. Understanding why relapses happen is the first step toward overcoming them. It's not about blaming yourself but about recognizing the triggers and building a plan to handle them more effectively next time.

Reframing Slip-Ups: From Setbacks to Learning Opportunities

One of the most important shifts in dealing with relapses is learning to reframe them as opportunities for growth rather than evidence of failure. This mindset allows you to move past feelings of guilt and instead focus on what you can learn from the experience. When you approach slip-ups with curiosity instead of self-criticism, you can uncover valuable insights about what caused the setback and how to strengthen your new habit.

For Alex, a freelance writer who was trying to build a habit of regular exercise, this shift in mindset was crucial. He had managed to stick with his morning runs for two months, but then a busy workweek disrupted his routine, and he found himself skipping workouts for several days in a row. Initially, Alex felt like he had lost all his progress. He berated himself for "falling off the wagon" and questioned whether he would ever manage to maintain a consistent exercise habit.

But after talking with a mentor, Alex realized that his setback was a chance to reevaluate his approach. He asked himself what had made it so hard to keep up with his routine during that busy week and realized that he had been trying to maintain the same intensity of workouts despite having less time. With this insight, he adjusted his plan, allowing himself shorter, more manageable workouts on days when work was demanding. This change made it easier for him to get back into his routine without feeling overwhelmed.

Alex's story shows how reframing a slip-up can turn a setback into a learning opportunity. By shifting from self-blame to self-reflection, he was able to identify what wasn't working and make adjustments that set him up for long-term success. This approach helps to build resilience, making it easier to recover from future challenges with greater confidence and self-compassion.

Developing a Recovery Plan: Bouncing Back from Relapses

When a relapse or slip-up occurs, having a plan in place for how to recover can make all the difference. A recovery plan involves acknowledging the setback, reflecting on what triggered it, and taking proactive steps to get back on track. The goal is not to punish yourself but to focus on regaining momentum as quickly as possible, turning a brief lapse into a temporary detour rather than a permanent setback.

For Marcus, a young professional working to cut down on his social media use, creating a recovery plan was a game-changer. He had been doing well with limiting his screen time until one weekend when he found himself spending hours scrolling through social media, losing track of time. Frustrated with himself, he considered giving up on his goal altogether. But instead of letting the setback derail him, he decided to put his recovery plan into action.

Marcus's plan involved three steps: first, he acknowledged what had happened without judgment, reminding himself that one weekend didn't define his overall progress. Next, he reflected on what had triggered the relapse and realized that boredom and loneliness had led him to reach for his phone more often. Finally, he decided to adjust his approach, planning a few offline activities he could turn to during the weekends, such as reading or going for a walk in the park.

By following his recovery plan, Marcus was able to get back on track quickly, turning what could have been a major setback into a minor hiccup. He found that each time he recovered from a slip-up, his commitment to his goal grew stronger, and he became better at recognizing and managing the triggers that led to overusing social media.

Marcus's story highlights how a recovery plan can provide a roadmap for navigating relapses with resilience. By focusing on actionable steps, he was able to maintain his progress and build a stronger foundation for lasting change. A well-crafted recovery plan empowers you to respond to setbacks with confidence, knowing that you have the tools to get back on course.

Practicing Self-Compassion: The Key to Resilience

One of the most challenging aspects of dealing with relapses is the tendency to be overly harsh on ourselves when we fall short of our goals. The internal dialogue that follows a slip-up can often be filled with negative self-talk, reinforcing feelings of failure and making it even harder to get back on track. Practicing self-compassion is essential for breaking this cycle, allowing you to treat yourself with the same kindness you would offer a friend.

For Sophia, a small business owner trying to quit smoking, self-compassion was the missing piece in her journey. After three months without a cigarette, she experienced a stressful day that ended with her lighting up again. The guilt hit her immediately, and she found herself thinking, "I'll never be able to do this. I'm just not strong enough." But after reflecting on how harsh she was being with herself, Sophia decided to try a different approach.

She reminded herself that change is difficult and that it was okay to struggle along the way. She focused on how far she had come rather than on this single setback. She wrote a letter to herself, acknowledging the difficulty of the journey and expressing pride in her progress so far. This act of self-compassion helped Sophia shift her perspective, allowing her to recommit to her goal without the weight of shame holding her back.

Sophia's story shows that self-compassion can be a powerful tool for overcoming the emotional toll of a relapse. By treating herself with understanding and kindness, she was able to recover more quickly and with greater determination. Self-compassion doesn't mean excusing slip-ups—it means recognizing that they are a natural part of the process and that you are worthy of patience and encouragement as you continue to strive for change.

Embracing the Journey: Relapses as Part of the Process

Ultimately, relapses and slip-ups are not barriers to habit change - they are part of the journey. For many, like Sarah, Alex, Marcus, and Sophia, the path to lasting transformation involved learning to navigate these challenges with resilience and self-awareness. They discovered that each setback was an opportunity to understand themselves better, refine their approach, and strengthen their commitment to their goals.

<u>Strategies to Stay Motivated</u>

one of the most crucial aspects of sustaining long-term habit change is maintaining motivation through the inevitable challenges and plateaus. The initial excitement of starting a new habit can fade, leaving you in a phase where progress feels slow, and the temptations to revert to old behaviors grow stronger. However, by employing specific strategies to stay motivated, you can navigate these dips in enthusiasm, keep your momentum alive, and continue moving toward your goals. Motivation, after all, isn't something you either have or don't have - it's something that can be cultivated, nurtured, and sustained through intentional effort.

Reconnecting with Your "Why": Remembering the Deeper Purpose

One of the most powerful ways to maintain motivation is to continually reconnect with the underlying reasons that inspired your desire for change in the first place. When the day-to-day effort of building a new habit starts to feel tedious, it's easy to lose sight of the bigger picture. But by revisiting your "why" - the deeper purpose behind your habit—you can reignite the emotional drive that keeps you going.

Take the story of Emily, a social worker who wanted to build a habit of daily meditation to manage her stress and improve her well-being. At first, she was diligent, waking up each morning to spend ten minutes in mindful breathing. But as weeks turned into months, the initial peace she felt after each session began to fade, replaced by the sense that meditation was just another item on her to-do list.

Recognizing that her motivation was waning, Emily decided to revisit the reasons she had started meditating in the first place. She journaled about the anxiety attacks she used to experience and how she hoped meditation would help her feel more grounded and in control of her emotions. She also wrote about her desire to be more present with her clients and her family, knowing that mindfulness could help her be a better listener and a calmer presence.

Reading over her own words, Emily felt a renewed sense of purpose. She remembered that meditation wasn't just about the practice itself - it was about building a life where she felt more at peace with herself and more connected to the people around her. This reminder of her "why" gave her the boost she needed to recommit to her daily meditation practice with a fresh perspective.

Emily's experience shows that reconnecting with your deeper purpose can transform the daily grind of habit-building into a meaningful journey. By focusing on the impact that change can have on your life and the lives of those you care about, you can reignite the motivation that carried you through the initial stages and find the strength to keep going.

Celebrating Small Wins: Finding Joy in Progress

Another powerful strategy for staying motivated is to celebrate small wins along the way. Building a new habit is often a long and challenging process, and it's easy to become discouraged if you're constantly focused on the gap between where you are and where you want to be. By recognizing and celebrating even the smallest signs of progress, you can maintain a sense of momentum and boost your motivation.

For Miguel, a college student working to improve his study habits, celebrating small wins was a game-changer. He had always struggled with procrastination, and when he first started using a daily study schedule, he found it difficult to stick with it consistently. But instead of focusing on the times he fell short, Miguel made a point of celebrating each time he completed a study session, no matter how small. He would reward himself with a short walk outside or treat himself to a favorite snack after a focused hour of work.

As he celebrated these small victories, Miguel found that his perspective began to shift. He no longer saw his study habit as a daunting challenge - he saw it as a series of small achievements that added up over time. Each celebration gave him a burst of positive energy, helping him to look forward to his next study session rather than dreading it. Over time, his confidence grew, and he began to see himself as someone capable of following through on his commitments.

Miguel's story highlights how celebrating small wins can turn the process of habit change into a more rewarding experience. These celebrations don't have to be elaborate; even a moment of acknowledging your progress can make a big difference. By focusing on what you've accomplished rather than what you have yet to do, you can maintain a sense

237

of pride and motivation, keeping your focus on the positive changes you're making.

Visualizing Success: Harnessing the Power of Imagination

Visualization is another effective technique for maintaining motivation during the ups and downs of habit change. This strategy involves imagining yourself achieving your goals and experiencing the positive outcomes of your new habits. Visualization can help bridge the gap between the effort you're putting in today and the future results you hope to achieve, making it easier to stay committed during the more challenging phases.

For Nathan, a high school teacher working to build a habit of daily exercise, visualization became a crucial tool. He had struggled with maintaining a workout routine for years, often losing motivation after the first few weeks. This time, he decided to try a different approach. Each night before going to bed, Nathan took a few minutes to close his eyes and imagine himself feeling strong and energetic after a morning run. He pictured himself playing basketball with his students without feeling winded and imagined the sense of accomplishment he would feel as his stamina improved.

This nightly visualization practice helped Nathan stay focused on the long-term benefits of his exercise routine, even on mornings when he would rather sleep in. By picturing the version of himself that he was working toward, he found it easier to push through moments of resistance and keep up with his workouts. The mental image of his future self became a powerful motivator, reminding him that the effort he put in today would pay off in the weeks and months to come.

Nathan's experience shows that visualization can make future rewards feel more real and tangible, providing a sense of motivation that keeps you engaged with the process. By focusing on the positive outcomes you're working toward, you can transform abstract goals into a vivid picture of success, making it easier to stay committed through the ups and downs.

Adjusting Your Approach: Staying Flexible in the Face of Challenges

Motivation can also be sustained by allowing yourself to adapt your approach when you encounter obstacles. When a habit starts to feel stale or overly difficult, it's easy to become discouraged. But instead of giving up, adjusting your strategy can help reignite your enthusiasm and make the process feel fresh again.

For Jasmine, a young professional trying to cut down on her screen time, adjusting her approach helped her stay motivated when her initial plan started to feel restrictive. At first, she set a goal to limit her phone use to 30 minutes per day outside of work. But after a few weeks, she found herself feeling deprived and frustrated, often breaking her own rules and then feeling guilty about it.

Instead of abandoning her goal, Jasmine decided to experiment with a different strategy. She shifted her focus from strict time limits to finding enjoyable activities that didn't involve screens, like reading, cooking new recipes, and taking up a pottery class. This change made her screen-time reduction feel less like a restriction and more like an opportunity to explore new interests. As she became more engaged with these offline activities, her phone use naturally decreased, and she felt more satisfied with her progress.

Jasmine's story highlights the importance of staying flexible in your approach to habit change. Sometimes, the key to staying motivated is not forcing yourself to stick with a rigid plan but being willing to adapt and find what works best for you. By remaining open to new strategies, you can make the journey of habit change feel more sustainable and enjoyable, keeping your motivation alive even when challenges arise.

Embracing a Growth Mindset: Seeing Progress, Not Perfection

At the heart of all these strategies is the importance of embracing a growth mindset—the belief that improvement comes through effort and learning rather than expecting perfection. A growth mindset helps you view setbacks as opportunities to grow rather than as evidence that you aren't capable of change. This perspective is essential for maintaining motivation, especially when the path to habit change is longer and more challenging than expected.

For Oliver, an entrepreneur working to build better time management skills, adopting a growth mindset was the key to staying motivated. He often felt overwhelmed by the demands of running his own business, and he struggled to stick to his plans for managing his schedule. But instead of beating himself up each time he had an unproductive day, Oliver began to see each day as a chance to learn more about what worked and what didn't.

He started tracking his time, analyzing which activities drained his energy and which ones helped him stay focused. On days when he fell short of his goals, he asked himself what he could do differently rather than dwelling on his mistakes. This shift in mindset helped him maintain a sense of progress, even when the changes were small.

Over time, Oliver found that his focus improved, and his time management skills became more consistent. He learned that motivation wasn't about getting everything right—it was about being willing to learn and adapt along the way.

Oliver's story shows that a growth mindset can sustain motivation by helping you focus on progress rather than perfection. By seeing each step as a part of your journey, you can maintain a sense of purpose and momentum, even when the path to change is challenging.

The Journey of Sustained Motivation

Staying motivated during the process of habit change requires more than just willpower - it requires strategies that help you maintain focus, celebrate progress, and adapt to challenges. For many, like Emily, Miguel, Nathan, Jasmine, and Oliver, these strategies transformed the journey of habit change from a struggle into a process of self-discovery and growth. They learned that motivation isn't something that comes and goes - it's something that can be cultivated through intentional practices and a commitment to the deeper purpose behind their goals.

Adapting to Life Changes and Stressors

sustaining long-term habit change often requires the ability to adapt when life takes unexpected turns. Life changes and stressors - like a new job, a move, a health challenge, or personal crises - can disrupt even the most established routines, making it challenging to maintain the habits you've worked so hard to build. These moments test not only your commitment to change but also your flexibility and resilience. Learning how to adapt your habits during times of upheaval is key to ensuring that progress doesn't unravel but instead continues to evolve with you.

Navigating Life Changes: Adjusting Habits to New Routines

Major life changes, such as a new job or moving to a different city, can significantly disrupt your daily rhythms. The routines that once supported your habits might no longer be feasible, requiring you to adjust your approach. Yet, these periods of transition can also be opportunities to create new structures that align with your evolving needs and circumstances.

Consider the story of James, an accountant who had developed a solid habit of going to the gym after work. For over a year, his routine was steady - he'd finish work at 5 p.m., head to the gym, and then go home for dinner. But when he took a new job that required longer hours and a longer commute, his routine was suddenly upended. By the time he got home, he was exhausted, and the thought of heading back out to the gym felt impossible.

At first, James struggled to adjust. He skipped workouts more often than not, and the frustration of losing his routine weighed heavily on him. But after some reflection, he realized that the problem wasn't his lack of commitment - it was that he was trying to force his old routine into a new situation that no longer fit. Instead of giving up, he decided to experiment with different approaches.

James started getting up 30 minutes earlier to do a quick workout at home before his commute. It wasn't as intense as his gym sessions, but it was something he could realistically manage with his new schedule. He also discovered that his office building had a small gym that he could use during lunch breaks, allowing him to squeeze in a more complete workout on days when he had a little extra time. By adapting his routine to his new reality, James found a way to keep fitness in his life, even if it looked different from before.

James's story highlights the importance of being flexible when life changes disrupt your habits. Instead of clinging to an old routine that no longer fits, he embraced the opportunity to create a new structure that worked with his current lifestyle. This adaptability allowed him to maintain his commitment to fitness, even as his life evolved.

Managing Stressors: Finding Stability Amidst Chaos

Stress is one of the most common obstacles to maintaining habits, as it can drain the mental and emotional energy needed to stick with new behaviors. When stress levels rise - whether due to work pressures, family responsibilities, or unexpected crises - it's natural to revert to familiar patterns, even if those patterns don't align with your goals. Yet, with the right strategies, it's possible to adapt your habits to provide stability during times of uncertainty.

For Emma, a nurse who had worked hard to build a habit of healthy eating, stress became a major challenge when the COVID-19 pandemic hit. Suddenly, her workdays grew longer and more exhausting, and the emotional toll of caring for patients during a crisis left her feeling drained. The healthy meals she had once enjoyed preparing after work felt like an impossible task, and she found herself turning to fast food for convenience and comfort.

Emma knew that her eating habits were slipping back into old patterns, but she also understood that she needed to give herself grace during such a difficult time. Instead of expecting herself to cook elaborate meals, she focused on finding small, manageable ways to maintain her habit. She started keeping simple, nutritious snacks in her work bag - things like almonds, fruit, and yogurt - that she could eat during short breaks. She also began prepping a few basic meals on her days off, so she'd have something healthy to heat up after a long shift.

These small adjustments allowed Emma to continue prioritizing her well-being without overwhelming herself with unrealistic expectations. She learned that during times of high stress, habits don't have to be perfect - they just need to be sustainable. Her flexibility helped her maintain a sense of control over her health, even when the world around her felt chaotic.

Emma's experience shows that adapting habits during stressful times isn't about maintaining the same level of intensity - it's about finding small, achievable actions that help you stay connected to your goals. By focusing on what she could realistically manage, she was able to preserve the essence of her habit, providing herself with stability when she needed it most.

Embracing a Flexible Mindset: Letting Go of Perfection

A flexible mindset is crucial when adapting to life changes and stressors. This mindset allows you to see adjustments not as failures but as necessary adaptations that keep you moving forward. It involves letting go of rigid expectations and understanding that the path to change is rarely a straight line.

For Luis, an artist who had built a habit of daily drawing, the need for flexibility became clear when he welcomed his first child. Suddenly, his days revolved around feedings, diaper changes, and trying to get some sleep whenever he could. The uninterrupted hours he used to dedicate to his art disappeared, and he found himself feeling frustrated by his inability to maintain his creative routine.

But instead of giving up on drawing altogether, Luis decided to shift his perspective. He realized that he could adapt his habit to fit his new role as a father. Instead of expecting himself to spend an hour at his drawing desk each day, he started carrying a small sketchbook with him, doodling during nap times or while sitting with his baby. He also experimented with shorter, quicker drawing sessions—five or ten minutes at a time—focusing on capturing simple moments from his new life.

This adjustment allowed Luis to continue nurturing his creativity, even though his life looked completely different from before. He learned that his habit didn't have to stay the same to be valuable - it could evolve alongside his changing circumstances. This shift in mindset helped him embrace the beauty of imperfect progress, finding joy in the small moments of creativity he managed to carve out each day.

Luis's story demonstrates that a flexible mindset is key to adapting habits during times of change. By letting go of the need for perfection, he was able to find a new way to pursue his passion, allowing his habit to thrive in a new context. This mindset helps you stay committed to your goals, even when life requires you to adjust your approach.

Building Habits That Adapt: Creating Resilient Routines

Building habits that can withstand life's ups and downs involves creating routines that are inherently adaptable. This means designing habits that can be scaled up or down depending on your circumstances, so that when life gets busy or stressful, you can still maintain the core of your practice without feeling like you're starting over.

For Angela, a marketing manager who had worked hard to build a habit of daily journaling, resilience was the key to sustaining her practice. She knew that some days she would have more time and energy to reflect deeply in her journal, while other days, a few quick notes would be all she could manage. So she created a habit that allowed for flexibility: on days when she had time, she would write a full page; on busy days, she would jot down three things she was grateful for or a few thoughts about her day.

This approach helped Angela maintain her journaling habit even when her schedule became unpredictable. It allowed her to keep the essence of her habit alive, even when her routine had to change. By designing her habit with built-in flexibility, she could adapt to whatever life threw her way without losing her connection to her practice.

Angela's story shows that building resilient habits is about creating routines that can adjust to different circumstances. It's about recognizing that some days will be easier than others, and that maintaining consistency doesn't always mean maintaining the same level of effort. By designing habits that can be scaled to fit your needs, you can stay committed to your goals, even when life changes.

Embracing Change as Part of the Journey

Adapting to life changes and stressors is a natural part of the journey toward long-term habit change. For many, like James, Emma, Luis, and Angela, these moments of adaptation became opportunities for growth and self-discovery. They learned that while life's changes might disrupt routines, they don't have to derail progress. Instead, with a flexible mindset and a willingness to adjust, these challenges can become stepping stones to deeper resilience and understanding.

Chapter 14: Optimizing Your Environment

Designing a Habit-Friendly Space

The concept of optimizing your environment to sustain long-term habit change is central to creating a lifestyle that supports your goals. While motivation and willpower are important, they are often fleeting. What truly influences our ability to maintain habits over time is the environment we inhabit every day. Designing a habit-friendly space means intentionally arranging your surroundings in a way that makes positive habits easier to follow and negative habits harder to engage in. This approach turns habit change from a constant struggle into a natural, almost effortless part of your daily life.

Creating a Space that Encourages Success

The spaces we live and work in have a profound effect on our behavior. Our environments subtly shape our actions, nudging us toward certain choices without us even realizing it. A cluttered desk might make it harder to focus, while a gym bag left by the door can make it easier to head out for a workout. By designing a space that aligns with the habits you want to cultivate, you can reduce the friction between intention and action, making it more likely that you'll stick with new routines.

Consider the story of Rachel, a graphic designer who wanted to build a habit of practicing yoga each morning. She had tried several times before but often found herself skipping sessions because her mat and equipment were tucked away in a closet. Each time she thought about unrolling her mat and finding her yoga blocks, it seemed like a hassle, and she would opt for a few more minutes of sleep instead.

One weekend, Rachel decided to redesign a corner of her living room into a dedicated yoga space. She cleared away some old furniture, laid down her mat, and placed her yoga blocks, strap, and a small plant in the corner. Now, every morning when she walked into the living room, her yoga mat was there, inviting her to begin her practice. The change was immediate: she found herself more motivated to stretch and move as soon as she saw the space she had created.

Rachel's experience illustrates the power of a habit-friendly space. By removing the barriers that made her practice feel like a chore, she turned her living room into a physical reminder of her commitment to her well-being. The presence of her yoga mat became a visual cue that made it easier to follow through on her intention. Her new environment didn't just support her habit - it inspired it.

Reducing Friction: Making Positive Habits Easy

One of the core principles of designing a habit-friendly space is reducing friction - the small barriers that make it harder to perform the actions you want to make a part of your routine. These barriers might seem insignificant on their own, but together they can create enough resistance to derail even the most motivated efforts. By identifying and minimizing these sources of friction, you can make positive habits easier to follow through on.

For Daniel, an aspiring writer, friction came in the form of distractions in his home office. He wanted to develop a habit of writing for an hour each morning, but he often found himself scrolling through social media or tidying up his desk instead. After reading about the concept of reducing friction, Daniel decided to take a closer look at his workspace.

He rearranged his office, moving his phone charger out of reach and turning his desk to face a blank wall rather than the window, where he often found himself daydreaming. He also set up his writing software to open automatically when he turned on his computer, so that he was ready to write as soon as he sat down. These changes made it easier for him to focus on his writing, removing the distractions that had been sapping his time and attention.

Daniel's story shows that reducing friction doesn't have to involve major changes - sometimes, small adjustments can have a big impact. By making his environment less conducive to distraction, he found it easier to stay on track with his writing habit. The reduced friction between his intention and action allowed him to use his mental energy on his craft rather than on resisting distractions.

Creating Triggers: Using Visual Cues to Reinforce Habits

Another powerful aspect of designing a habit-friendly space is the strategic use of visual cues - objects or arrangements that serve as reminders to practice your desired habit. Visual cues work by tapping into the brain's natural tendency to respond to environmental stimuli, making it easier to remember and follow through on your goals.

For Mia, a young professional trying to drink more water throughout the day, visual cues became a key part of her strategy. She had always struggled with staying hydrated, often getting caught up in work and forgetting to reach for her water bottle. To address this, Mia placed a large glass pitcher of water on her desk each morning, along with a glass. The sight of the pitcher served as a constant reminder to take a sip, making it easier for her to stay on track with her hydration goals.

After a few weeks, drinking water throughout the day became second nature for Mia. She no longer had to remind herself to reach for the glass - the presence of the water pitcher was enough to trigger the habit automatically. This small change in her environment helped her overcome a habit she had struggled with for years, simply by making the desired behavior more visible and accessible.

Mia's experience demonstrates how visual cues can transform a habit from something you have to remember into something you naturally do. By placing reminders in your environment, you can keep your goals top of mind, making it easier to build consistency over time. Whether it's a water pitcher, a gym bag by the door, or a gratitude journal on your bedside table, visual cues help create an environment that supports the habits you want to cultivate.

Designing Spaces to Discourage Bad Habits

Just as a habit-friendly space can make positive behaviors easier, it can also help to discourage habits you're trying to change. This involves adding friction or removing triggers for unwanted behaviors, making it less convenient to engage in them. The goal is not to rely solely on willpower but to design an environment where the path of least resistance aligns with your desired habits.

For Olivia, a marketing executive trying to cut down on her nightly screen time, designing her environment to discourage her habit of late-night scrolling was key. She had developed a habit of checking her phone in bed, which often kept her awake for hours and left her feeling tired the next morning. Recognizing that her environment was contributing to her habit, she decided to make some changes.

Olivia set up a charging station for her phone outside her bedroom and replaced her habit of checking her phone with reading a book. She bought a small bedside lamp and placed a stack of books she'd been wanting to read on her nightstand. The change wasn't easy at first - she missed the instant gratification of scrolling through social media. But over time, she found that the new arrangement helped her wind down more effectively, and she began to look forward to her reading time each night.

Olivia's story highlights how designing an environment that discourages bad habits can create space for healthier alternatives. By adding friction to her old routine - making it less convenient to access her phone - she was able to create a new bedtime habit that aligned better with her goals. This approach helped her rely less on willpower and more on the structure of her environment to support her desired change.

Personalizing Your Space: Making It Work for You

Designing a habit friendly space is not a one-size-fits-all approach; it's about creating an environment that fits your unique needs and preferences. What works for one person might not work for another, and the key is to experiment and find what feels natural and supportive for you.

For Alex, a musician who wanted to build a habit of practicing the piano each day, the key to creating a habit-friendly space was accessibility. He realized that one of the reasons he struggled to practice was that his keyboard was tucked away in a closet, making it a hassle to set up each time he wanted to play. So he rearranged his living room to create a small music corner, with his keyboard set up and ready to use. He also placed his sheet music in a nearby drawer and added a comfortable chair where he could sit and play.

The change made a world of difference for Alex. Having his keyboard out in the open served as a reminder to practice, and the ease of access made it more likely that he would sit down to play, even for just a few minutes. He found that he no longer needed to push himself to practice - it became a natural part of his day, simply because the environment made it easy to do so.

Alex's story shows that personalizing your space to fit your habits can make the process of change feel more organic and enjoyable. By designing an environment that supports your goals, you can create a space where positive habits flourish naturally, without constant effort or reminders.

The Long-Term Impact of a Habit-Friendly Environment

Designing a habit-friendly space is more than just a short-term strategy - it's an investment in a lifestyle that aligns with your values and aspirations. For many, like Rachel, Daniel, Mia, Olivia, and Alex, these adjustments to their environments were not just about making habits easier in the moment - they were about creating a physical space that reflected the person they wanted to become. They learned that by shaping their surroundings, they could shape their behaviors, making habit change feel like a natural extension of their daily lives.

Minimizing Negative Influences

The concept of optimizing your environment for sustaining long-term habit change extends beyond creating spaces that encourage positive behaviors - it also involves minimizing negative influences that can derail your progress. Negative influences come in many forms: people, objects, or even digital distractions that subtly pull you away from your goals. Recognizing and reducing these influences is key to maintaining focus and ensuring that the environment around you supports your intentions rather than undermines them. This approach allows you to create a space where your desired habits have room to thrive, free from the subtle but persistent pull of old patterns.

Identifying the Subtle Saboteurs: Recognizing Negative Influences

Negative influences can be difficult to recognize because they often blend seamlessly into our daily lives. They might come in the form of a friend who habitually encourages you to skip your workouts, a phone that constantly buzzes with notifications, or a pantry stocked with snacks that tempt you late at night. While these influences might seem harmless on their own, over time, they can chip away at your resolve and make it harder to stick with your new habits.

Consider the story of Mark, a sales manager who was working to cut back on his alcohol consumption. He found that his efforts were often undermined by social gatherings with friends, where drinking was the norm. At first, he tried to resist the pressure to join in, but each time, the environment made it difficult for him to stick to his intentions. Even though he didn't want to disappoint his friends or miss out on the fun, he realized that these situations were making it harder for him to achieve his goal.

After reflecting on the impact of these gatherings, Mark decided to take a different approach. Instead of completely isolating himself, he had honest conversations with his close friends, letting them know about his goal and asking for their support. He suggested alternative activities that didn't revolve around drinking, like hiking, game nights, or movie marathons. To his surprise, many of his friends were open to the idea, and he found that creating a social environment that aligned with his goals made it much easier to reduce his alcohol intake.

Mark's story shows that sometimes, minimizing negative influences involves adjusting the dynamics of your social circle. It's not always about cutting ties but about reshaping relationships in ways that support your growth. By addressing the influence that his social environment had on his behavior, Mark was able to create a more supportive space for his habit change.

Reducing Temptations: Adjusting Your Physical Space

The physical objects around us can also act as negative influences, subtly nudging us toward behaviors we're trying to change. Reducing these temptations can make it easier to maintain focus on your new habits, ensuring that your environment is a reflection of your priorities.

For Lily, a software developer who wanted to cut back on her late-night snacking, the temptation came in the form of a pantry filled with chips, cookies, and other snacks that she would often reach for while watching TV. She knew that her habit of snacking wasn't about hunger but about convenience - when the snacks were within arm's reach, it was easy to grab them without thinking.

Instead of relying on willpower alone, Lily decided to make some changes to her environment. She removed the snacks from her pantry and replaced them with healthier options, like nuts, dried fruit, and air-popped popcorn. She also put a bowl of fresh fruit on the kitchen counter, making it the first thing she saw when she walked into the kitchen.

The change wasn't about depriving herself but about making it more difficult to engage in the habit she wanted to break. If she really wanted a snack, she would have to go out of her way to get it, which gave her time to reconsider whether she was truly hungry or just eating out of habit. Over time, she found that her late-night snacking decreased, and she started reaching for healthier options more naturally.

Lily's story highlights how adjusting your physical environment can help you minimize the influence of old habits. By creating a space where the behaviors she wanted to avoid were less convenient, she made it easier to stick with her new routine. Reducing temptations isn't about removing all enjoyment from your life - it's about designing a space where making healthy choices feels like the easiest option.

Managing Digital Distractions: Reclaiming Your Focus

In the digital age, one of the most pervasive negative influences is the constant presence of screens and notifications that pull our attention away from what matters most. From social media alerts to endless news feeds, these distractions can sap your focus and make it difficult to maintain new habits. Managing digital distractions is an essential part of creating an environment that supports long-term change, allowing you to reclaim your time and energy for the habits you want to build.

For Jasmine, a writer trying to build a habit of reading for 30 minutes each night, the allure of her phone often got in the way. She would sit down with a book, but before long, she'd find herself scrolling through Instagram or responding to emails instead. Each time, she felt frustrated with herself, wondering why it was so hard to stay focused on something she genuinely enjoyed.

Determined to regain control of her evenings, Jasmine made a few changes to her digital environment. She set up a "do not disturb" mode on her phone that automatically activated at 8 p.m., silencing all notifications. She also created a charging station outside her bedroom, making it easier to leave her phone behind when she went to bed with her book. Within a few weeks, she noticed that she was reading more and scrolling less, and the sense of accomplishment she felt from finishing books helped her stay committed to her new habit.

Jasmine's story shows that managing digital distractions can be a simple yet powerful way to minimize negative influences. By creating a space where screens were less accessible, she was able to shift her focus back to the activities that aligned with her goals. This approach helped her turn her evenings into a time for relaxation and personal growth, rather than a time for endless scrolling.

Setting Boundaries: Protecting Your Energy and Time

Minimizing negative influences also involves setting boundaries that protect your energy and time from demands that don't serve your goals. These boundaries can be physical, like creating a quiet space for meditation, or social, like limiting time spent with people who discourage your progress. Boundaries are not about shutting people out or avoiding responsibilities - they're about creating space for the habits that are important to you.

For Kevin, a young father who wanted to build a habit of daily exercise, setting boundaries with his time was crucial. After the birth of his daughter, he found it challenging to carve out time for his workouts, often feeling pulled in different directions by work, family, and social obligations.

His evenings were filled with visits from friends, late-night work emails, and TV shows he watched to unwind.

Realizing that his time was being consumed by activities that left him feeling drained, Kevin decided to set some boundaries. He communicated with his friends about limiting social visits to weekends, and he set a rule for himself: no work emails after 7 p.m. He also created a small corner of the living room as his exercise space, where he kept a yoga mat and some weights, ready for a quick workout before dinner.

These boundaries allowed Kevin to reclaim time for his physical health, making it easier to stick to his exercise habit. By creating space in his life that was dedicated to his goal, he found that his energy levels improved, and he was better able to balance his roles as a father, husband, and professional. His boundaries weren't about isolating himself—they were about making room for what mattered most.

Kevin's story highlights how setting boundaries can help you minimize the negative influences that drain your time and energy. By protecting his space for exercise, he was able to maintain a routine that supported his well-being, even amidst the demands of a busy life. Boundaries give you the power to prioritize your habits and ensure that the environment around you supports your growth.

Embracing a Mindful Approach: Awareness of Influences

Ultimately, minimizing negative influences is about cultivating a sense of mindfulness regarding how your environment shapes your behavior. It's about recognizing the ways in which your surroundings affect your decisions and being willing to make adjustments that align with your values and goals. This awareness allows you to become an active participant in your own habit change, rather than a passive observer of your circumstances.

For many, like Mark, Lily, Jasmine, and Kevin, the journey to minimizing negative influences involved a process of trial and error - identifying what was holding them back and finding ways to create a more supportive environment. They learned that habit change isn't just about the actions you take - it's about creating a space where those actions feel like a natural choice.

The Impact of Social Circles on Habit Formation

The role of social circles in shaping our habits is a critical, yet often overlooked, aspect of habit formation and long-term change. While we often think of habits as highly personal, the truth is that our behavior is deeply influenced by the people we interact with daily. Our social circles - comprising friends, family, colleagues, and even casual acquaintances - can either support or hinder our efforts to change. Understanding the impact of these social dynamics allows us to make more conscious choices about how to shape our environments, leveraging the power of social influence to foster positive change.

The Subtle Power of Social Influence: How Behavior Spreads

Human beings are inherently social creatures, wired to observe and emulate the behaviors of those around them. This tendency is a fundamental part of our evolution, allowing us to learn from others and adapt to our environment. But in the context of habit formation, this means that the habits of our social circles can become our own—often without us even realizing it.

Take the story of Paul, an advertising executive who decided to cut down on his alcohol consumption. He made this decision after realizing that his weekend drinking habit was taking a toll on his health and productivity. But Paul quickly found that his efforts to drink less clashed with his social life. Many of his friends loved to gather at bars on Friday nights, and the expectation was that everyone would have a drink in hand. Whenever he tried to order a non-alcoholic option, his friends would playfully tease him or encourage him to "just have one."

At first, Paul tried to stick to his goal, but the subtle pressure from his friends made it difficult. He often found himself giving in, thinking that one drink wouldn't hurt. But as the weeks went by, he realized that the influence of his social circle was keeping him tied to a habit he no longer wanted. It wasn't that his friends intended to undermine him - they just didn't share his goal.

Paul's story illustrates how the habits of those around us can influence our own. In many social situations, there is an unspoken norm that guides behavior, and deviating from that norm can feel uncomfortable or isolating. Even without explicit pressure, the desire to fit in can make it challenging to break away from habits that are deeply embedded in our social routines.

Shaping Your Social Environment: Finding Supportive Influences

While social circles can reinforce old habits, they can also be a powerful force for positive change. By surrounding ourselves with people who share our values and goals, we can create a social environment that supports our efforts to build new habits. Finding or creating a network of like-minded individuals can make the process of habit change feel less isolating and more like a shared journey.

For Anna, a recent college graduate trying to establish a habit of running, the turning point came when she joined a local running club. She had struggled to stick with her running routine on her own, often finding excuses to skip her workouts. But when she started meeting up with a group of runners every Saturday morning, everything changed. The club's members encouraged each other, shared tips, and celebrated each other's progress, creating an atmosphere of camaraderie.

What Anna loved most was the sense of accountability that came with being part of the group. On days when she felt tempted to skip a run, the thought of letting her new friends down motivated her to show up. She found that the positive energy of the group made running more enjoyable, transforming it from a solitary struggle into a social experience that she looked forward to.

Anna's experience shows how a supportive social circle can provide the motivation and accountability needed to sustain new habits. The encouragement and shared commitment of her running group made it easier for her to push through the difficult days and maintain her routine. By aligning herself with people who valued fitness, she created a social environment that naturally reinforced her own goals.

Social Contagion: How Habits Spread Through Networks

The concept of social contagion - the idea that behaviors, emotions, and even habits can spread through social networks - plays a significant role in how our social circles influence habit formation. Research has shown that when one person in a social network adopts a new behavior, it can ripple through their friends, family, and acquaintances, influencing others to adopt similar habits.

For example, when Sophia, a high school teacher, decided to start eating healthier, she didn't anticipate that her choice would impact her entire family. She began by packing balanced lunches for herself, including fresh fruits and vegetables, lean proteins, and whole grains. Her colleagues noticed her new lunches and began asking her for recipes. At home, her husband and kids became curious about her meals, and before long, she started preparing healthier dinners for the whole family.

As her family began to enjoy the new recipes, they started making healthier choices on their own. Her husband began swapping out sugary drinks for water, and her kids started snacking on fruit instead of chips. What began as Sophia's personal goal evolved into a family-wide shift toward better nutrition.

Sophia's story illustrates the power of social contagion. Her efforts to change her own eating habits didn't stay confined to her - they spread to the people closest to her, creating a ripple effect of positive change. This kind of influence can work both ways: just as positive behaviors can spread, negative habits can also become contagious, emphasizing the importance of being mindful about the social environments we engage with.

Navigating Challenging Social Dynamics: Balancing Relationships and Change

One of the challenges of changing habits in the context of social circles is finding a balance between maintaining relationships and staying true to your goals. When your efforts to change don't align with the habits of your friends or family, it can create tension or even feelings of isolation. Learning how to navigate these dynamics is essential for maintaining both your habits and your relationships.

For Maya, a software developer who decided to cut back on her screen time, this balance was difficult to find. She realized that many of her friendships revolved around online gaming, and while she enjoyed the social aspect, she wanted to spend less time on screens. When she started pulling back from the gaming sessions, some of her friends noticed and questioned her about it, making her feel like she was abandoning the group.

Rather than letting this tension undermine her goal, Maya decided to be honest with her friends about her intentions. She explained that she wanted to focus on other hobbies, like hiking and reading, and invited them to join her for those activities. While some friends weren't interested, a few were willing to try new things, and they started meeting up for weekend hikes.

This shift allowed Maya to maintain her relationships while staying true to her desire to reduce screen time. It wasn't easy, and she faced moments of doubt about whether she was making the right choice. But over time, she found that the friends who supported her new interests became a core part of her life, providing a social circle that aligned better with her goals.

Maya's experience shows that navigating social dynamics during habit change often requires open communication and a willingness to adapt. It's not always about leaving behind old friends but about finding ways to integrate new habits into your social life. This approach allows you to build a network that supports your growth without sacrificing meaningful connections.

Choosing Your Circle: The Importance of Intentional Relationships

Ultimately, the impact of social circles on habit formation comes down to making intentional choices about the people you spend time with. This doesn't mean cutting ties with anyone who doesn't share your goals, but it does mean being mindful about who you allow to influence your behavior. Surrounding yourself with people who inspire and uplift you can make the process of habit change feel less like a solitary struggle and more like a collective journey toward a better version of yourself.

For David, a business consultant working to develop a habit of daily gratitude journaling, this realization made all the difference. He noticed that some of his friends tended to focus on negativity, often complaining about their jobs, relationships, and daily challenges. While he valued these friendships, he found that their conversations left him feeling drained and made it harder for him to focus on gratitude.

David decided to seek out new connections with people who shared his interest in personal growth. He joined a local mindfulness group and started attending weekly meetups, where participants shared their reflections and practices. This group became a source of positive energy and encouragement for him, helping him stay committed to his gratitude journaling practice. He still maintained his old friendships but balanced them with new connections that aligned with his values.

David's story shows that choosing your circle is about finding a balance that allows you to maintain your relationships while also seeking out influences that support your goals. By being intentional about who you allow into your life, you can create a social environment that naturally reinforces the habits you want to build.

The Social Dimension of Habit Change: A Journey Shared

The journey of habit change is not just about individual effort - it's also about the communities and relationships that shape us. For many, like Paul, Anna, Sophia, Maya, and David, the influence of their social circles played a pivotal role in their ability to build and sustain new habits. They learned that while habits might begin with a personal decision, they are sustained by the support, accountability, and encouragement of others.

Chapter 15: Measuring and Celebrating Progress

<u>Tracking Tools and Techniques</u>

The importance of measuring and celebrating progress is highlighted as a crucial aspect of sustaining long-term habit change. It's one thing to set a goal or start a new habit, but to keep that momentum alive over weeks, months, or even years requires a way to track your efforts. Tracking tools and techniques serve as a mirror, reflecting back the progress you've made, identifying areas for improvement, and providing tangible evidence of your commitment. This practice not only keeps you accountable but also allows you to appreciate the journey, making the process of change more rewarding and motivating.

The Power of Tracking: Turning Invisible Progress into Visible Wins

One of the most compelling reasons to use tracking tools is that they transform the often invisible nature of progress into something you can see and measure. Habits build incrementally - day by day, one small action at a time - and it's easy to lose sight of how far you've come when each step forward feels so subtle. Tracking helps bridge that gap, making the small wins more visible and giving you a sense of achievement that fuels further efforts.

Take the story of Clara, a marketing consultant who was working to build a habit of writing in her gratitude journal each evening. At first, she enjoyed the process, but after a few weeks, her initial enthusiasm began to wane. It started feeling like just another task on her to-do list, and she questioned whether the habit was really making a difference in her life.

That's when Clara decided to start using a habit-tracking app on her phone. Each night after writing in her journal, she would check off a box in the app. The simple act of marking her progress gave her a small burst of satisfaction. As the days turned into weeks, she could see her progress in the form of a streak, a growing chain of completed days that made her efforts feel tangible. On the days when she felt tempted to skip journaling, the sight of her streak motivated her to keep going - she didn't want to break the chain.

Over time, Clara began to see a deeper impact. She could look back over her entries and see how her mindset had shifted, how her focus had moved from daily frustrations to moments of appreciation. The habit tracker had turned a routine that once felt tedious into a daily ritual that she was proud of. It gave her a sense of accomplishment and made her progress visible, allowing her to celebrate the consistency that she might have otherwise overlooked.

Clara's experience shows that tracking tools can transform abstract progress into something you can see and celebrate. The act of recording your efforts, whether through a digital app or a simple calendar, provides a concrete way to measure your journey, turning invisible progress into visible wins.

Choosing the Right Tools: Finding What Works for You

There are many different tools and techniques available for tracking habits, and finding the right one is about discovering what aligns with your preferences and lifestyle. Some people thrive with the simplicity of a physical habit tracker, like a wall calendar where they can mark each completed day. Others prefer digital solutions that offer reminders, graphs, and the ability to track multiple habits at once.

For Raj, a data analyst working to establish a daily exercise routine, digital tracking tools made all the difference. He tried keeping a paper journal at first, but he often forgot to update it, and it quickly fell out of use. Then he discovered a fitness app that allowed him to log each workout, track his progress, and set daily goals. The app sent him reminders when he hadn't logged a session, and it provided weekly summaries of his performance.

Seeing his progress laid out in graphs and charts gave Raj a new perspective on his journey. He could see how his stamina had improved over time, how he was able to lift more weight or run longer distances than he could a month ago. The app also allowed him to set milestones, like completing his first 5K run, and celebrated each achievement with digital badges and encouraging messages.

For Raj, the app became more than just a tool - it became a source of motivation. Each time he reached a milestone or received a new badge, it reinforced his sense of progress and made him eager to keep pushing forward. The ability to look back at his data gave him a tangible reminder of how far he had come, making the effort feel worthwhile even on the days when he didn't feel like exercising.

Raj's story highlights the importance of finding a tracking method that fits your style. For him, the app provided the structure and feedback he needed to stay motivated. But for others, like Clara, a simpler method might be more effective. The key is to find a tool that makes tracking feel like a rewarding part of the process rather than a chore.

The Art of Self-Reflection: Turning Data into Insight

Tracking your habits is not just about collecting data - it's about using that data to gain insight into your patterns and make adjustments as needed. Self-reflection is an essential part of the tracking process, allowing you to understand why certain habits are working well and where you might be struggling. This reflection turns raw numbers into actionable insights, helping you refine your approach and stay on the path to success.

For Lena, a small business owner working to improve her sleep habits, tracking provided the clarity she needed to make meaningful changes. She struggled with going to bed at a consistent time and often found herself staying up late, feeling groggy and unproductive the next day. She started using a sleep-tracking app that recorded her bedtime, wake-up time, and sleep quality.

After a few weeks of tracking, Lena reviewed her data and noticed a clear pattern: on the nights when she stayed up watching TV or using her phone, her sleep quality was significantly lower, and she felt more tired in the morning. Armed with this insight, she decided to set a screen-time limit in the evenings and started using a physical book to wind down instead of her phone.

The change wasn't immediate - there were still nights when she slipped back into old habits - but over time, Lena saw her sleep scores improve. The tracking data gave her a way to measure the impact of her changes, reinforcing the connection between her evening habits and the quality of her sleep. It helped her turn abstract concepts like "better sleep" into concrete actions that she could control.

Lena's story shows how tracking tools can be a powerful aid in self-reflection. By reviewing her data and making adjustments, she was able to align her habits with her goals. Tracking gave her the ability to see the cause-and-effect relationships between her behaviors and their outcomes, turning her journey toward better sleep into a process of continuous improvement.

Celebrating Milestones: Turning Progress into Motivation

One of the most rewarding aspects of tracking your habits is the opportunity to celebrate milestones along the way. These celebrations serve as powerful motivators, reminding you of how far you've come and giving you the energy to keep pushing forward. Whether it's a small achievement like completing a week of consistent workouts or a larger milestone like reaching a weight-loss goal, taking time to acknowledge your progress makes the journey more enjoyable.

For Damien, a graphic designer who wanted to learn a new language, celebrating milestones became a key part of his tracking process. He used a language-learning app that allowed him to set daily goals and track his streaks. Each time he completed a lesson, the app would celebrate with encouraging messages and virtual rewards, like unlocking new levels or earning points.

Damien found that these small celebrations made a big difference in his motivation. He looked forward to the little animations that popped up when he completed a lesson, and he felt a sense of accomplishment each time he hit a new milestone, like mastering a set of vocabulary words or completing his first conversation practice. On days when he felt too tired to study, the thought of maintaining his streak or unlocking the next level gave him the push he needed to stay consistent.

As the months went by, Damien realized that the celebrations were more than just digital rewards—they were reminders of his commitment to himself. Each milestone was a marker of progress, a way of acknowledging that his efforts were adding up, even when the journey felt slow.

Damien's experience highlights how celebrating progress can transform the process of habit tracking into a source of joy. The act of acknowledging milestones turns the focus from how far you still have to go to how much you've already accomplished, making it easier to stay motivated and engaged with your goals.

The Role of Consistency: Making Tracking a Habit Itself

For tracking to be effective, it needs to become a habit in its own right - a regular part of your daily or weekly routine. Consistency in tracking ensures that you have a clear record of your progress, making it easier to identify patterns and celebrate achievements. But like any habit, tracking requires commitment and patience, especially during the times when progress feels slow or uncertain.

For Tom, a university student working to build a habit of studying for an hour each day, making tracking a habit itself was a game-changer. He used a simple notebook where he recorded each study session, noting what he worked on and how focused he felt. At the end of each week, he reviewed his entries, looking for patterns in his concentration levels and the subjects he struggled with.

At first, keeping up with the notebook felt like an extra task, but as Tom saw the weeks fill up with his study sessions, he began to appreciate the sense of accomplishment it gave him. The notebook became a physical reminder of his dedication, and he found that even on days when he didn't feel like studying, the act of writing in his notebook motivated him to keep going. It made him feel like each study session was part of a bigger picture - a commitment to his academic goals.

Tom's story shows that making tracking a habit itself can help you stay consistent, turning the process of measurement into a source of accountability and motivation. By building a routine around tracking, he created a system that kept him engaged with his progress, making it easier to stay on course even when the journey felt challenging.

Reflecting on Milestones Achieved

Reflecting on milestones achieved is emphasized as a critical practice for sustaining long-term habit change. While building new habits often focuses on daily consistency and the steady progression toward a goal, it's equally important to pause and look back on the milestones that mark the journey. Reflecting on these achievements allows you to appreciate your progress, reinforcing the positive changes you've made and offering a sense of closure for each phase of your journey. This practice transforms the pursuit of change from a relentless forward push into a balanced experience that honors both the process and the progress.

The Power of Reflection: Turning Achievements into Motivation

When you reflect on milestones, you transform each achievement into a source of motivation for the next phase of your journey. This process is about more than just recognizing that you've reached a goal - it's about understanding the effort, determination, and small victories that led to that moment. By looking back on what you've accomplished, you create a narrative of success that can sustain you through the inevitable challenges that come with long-term change.

Take the story of Aaron, a high school teacher who set out to lose 20 pounds over the course of a year by developing healthier eating habits and exercising regularly. The first few months were challenging as he adjusted to a new diet and workout routine. But he tracked his progress diligently, and after six months, he hit the milestone of losing 10 pounds. Instead of immediately shifting his focus to the next 10 pounds, Aaron took a weekend to reflect on how far he had come.

He went through his journal, rereading the entries where he had celebrated small wins - like completing his first 5K run or learning how to cook a healthy version of his favorite meal. He noticed how his mindset had changed, how what once felt like sacrifices had become a source of pride. This reflection allowed him to see the journey as a series of accomplishments rather than a never-ending climb.

The act of reflection gave Aaron a renewed sense of motivation. He realized that if he had been able to reach this milestone, there was no reason he couldn't reach the next one. It reminded him that change was possible and that he had the resilience to keep going. For Aaron, reflecting on his milestone didn't just acknowledge his progress - it reignited the fire that kept him moving forward.

Aaron's story shows that reflecting on milestones allows you to draw strength from your achievements. It's a chance to recognize that every step of the journey matters, that each small victory contributes to the larger goal. This sense of appreciation can be a powerful antidote to the moments of doubt and fatigue that often accompany long-term change.

Acknowledging Growth Beyond the Numbers

While milestones often come with tangible measures of success, such as pounds lost or weeks of consistency, the true value of reflection lies in recognizing the growth that isn't always quantifiable. This includes shifts in mindset, newfound resilience, and the development of skills that make future challenges more manageable. Reflecting on these deeper changes can provide a sense of fulfillment that goes beyond the surface-level metrics.

For Maya, a software developer who had spent a year working on reducing her stress levels through meditation and mindfulness, her biggest milestone wasn't about the number of sessions completed or minutes spent meditating. Instead, it was the realization that she had learned how to navigate stressful situations with greater calm and clarity. She could handle a busy day at work or a disagreement with a colleague without immediately feeling overwhelmed.

When she reached the one year mark of her meditation practice, Maya decided to reflect on how far she had come. She spent an afternoon journaling about the moments when she had felt her new skills make a difference - like the time she calmed herself before a big presentation or managed to focus on her breathing during a sleepless night. She realized that the milestone wasn't just about reaching a year of daily practice; it was about becoming someone who could face stress with greater resilience.

Maya's reflection helped her appreciate the transformation she had undergone. It wasn't just about checking off another day on her meditation app - it was about recognizing that she had changed how she approached the world. This deeper sense of growth made her more committed to continuing her practice, even though she no longer felt the same urgency to track every session.

Maya's story highlights the importance of reflecting on growth that goes beyond numbers. By acknowledging the shifts in her mindset and the skills she had developed, she found a sense of fulfillment that kept her practice meaningful. This kind of reflection allows you to see the bigger picture of your journey, reminding you that the true reward of habit change is not just achieving a goal but becoming a better version of yourself.

Turning Reflection into Ritual: Celebrating Your Journey

Reflection on milestones can become a powerful ritual that you incorporate into your life, turning each milestone into a moment of celebration and gratitude. This practice helps to create a sense of closure for each phase of your journey, allowing you to savor the progress you've made before moving on to the next challenge. Celebrating these moments doesn't have to be elaborate - it can be as simple as treating yourself to a favorite activity or sharing your success with a friend.

For Ben, an aspiring novelist, this ritual became a cornerstone of his writing habit. He had set a goal to write 500 words a day, and after three months, he reached the milestone of completing the first draft of his novel. Instead of immediately diving into revisions, he took a few days to reflect on what he had accomplished. He reread some of his favorite scenes, remembering the excitement he had felt while writing them. He also wrote a letter to himself, capturing the challenges he had overcome - like the days when writer's block had made each word feel like a struggle.

To celebrate, Ben treated himself to a weekend away at a small cabin, where he spent time hiking, reading, and thinking about what his next steps would be. This break allowed him to appreciate the journey he had been on and to see the draft as a meaningful achievement rather than just a step toward a finished book. It gave him the mental space to feel proud of himself before tackling the work of editing.

Ben's story shows that turning reflection into a ritual can deepen your appreciation for each milestone. By taking time to savor his progress, he found a way to make the journey more joyful and rewarding. This ritual of celebration provided a sense of closure for the first draft, allowing him to approach the next phase of his writing with fresh energy and enthusiasm.

Learning from Setbacks: Embracing Imperfect Milestones

Reflection is not only for the moments when everything goes according to plan - it's also an opportunity to learn from setbacks and imperfect milestones. When you fall short of a goal, reflecting on what went wrong and what you can do differently helps turn disappointment into a learning experience. This approach allows you to celebrate progress even when the outcome isn't exactly what you hoped for, fostering a mindset of resilience.

For Leah, a graphic designer trying to build a habit of running three times a week, setbacks were part of the process. She had set a goal to complete a half-marathon after six months of training, but a minor injury forced her to take a break from running just a few weeks before the race. At first, she felt discouraged, believing that she had failed to reach her milestone.

But after some time, Leah decided to reflect on her journey. She realized that even though she hadn't been able to run the half-marathon, she had built a habit of regular exercise, improved her endurance, and discovered a love for running that she never thought she'd have. She wrote down all the positive changes she had experienced, like feeling more energetic and less stressed, and reminded herself that these gains were worth celebrating, even if the race didn't happen.

This reflection helped Leah reframe her perspective. She decided to focus on healing her injury and signed up for a shorter race a few months later. The setback became a part of her story, not the end of it. By celebrating the progress she had made, she found the motivation to keep running, even though the path had been different from what she initially imagined.

Leah's experience shows that reflecting on milestones isn't just about celebrating the perfect moments - it's about finding meaning in the journey, even when it takes unexpected turns. By embracing the lessons learned from setbacks, she turned what could have been a source of frustration into an opportunity for growth. This kind of reflection fosters a sense of resilience, reminding you that every step forward, even a difficult one, contributes to the bigger picture of your progress.

The Value of Looking Back: Honoring the Journey

Ultimately, reflecting on milestones is about honoring the journey you've been on and recognizing that each step, big or small, has value. For many, like Aaron, Maya, Ben, and Leah, this practice transformed the way they viewed their progress. They learned that milestones are not just markers of achievement but opportunities to connect with their own resilience, celebrate their growth, and find meaning in the process of change.

The Importance of Rewarding Yourself

The practice of rewarding yourself is highlighted as an essential element in sustaining long-term habit change. While consistency, effort, and discipline are vital, the role of rewards cannot be underestimated. Rewards act as positive reinforcement, providing a sense of gratification that makes the process of change feel rewarding rather than purely effortful. They help to transform the daily grind of building new habits into a journey filled with moments of joy and satisfaction, turning the hard work of self-improvement into an experience that is not only sustainable but enjoyable.

Why Rewards Matter: Rewiring the Brain for Positive Change

When we reward ourselves for making progress, we are not merely indulging in a pleasant moment - we are engaging in a powerful process of psychological conditioning. Rewards help to solidify new behaviors in the brain, reinforcing the connection between the habit and a sense of pleasure. This is because the brain is wired to seek out behaviors that lead to positive outcomes, making it more likely that we will repeat those behaviors in the future.

Take the story of Isabel, a young architect who wanted to build a habit of reading every night before bed. Initially, her motivation was strong - she enjoyed the idea of winding down with a good book. But as the weeks went on, she found herself tempted to scroll through her phone or watch another episode of her favorite show instead. The pull of these easier, more immediately gratifying habits made it hard for her to stick with her reading routine.

Isabel realized that what her phone and TV offered - instant rewards in the form of entertainment - was something her reading habit lacked. To counter this, she decided to create a reward system for herself. She promised that if she read for 30 minutes each night for a week, she would treat herself to a visit to her favorite bookstore and pick out a new novel. This small but meaningful reward gave her something to look forward to, turning her reading habit into an experience that came with a sense of anticipation and pleasure.

As Isabel kept up with her reading routine, she found that the promise of a reward kept her on track even on nights when she felt tired or tempted by her phone. Each time she reached her goal and earned her reward, the satisfaction she felt made her more excited to continue the habit. Over time, the act of reading itself became more rewarding, as she discovered new authors and stories that enriched her evenings.

Isabel's story shows that rewards can play a crucial role in making new habits more appealing. By associating her reading habit with a positive outcome - a new book to explore - she was able to create a sense of joy and satisfaction that helped her stay committed. This process of linking effort to reward can rewire the brain to see the habit as something desirable, making it easier to maintain over the long term.

Finding the Right Rewards: Balancing Pleasure and Progress

Choosing the right rewards is key to making this strategy effective. The best rewards are those that align with your goals and values, providing a sense of pleasure without undermining the progress you've made. This balance ensures that rewards enhance your journey rather than derail it, making it more likely that you'll stick with your habit over time.

For Max, a project manager working to build a habit of daily exercise, finding the right rewards made all the difference. He initially tried using food as a reward, treating himself to a dessert after each week of consistent workouts. But he soon found that this approach wasn't helping him reach his overall health goals - it left him feeling like he was undoing some of his hard work.

Max decided to rethink his reward system, looking for incentives that would support rather than undermine his progress. He started setting aside a small amount of money each time he reached a fitness milestone, like completing a month of regular workouts or running a new personal best. At the end of three months, he used the money to buy himself a new pair of running shoes that made his workouts more comfortable and enjoyable.

This new reward system had a dual effect: it made him look forward to his workouts, knowing that he was working toward something tangible, and it also reinforced his commitment to his fitness journey by rewarding him with something that would enhance his progress. The satisfaction of earning a new pair of shoes after months of effort made him proud of what he had achieved and motivated him to keep pushing forward.

Max's experience shows that the most effective rewards are those that align with your values and support your long-term goals. By choosing rewards that enhanced his fitness journey rather than detracting from it, he found a way to celebrate his progress while staying true to his commitment to health.

Turning Rewards into Rituals: Making the Journey Enjoyable

Incorporating rewards into your routine can turn the process of habit change into a more enjoyable experience. By turning rewards into small rituals, you create moments of celebration that break up the monotony of daily effort. These rituals can make the journey of building new habits feel less like a grind and more like a series of small adventures.

For Elena, a graphic designer trying to establish a habit of journaling about her creative process, the ritual of rewarding herself became a source of joy. She struggled with consistency at first, often finding it hard to sit down and write after a long day of work. But she decided to treat herself to a small, favorite coffee shop visit every Sunday if she managed to journal for at least 15 minutes each day throughout the week.

This simple ritual gave her something to look forward to, turning her Sunday mornings into a time of celebration and reflection. She would take her journal to the coffee shop, order her favorite latte, and spend time reading over her entries from the week. This ritual not only made her feel proud of her consistency but also allowed her to see how her creative thoughts had evolved over time.

Elena's reward became more than just a treat - it became a ritual that made her journaling habit feel like a part of her identity. It gave her a way to mark the end of each week with a moment of reflection, turning her progress into a source of pride and pleasure. This transformation helped her stay committed to her journaling practice, even when the initial excitement had faded.

Elena's story shows that turning rewards into rituals can create a sense of joy that sustains long-term habit change. By making her rewards a regular part of her routine, she created a positive association with her journaling habit, making it easier to maintain. This approach helps to shift the focus from the effort required to the enjoyment of the journey, making habit change feel more like a series of meaningful experiences.

Overcoming Challenges with Rewards: Maintaining Momentum

Rewards also play a crucial role in overcoming the challenges and setbacks that are a natural part of any long-term habit change. When progress slows or motivation wanes, rewards can provide the extra push needed to keep moving forward. They act as reminders that effort is worthwhile, even when the results aren't immediately visible.

For Jordan, a software developer working to build a habit of learning a new programming language, rewards helped him push through a difficult phase. He had been making steady progress for a few months, but as he reached more complex concepts, he found himself feeling overwhelmed and frustrated. The excitement of starting something new had worn off, and the daily study sessions began to feel like a chore.

To maintain his momentum, Jordan decided to set up a reward for himself: if he completed a challenging online course on the new language, he would treat himself to a weekend trip to the mountains - a place where he always felt refreshed and inspired. This reward gave him something tangible to look forward to, turning his study sessions into steps toward a meaningful experience.

Knowing that a reward awaited him at the end of the course helped Jordan push through the tough days. It gave him a reason to keep going when he felt like giving up. And when he finally completed the course and took his trip, the sense of accomplishment he felt made the reward even sweeter. It reminded him that his hard work had paid off, making him eager to continue learning.

Jordan's experience shows that rewards can be a powerful tool for maintaining momentum during difficult times. By providing a sense of hope and anticipation, they make the process of overcoming challenges feel more manageable. Rewards help to bridge the gap between effort and achievement, reminding us that even the toughest parts of the journey can lead to moments of joy.

The Emotional Reward: Celebrating Yourself

Beyond tangible rewards, the most important reward of all is the sense of self-appreciation that comes from acknowledging your efforts. Celebrating yourself for the progress you've made - even if it's imperfect - creates a positive emotional connection to the habit. It reinforces the belief that you are capable of change, that your efforts matter, and that you are worthy of the goals you've set for yourself.

For Layla, a new mother trying to build a habit of taking daily walks with her baby, the most meaningful reward was the pride she felt when she reflected on her consistency. She didn't set up elaborate rewards or treat herself to special gifts - she simply made a point of acknowledging each week that she had made time for herself and her health amidst the challenges of new parenthood.

She would sit down each Sunday and write a short note to herself, reflecting on the moments when she had pushed through tiredness or braved the weather for the sake of her walk. These notes became a collection of small celebrations, reminding her that even in the busyness of life, she had made herself a priority. The act of writing these reflections became a reward in itself - a moment to pause and appreciate how far she had come.

Layla's story shows that the most valuable rewards aren't always material - they are the moments when we take time to honor our own efforts. By creating a space to celebrate herself, she turned her walking habit into a source of pride and self-respect. This emotional reward made the habit feel meaningful, giving her the motivation to continue even when the journey was difficult.

Conclusion

Embracing a Lifestyle of Continuous Improvement

The journey culminates in an essential realization: that the process of habit change is not merely about reaching a specific goal or overcoming a single challenge - it is about embracing a lifestyle of continuous improvement. This shift in perspective transforms habit change from a one-time effort into a lifelong journey of growth and self-betterment, where each day becomes an opportunity to refine, evolve, and align more closely with the person you aspire to be.

The Journey of Growth: A Commitment to Evolving

Embracing a lifestyle of continuous improvement means recognizing that the journey of self-transformation is ongoing. It's about understanding that even as you reach one milestone, there is always room to deepen your skills, expand your understanding, and adjust your habits to new circumstances. Rather than seeing habit change as a linear path with a fixed endpoint, this mindset encourages you to see each goal as a stepping stone toward a richer, more fulfilling life.

Take the story of Sam, a financial analyst who initially set out to improve his time management skills. He began with a simple goal: to organize his workday better, reducing the time he spent on emails and distractions so that he could focus on deep, meaningful tasks. After months of refining his routine, using time-blocking techniques, and eliminating digital distractions, he found himself achieving more during his workdays than he ever had before. But rather than stopping there, Sam began to ask himself what else he could improve in his life.

With the momentum he had gained, he turned his attention to his physical health, setting new fitness goals that challenged him in ways he hadn't considered before. He started learning about nutrition, experimented with different workout routines, and even tried his hand at mindfulness practices to reduce stress. As he continued to explore new areas of growth, he realized that each success in one area of his life gave him the confidence to tackle the next. He became less focused on the idea of "finishing" his journey of self-improvement and more interested in the endless possibilities that lay ahead.

Sam's story shows that the essence of continuous improvement is the willingness to keep moving forward, even after you've achieved your initial goals. It's about seeing every accomplishment as a doorway to new challenges and opportunities, and recognizing that true fulfillment comes not from reaching a destination but from enjoying the process of getting better each day.

Learning from the Process: Celebrating Small Gains

When you embrace a lifestyle of continuous improvement, you learn to appreciate the value of small, incremental gains. Rather than focusing solely on the major breakthroughs, you begin to see the beauty in the small steps that build upon each other over time. This perspective allows you to stay motivated and engaged, even when progress feels slow or difficult. It teaches you that the act of showing up, day after day, is where real change happens.

For Clara, a graphic designer who initially worked to reduce her stress through daily meditation, this mindset shift was transformative. She started her practice with the hope of finding more peace in her busy life. At first, her progress seemed slow - there were days when her mind raced, and the quiet moments felt like a struggle. But over time, she began to notice subtle changes: she was quicker to let go of negative thoughts, more patient with herself and others, and more attuned to the present moment.

As Clara continued her meditation practice, she realized that the benefits extended beyond her stress levels. She became more mindful in her interactions, more intentional about her work, and even began exploring new creative outlets she had always been curious about. The small, daily practice of meditation became a gateway to a broader journey of self-discovery and growth.

Clara's experience illustrates that a lifestyle of continuous improvement is about more than chasing after big wins - it's about appreciating the small moments of progress that add up over time. It's about recognizing that each day you invest in your habits, no matter how imperfectly, contributes to a richer, more meaningful life. This perspective allows you to stay engaged with your journey, knowing that each step forward is a step worth celebrating.

Embracing Change: Adapting as You Grow

A lifestyle of continuous improvement also involves embracing the inevitability of change. As you grow, your goals, interests, and even the habits that once served you may evolve. This mindset encourages you to stay open to new possibilities, to adapt your habits to the changing seasons of your life, and to continually reassess what it means to live in alignment with your values.

For Nadia, a nurse who had built a solid habit of running every morning, adapting to change became crucial when she transitioned into a new role that required longer hours and more responsibilities. Her morning routine no longer fit with her new schedule, and she found herself feeling frustrated and disconnected from the habit she had worked so hard to build. But instead of clinging to her old routine, Nadia decided to see this transition as an opportunity for growth.

She explored new ways to integrate fitness into her day, experimenting with evening yoga sessions and short runs during her lunch breaks. She also started reading about nutrition and stress management, realizing that her new role required her to think about her well-being in a more holistic way. While her habits looked different than they had before, Nadia found that they still provided her with a sense of fulfillment and balance.

Nadia's story shows that continuous improvement is not about sticking rigidly to a plan but about being willing to adapt as you grow. It's about recognizing that as your life changes, so too can the habits that support you. This flexibility allows you to remain committed to your well-being, even as your circumstances shift.

The Joy of the Journey: Finding Meaning in Growth

At its core, embracing a lifestyle of continuous improvement is about finding joy in the journey of growth. It's about recognizing that each moment of effort, each small adjustment, and each new habit is a part of a larger story that you are writing for yourself. This mindset turns the process of self-improvement into a source of fulfillment, where the act of striving becomes a reward in itself.

For Alex, a young entrepreneur who had worked to develop a habit of journaling, the joy of continuous improvement became most evident in the quiet moments of reflection. As he wrote about his experiences each evening, he realized that his goals had shifted over time - from building a successful business to creating a life where he felt balanced, connected, and true to himself. He found that the act of journaling, which had started as a simple habit, had become a way to track his own evolution and to appreciate the progress he had made, both professionally and personally.

Alex discovered that the most meaningful part of his journey wasn't the external achievements - though he had plenty to be proud of - but the sense of inner growth he felt along the way. He learned to value the process of setting new goals, exploring new interests, and becoming more attuned to his own needs and desires. Each entry in his journal became a reminder that he was not just building a business but building a life that reflected who he wanted to be.

Alex's story highlights that the true reward of continuous improvement lies in the sense of meaning it brings to your life. It's about realizing that the process of becoming is just as valuable as the achievements themselves. This mindset allows you to appreciate the journey of habit change as a continuous unfolding, where each chapter holds its own lessons and joys.

A Life of Possibilities: Looking Ahead with Confidence

As you reach the end of this book, the idea of embracing a lifestyle of continuous improvement serves as an invitation to keep exploring, learning, and growing. It's a reminder that the work you've put into transforming your habits has prepared you not just for a specific goal but for a life where change is a welcome companion. It's about approaching each new challenge with curiosity and each success with gratitude, knowing that the path of self-improvement is never truly finished.

For many, like Sam, Clara, Nadia, and Alex, this journey has been one of discovery - both of their own potential and of the infinite possibilities that come with a commitment to growth. They learned that each habit they built, each setback they overcame, and each milestone they celebrated was part of a larger story of becoming. They discovered that true power lies not in reaching the end but in finding the strength to keep going, to keep learning, and to keep embracing the process of change.

The Ongoing Journey of Habit Mastery

The theme of *The Ongoing Journey of Habit Mastery* emerges as a profound reminder that the pursuit of self-transformation is never truly complete. Rather than a fixed destination, the mastery of habits unfolds like a story, one that is written day by day, page by page. It is a narrative in which the protagonist – you - continually faces new challenges, discovers unexpected strengths, and finds meaning in the act of striving, even when the path ahead is uncertain.

The Ever-Turning Wheel of Change

In this story, each habit you cultivate, each moment of progress you achieve, is like a chapter that adds richness to the tale of your life. Yet, even as one chapter ends, another begins, demanding fresh energy, new perspectives, and a willingness to embrace the unknown. Mastery, in this sense, is not a static state. It is an ever-turning wheel - one that turns through seasons of success and struggle, through days when everything clicks into place, and through those when old patterns reemerge, testing the resilience of your resolve.

Consider the experience of Eleanor, a pianist who, after years of practice, felt she had finally mastered her instrument. She could glide through complex pieces with grace, her fingers moving across the keys as if they were dancing. Yet, just as she began to feel secure in her abilities, she found herself drawn to a new challenge - jazz improvisation. In the world of classical music, she had thrived on precision and structure, but improvisation demanded a different kind of mastery - one that required spontaneity, intuition, and a willingness to explore uncharted territory.

At first, Eleanor struggled. The freedom that jazz offered felt chaotic compared to the order she was used to. But as she continued to practice, she discovered a new kind of joy - a thrill in the unpredictability, a beauty in the imperfect notes that emerged from her exploration. Her journey through jazz reminded her that mastery was not a final achievement but a constant expansion of her horizons. Each new challenge deepened her understanding of music, and in the process, she realized that the true essence of mastery was to remain a student, always eager to learn.

Eleanor's story reflects the nature of the ongoing journey of habit mastery. It teaches us that even as we achieve one level of proficiency, there is always another layer to uncover, another dimension to explore. Mastery, therefore, is a commitment to perpetual growth, an embrace of the unfolding mystery that each new day brings.

The Seasons of Growth: Embracing the Cycles of Habit Mastery

The journey of habit mastery is not a straight line; it moves in cycles, like the changing of the seasons. There are moments of spring, when new habits take root with enthusiasm and promise. These are the times when the air is filled with the excitement of possibility, when the small steps you take each day seem to bloom with potential. But just as spring gives way to summer, when the heat of sustained effort is required to nurture those habits, so too does the journey move through autumn, when the initial excitement fades, and you must find the discipline to keep going even as progress slows.

And then, inevitably, comes winter - a time when the darkness of doubt creeps in, when setbacks make you question whether the effort is worth it. These are the moments when the familiar pull of old habits feels strongest, when the cold of failure chills your spirit. Yet, it is in these times of winter that the seeds of new growth are planted, lying dormant beneath the surface, waiting for the warmth of renewed commitment to bring them back to life.

For Daniel, a schoolteacher who had spent years working to build a habit of regular exercise, the cycles of growth became a familiar rhythm. He experienced many winters, times when an injury or a demanding school year made it difficult to maintain his routine. But each time, he learned to wait for spring - to trust that even when he felt stuck, the effort he had put in before would carry him through. When the new season came, he would feel his strength return, and the habit that had withered in the cold would bloom once more, stronger for having survived the winter.

Daniel's experience teaches us that mastery is about understanding the natural cycles of change. It is about learning to endure the winters, to celebrate the springs, and to recognize that each season has its place in the journey. Mastery is not the absence of struggle but the willingness to continue through every phase, knowing that growth is always on the horizon.

The Dance Between Discipline and Compassion

As you travel this path of ongoing habit mastery, you come to realize that the dance between discipline and compassion is what keeps you balanced. Discipline drives you to show up each day, to push through the resistance, and to reach for new heights. It is the force that keeps you moving when the initial excitement fades, that helps you maintain the integrity of your commitments.

But alongside discipline, compassion is the gentle hand that guides you when you stumble. It is the voice that reminds you that setbacks do not define you, that mistakes are not failures but opportunities for learning. Compassion allows you to forgive yourself when old habits resurface, to recognize that change is rarely linear, and to offer yourself the patience you would extend to a dear friend.

For Mia, a business consultant who struggled with perfectionism, this balance became her greatest lesson in the journey of habit mastery. She had always relied on discipline to achieve her goals, pushing herself relentlessly until burnout forced her to stop. But as she worked to develop healthier habits, like daily mindfulness and setting boundaries at work, she realized that what she needed most was not more discipline but more self-compassion.

She learned to celebrate her small wins, even when they fell short of her expectations, and to offer herself kindness when she missed a day or slipped back into old patterns. This compassion became a source of resilience, allowing her to return to her habits with renewed energy rather than abandoning them in frustration. It taught her that mastery was not about never making mistakes but about always finding the courage to begin again.

Mia's story reveals that true mastery is found not in rigid adherence to a plan but in the grace with which you navigate the inevitable ups and downs. It is the ability to hold yourself accountable while also understanding that you are human, imperfect, and beautifully capable of growth.

An Endless Horizon: The Beauty of the Unfinished

As you reach the end of this book, you may find that the path of habit mastery stretches out before you, endless and inviting. It is a path that leads not to a final destination but to an ever-expanding horizon, where each goal achieved opens the door to new possibilities. This realization is the essence of the ongoing journey: the understanding that life is a series of transformations, that every habit you build or change is a part of a greater unfolding.

For Elena, an artist who set out to develop a habit of sketching each day, this realization came when she looked back on her sketchbooks and saw not just the progress she had made but the way her art had evolved. What began as a simple desire to improve her technique had become a lifelong love affair with creativity. She discovered that the beauty of her journey lay not in the perfect lines she drew but in the act of drawing itself, in the quiet moments of connection between her hand and the page.

Elena learned that mastery is not about reaching a point where you no longer have to try - it is about falling in love with the process, with the discovery of what you can create when you keep showing up. She realized that each sketch, each brushstroke, was both a step toward improvement and a celebration of the moment she was in. It was a reminder that the pursuit of mastery is a dance, one that invites you to find joy in the movement, not just in the end result.

Elena's story is a testament to the beauty of the unfinished. It is a reminder that the journey of habit mastery is, in many ways, a work of art - one that you continue to shape with each new effort, each new choice. It is an invitation to see yourself not as a fixed being but as a work in progress, capable of endless transformation.

Embracing the Journey: A Life of Unfolding Potential

As you close this book and step back into your life, know that the journey of habit mastery is yours to continue. It is a path that will challenge you, inspire you, and sometimes test your patience. But it is also a path that will reveal the depths of your own resilience, the strength of your desire to grow, and the limitless potential that lies within you.

The story you are writing is one of courage - the courage to change, to face your fears, to push beyond your comfort zones, and to keep moving forward even when the way is unclear. It is a story of transformation, where each habit you cultivate becomes a thread in the tapestry of your life, weaving together a vision of who you are becoming.

So, as you embrace this ongoing journey, let it be a journey filled with curiosity and wonder. Let it be a journey where you learn to trust in the process, to find joy in the effort, and to celebrate each moment of growth along the way. And remember, above all, that the path of habit mastery is not about perfection - it is about becoming, about embracing the unfolding story of your life with all of its challenges, triumphs, and beautiful possibilities.

<u>Encouragement for the Road Ahead</u>

As *"Habits Unleashed: The Ultimate Guide to Transforming Bad Habits into Positive Power"* draws to a close, there is a final message to carry with you - a message of encouragement for the road ahead. This journey of transforming habits, of uncovering your potential, has been filled with revelations and challenges, triumphs and setbacks. But now, as you stand on the threshold of what comes next, know that the most important part of this journey lies in your hands, in the choices you will make after these pages have been turned.

A Beacon for the Future: Trusting in Your Own Strength

The road ahead is not always clear. It twists and turns, sometimes leading you through valleys of doubt and over mountains of effort. Yet, remember that every step you have taken to reach this point is proof of your strength. Each habit you have nurtured, each moment when you chose to try again rather than give up, has built within you a resilience that cannot be undone. This resilience is your beacon, a light that will guide you through the darker days when progress feels slow or when old habits try to pull you back.

Consider the way a lighthouse stands firm against the crashing waves, casting its light into the stormy sea. In the same way, your inner strength can serve as a lighthouse, guiding you back to your intentions whenever the currents of life threaten to sweep you off course. It is this strength that will remind you that you have faced challenges before, and that you have the power to face them again.

Remember the story of Marcus, who started his journey struggling with self-doubt, unsure if he could ever break free from the habits that had held him back for so long. He stumbled many times, questioned himself, and almost turned back. But he kept moving forward, one small step at a time, building new habits and letting go of old ones. And now, even as he looks toward new challenges, he knows that the strength he found during his journey is his to carry forward.

He knows that no setback is final, and no challenge insurmountable, because he has already proven to himself that he is capable of change.

Like Marcus, you have within you the power to navigate whatever lies ahead. Trust in the strength you have cultivated, and let it be the foundation upon which you continue to build.

Embrace the Unknown: An Adventure in Becoming

As you continue your journey beyond these pages, embrace the unknown with a sense of curiosity and adventure. The path you are on is one of becoming - becoming more in tune with your values, more aligned with your true self, and more capable of living the life you envision. But this path is not always predictable, and that is where its beauty lies. It offers the thrill of discovery, the chance to surprise yourself with what you can achieve when you step into the unfamiliar.

Imagine a traveler standing at the edge of a vast, uncharted landscape, the horizon stretching out endlessly before them. They do not know what lies beyond the next hill, but they feel a sense of excitement in their chest, a spark of anticipation for the adventures that await. In the same way, the journey of habit change invites you to step forward into the unknown, to explore new possibilities and to become a traveler in your own life.

For many, like Sarah, the thought of leaving the comfort of old routines can be daunting. She remembers how she used to cling to the safety of her habits, even when they no longer served her, because she feared the uncertainty that change might bring. But as she began to embrace new habits - building a daily writing practice, finding joy in evening walks, learning to set boundaries - she discovered that the unknown was not something to fear but something to welcome. It was a place where she could grow, where she could find new strengths within herself, and where she could become the author of her own story.

Sarah's journey reminds us that the road ahead is an invitation to adventure, a chance to explore the unexplored corners of your own potential. Embrace it with a spirit of openness, and let each new day become an opportunity to discover what lies within you.

Compassion for the Journey: Forgiving Yourself as You Grow

As you venture onward, remember that no journey is without its missteps, and no path is free from moments of doubt. There will be days when old habits resurface, when progress feels slow, or when the weight of change feels too heavy to bear. But in those moments, let compassion be your guide. Offer yourself the same understanding you would give to a friend, recognizing that growth is rarely a straight line, and that setbacks are a natural part of any transformation.

Think of it like a gardener tending to a garden. There will be days when the flowers bloom brightly, and others when they wilt under the heat of the sun. Yet, the gardener does not curse the flowers for their struggle - she waters them, tends to the soil, and trusts that with care and time, they will bloom again. In the same way, your compassion toward yourself can nourish your spirit, helping you to weather the challenges and come back stronger.

For Javier, a chef who spent years trying to break free from his perfectionism, learning to be compassionate with himself became the most transformative part of his journey. He had always held himself to impossible standards, berating himself for every mistake and flaw. But as he worked on building new habits - practicing mindfulness, embracing imperfection in his cooking - he learned to soften his inner voice. He learned that it was okay to stumble, to have days when he fell short of his goals, and that each setback was not a failure but a chance to begin again.

Javier's story is a testament to the power of self-compassion. It teaches us that when we forgive ourselves for our missteps, we create space for new growth. We give ourselves permission to be human, to embrace the messiness of change, and to find strength in our own vulnerability.

A Future Filled with Possibility: Writing the Next Chapter

Now, as you look to the road ahead, know that the story of your life is still being written. The habits you have transformed, the goals you have set, and the values you hold close to your heart are all threads in a tapestry that continues to unfold. And while this book may be ending, your journey is just beginning.

Each day offers a new page, a blank space where you can choose how the story will continue. Will you take a step toward a new habit that excites you? Will you revisit an old goal with a fresh perspective? Will you find new ways to bring joy, kindness, and purpose into your life? The possibilities are limitless, and they are yours to explore.

Think of Caroline, a retiree who found a new passion for painting in her sixties. She began with small, hesitant strokes, unsure if she could call herself an artist. But as she painted each day, she found herself falling in love with the process, with the way colors blended on the canvas and with the sense of calm that came from creating something new. Painting became more than a hobby - it became a way for her to write a new chapter in her life, one filled with creativity and self-expression.

Caroline's story reminds us that it is never too late to begin again, to find new passions, and to discover new sides of ourselves. It is never too late to turn the page and start writing a new chapter, one that reflects the person you are becoming.

So, as you step into the future, know that you carry with you the power to shape your life, to transform your habits, and to create a story that is uniquely yours. Let the lessons you have learned guide you, let the strength you have cultivated give you courage, and let the love you have found for yourself be the foundation upon which you build. This is your journey, your story, and the road ahead is filled with endless possibility.

And whenever you find yourself facing a crossroads, a moment of doubt, or a new challenge, remember this: you have already come so far. You have already faced the darkness and found the light within yourself. You have already proven that change is possible, that growth is within your reach, and that you are capable of becoming the person you aspire to be. Let this be your encouragement for the road ahead - a reminder that you are strong, you are worthy, and your journey of transformation has only just begun.

Appendices

Appendix A: Habit Change Worksheets and Templates

Habit Change Worksheets and Templates serves as a practical toolkit for readers, offering a structured and hands-on approach to applying the concepts discussed throughout the book. This appendix is designed to be a companion to your journey of habit transformation, providing you with the resources to plan, track, and reflect on your progress with clarity and intention. Each worksheet and template is crafted to help you break down complex habit change processes into manageable steps, ensuring that you have the support you need as you work to turn your goals into reality.

The Purpose of Habit Change Worksheets

The habit change worksheets are more than just forms to fill out - they are a means of translating your goals into actionable plans. They provide a space for introspection, encouraging you to reflect deeply on your motivations, challenges, and the steps needed to build lasting habits. These worksheets guide you through the key stages of habit formation, from identifying your goals and understanding your triggers to developing strategies for maintaining consistency and overcoming setbacks.

The worksheets are designed to be revisited regularly, allowing you to adjust your plans as you grow and learn. As you progress, you'll find that these templates become a record of your journey, capturing the insights, adjustments, and victories that shape your path to habit mastery. Whether you're working to build a new positive habit or break free from a negative one, these worksheets serve as a roadmap that keeps you focused on the steps ahead while celebrating the progress you've made.

Getting Started: The Habit Planning Template

One of the foundational tools in Appendix A is the Habit Planning Template, a detailed guide that helps you set clear intentions for the habits you want to cultivate or change. This template begins with a section where you can articulate your habit goals, breaking them down into specific, actionable steps. It prompts you to reflect on the *why* behind your goal—what motivates you to make this change and how achieving it will impact your life.

For example, if your goal is to develop a habit of daily exercise, the template encourages you to specify the type of exercise, the duration, and the frequency. It asks questions like: "What do you hope to gain from this habit?" and "What challenges might prevent you from sticking with it?" These prompts are designed to help you think through potential obstacles and to prepare strategies for overcoming them, such as identifying a time of day when you're most likely to follow through or choosing an accountability partner to support you.

The Habit Planning Template also includes a space for visualizing your success. This section invites you to imagine what your life will look like once the habit is fully integrated, helping to create a mental picture that serves as a source of motivation during challenging times. By completing this template, you'll have a comprehensive plan that not only outlines your goal but also prepares you for the practical realities of turning intention into action.

Daily and Weekly Habit Tracking Sheets

To maintain consistency, Appendix A includes Daily and Weekly Habit Tracking Sheets that allow you to monitor your progress in real-time. These sheets are designed with simplicity in mind, providing an easy-to-use format where you can record each time you complete your habit, track any missed days, and note the reasons behind them.

The Daily Habit Tracking Sheet is perfect for those who are focusing on habits that require consistent, day-to-day effort. It includes a section for each day of the week, where you can check off your habit completion and jot down a brief note about how you felt during the process. This space encourages you to pay attention to patterns - like noticing that you tend to skip your habit on particularly stressful days - so you can address these challenges proactively.

The Weekly Habit Tracking Sheet is ideal for habits that might not occur daily but require a broader view of progress. For example, if you're aiming to read three books a month or exercise four times a week, this template allows you to see how well you're meeting your goals over a longer period. It includes sections for summarizing your successes and challenges at the end of each week, prompting you to reflect on what went well and what adjustments might be needed. These tracking sheets help you stay accountable to your goals, providing a sense of accomplishment as you see your consistency grow over time.

Reflection and Review: The Monthly Habit Review Template

The Monthly Habit Review Template is a deeper dive into your progress, offering a structured way to evaluate your efforts over a longer time frame. This template is designed to help you step back and assess the overall impact of your habit, ensuring that it aligns with your evolving goals and needs.

In the first section of the template, you'll find prompts to reflect on what has worked well during the month and what challenges you encountered. It encourages you to think about how your habit has affected other areas of your life - perhaps your morning meditation routine has improved your focus at work, or your efforts to reduce screen time have led to more meaningful conversations with family. This reflection helps you recognize the broader benefits of your habit, reinforcing your motivation to continue.

The second section focuses on adjustments and adaptations. It asks questions like: "Are there any aspects of your habit that need to be adjusted?" and "What new strategies could help you overcome challenges?" This space is an invitation to refine your approach, whether that means adjusting the time of day you practice your habit, finding new ways to make it enjoyable, or seeking out additional support. The Monthly Habit Review Template serves as a tool for continuous improvement, ensuring that your habits remain aligned with your changing life circumstances and goals.

Overcoming Setbacks: The Habit Recovery Worksheet

Setbacks are a natural part of any habit change journey, and Appendix A includes the Habit Recovery Worksheet to help you navigate these moments with resilience. This worksheet is designed to guide you through the process of understanding why a setback occurred, how it affected your progress, and what steps you can take to get back on track.

The worksheet begins with a section for reflecting on the setback itself. It asks questions like: "What specific event or challenge led to the setback?" and "How did you feel in the moment?" This reflection helps you gain clarity about the factors that triggered the setback, allowing you to address them with greater awareness in the future.

Next, the worksheet guides you through a problem-solving process, encouraging you to brainstorm solutions for overcoming similar challenges in the future. It invites you to consider what resources or support you might need, such as seeking advice from a mentor, adjusting your environment, or revisiting your original motivation for the habit. The Habit Recovery Worksheet helps you see setbacks not as failures but as opportunities for growth, teaching you to approach obstacles with a mindset of learning and adaptation.

Celebrating Milestones: The Progress Reflection Template

The Progress Reflection Template in Appendix A is designed to help you celebrate the milestones you achieve along your habit journey. This template provides a space for reflecting on the progress you've made, acknowledging the effort it took to reach each milestone, and considering how far you've come since you began.

The first part of the template asks you to describe your milestone - whether it's completing a month of daily exercise, reading a set number of books, or successfully reducing a negative habit. It invites you to reflect on the emotions you felt when you reached this goal and to recognize the challenges you overcame along the way. This reflection helps you internalize the progress you've made, reinforcing your belief in your ability to change.

The second part of the template encourages you to think about how you would like to celebrate this achievement. It might be through a small reward, like treating yourself to a special meal or taking a day to relax and enjoy your favorite hobby. This section emphasizes the importance of marking your progress, making each milestone feel like a meaningful part of your journey rather than just a step toward the next goal.

Bringing It All Together: Creating a Personalized Habit Plan

Finally, Appendix A concludes with a template for creating a Personalized Habit Plan, a comprehensive document that ties together your goals, strategies, tracking methods, and reflections. This plan acts as a blueprint for your habit change journey, providing a clear path forward that you can adjust as needed.

The Personalized Habit Plan begins with a summary of your habit goals, motivations, and key strategies, offering a snapshot of your intentions. It then incorporates elements from the other worksheets, such as a section for tracking your progress, reflecting on monthly reviews, and noting any adjustments. By bringing all of these components together in one place, the Personalized Habit Plan ensures that you have a cohesive and well-organized approach to achieving your goals.

This final template is a testament to the idea that habit change is not just about willpower - it's about planning, reflection, and the willingness to adapt. It is a reminder that your journey is unique, and that the tools and templates provided in Appendix A are there to support you every step of the way.

Through these worksheets and templates, *Habits Unleashed* offers not just inspiration but practical guidance for turning your vision of change into a lived reality. Whether you're taking your first steps toward a new habit or looking to refine a practice that has been with you for years, Appendix A provides the structure, support, and encouragement you need to stay on course. As you use these tools, you'll find that each page becomes a part of your story - a story of growth, transformation, and the power to shape your life one habit at a time.

Appendix B: Recommended Resources and Further Reading

Recommended Resources and Further Reading serves as an essential guide for those seeking to deepen their understanding of habit formation, personal growth, and the science of behavior change. Below is a detailed breakdown of the key categories and resources included in this appendix:

1. Foundational Books on Habits and Behavior Change

Atomic Habits by James Clear:

- o Focuses on the power of small, incremental changes that compound over time.

- o Emphasizes the importance of systems over goals for creating lasting change.

- o Offers practical techniques for building positive habits and breaking negative ones, like habit stacking and identity-based habits.

The Power of Habit by Charles Duhigg:

- o Explores the habit loop—cue, routine, reward—and how it drives our behavior.

- o Blends scientific research with real-world examples, showing how habits shape our lives.

- o Provides insights into changing habits at individual, organizational, and societal levels.

The Brain That Changes Itself by Norman Doidge:

- o Delves into the concept of neuroplasticity, the brain's ability to rewire itself.

- o Highlights real-life cases of people transforming their habits through brain change.

- o Inspires readers by showing the potential for change even in deeply ingrained behaviors.

2. Articles and Research Papers on Habit Science

A Neural Basis for Habit Formation (Neuron):

- o Examines the role of the basal ganglia in converting conscious actions into automatic behaviors.

- o Provides insights into why habits become deeply ingrained and how they can be altered.

- o Useful for readers who want to understand the brain mechanisms behind habit loops.

The Role of Rewards in Behavior Change (Journal of Behavioral Decision Making):

- o Focuses on how rewards and reinforcement influence the formation and maintenance of habits.

- o Offers evidence-based strategies for using rewards effectively in habit-building.

- o Helps readers understand the balance between intrinsic and extrinsic motivation.

Social Influence and Habit Formation: The Role of Social Norms (Personality and Social Psychology Review):

- o Explores how social environments and norms shape our habits.

- o Discusses the impact of social contagion on behavior change.

o   Offers strategies for leveraging positive social influences in habit transformation.

3. Podcasts and Audio Resources

The Tim Ferriss Show:

o   Features interviews with high achievers sharing their routines, habits, and mindsets.

o   Provides practical advice and insights from leaders in various fields.

o   Ideal for those looking for actionable strategies to optimize their habits.

The Habit Coach by Ashdin Doctor:

o   Short, practical episodes offering tips for building and maintaining habits.

o   Covers a wide range of topics, including productivity, mindfulness, and health.

o   Perfect for listeners who prefer concise, easy-to-apply advice.

Hidden Brain by NPR:

o   Explores the psychological and neurological factors influencing our behavior.

o   Blends storytelling with scientific research to uncover why we do what we do.

o   Helps listeners understand the subconscious forces driving their habits.

4. Websites and Online Communities

Habitica:

o   A gamified habit-tracking app that turns habit-building into a role-playing game.

o   Users earn rewards and level up as they complete tasks and build consistency.

o   Includes community features for support and accountability.

Coursera:

o   Offers online courses on psychology, behavior change, and self-discipline from top universities.

o   Provides a structured way to deepen your understanding of habit science.

o   Ideal for learners who appreciate guided study and the opportunity to earn certificates.

Reddit Community: r/Habits:

o   A forum for sharing experiences, challenges, and tips related to habit formation.

o   Users can ask questions, seek advice, and find motivation from a supportive community.

o   Great for those who want to connect with others on similar habit journeys.

5. Recommended Reading for Personal Growth and Mindset

Mindset by Carol S. Dweck:

o   Introduces the concept of a growth mindset, emphasizing the belief that abilities can be developed.

o   Helps readers shift their perspective on challenges and setbacks.

o   Complements the habit-building process by fostering resilience and openness to learning.

Man's Search for Meaning by Viktor E. Frankl:

o   Explores the human search for purpose, even in the face of adversity.

o   Encourages readers to connect their habit goals with a deeper sense of meaning.

o   Offers a philosophical perspective on the importance of finding purpose in the process of change.

Grit by Angela Duckworth:

o   Focuses on the role of passion and perseverance in achieving long-term goals.

o   Highlights how sustained effort, rather than talent alone, leads to success.

o   Provides insights into maintaining commitment to habits over time.

6. Online Tools and Habit-Building Apps

Strides:

o A habit-tracking app that allows users to set goals and track progress with customizable reminders.

o Offers visual progress tracking, including charts and streaks.

o Suitable for those who prefer detailed tracking and goal-setting.

Streaks:

o A simple app focused on building and maintaining daily habit streaks.

o Encourages users to keep up consistency by visualizing their progress.

o Great for those who are motivated by the idea of not breaking a chain.

Notion Templates for Habit Tracking:

o Provides customizable templates for tracking habits, journaling, and reflecting.

o Allows users to create their own habit systems within the versatile Notion workspace.

o Ideal for those who like to combine habit tracking with other aspects of personal organization.

7. Videos and Online Courses

TED Talks on Habits and Behavior Change:

o   Features talks by experts like BJ Fogg and Kelly McGonigal, covering topics such as tiny habits and the power of willpower.

o   Offers inspiring and thought-provoking perspectives on self-discipline and habit change.

o   Great for visual learners who enjoy engaging content.

MasterClass with Robin Arzon: Mental Strength:

o   Focuses on building mental resilience and developing habits that support athletic and personal growth.

o   Provides practical advice on staying motivated and overcoming challenges.

o   Ideal for those seeking to improve their mindset alongside their physical habits.

Mindfulness-Based Stress Reduction (MBSR) Online Courses:

o   Offers structured programs for integrating mindfulness into daily life.

o   Helps build habits of focus, presence, and stress management.

o   Supports readers who want to enhance their mental and emotional well-being alongside habit change.

8. Research Journals and Websites for Ongoing Learning

Psychology Today:

o   A website featuring articles on the latest research in psychology, behavior change, and mental health.

o   Provides accessible explanations of complex psychological concepts.

o   Useful for readers who want to stay updated on new insights in habit science.

American Psychological Association (APA) Journals:

o   Offers access to peer-reviewed studies on behavior change, self-regulation, and motivation.

o   Useful for those seeking academic and research-based information.

o   Ideal for readers who enjoy deep dives into empirical evidence.

Greater Good Science Center:

o   A resource from UC Berkeley focused on research related to well-being, habits, and positive psychology.

o   Includes articles, videos, and podcasts on building habits that foster happiness and resilience.

o   Great for readers looking for scientifically-backed strategies for personal growth.

9. Audiobooks for Learning on the Move

Audible's Habit Building Collection:

- A curated list of audiobooks on habit change, motivation, and self-discipline.

- Allows readers to absorb key concepts while on the go.

- Ideal for those who prefer auditory learning or have a busy lifestyle.

Audiobook Version of *The Power of Habit*:

- Narrated by Charles Duhigg, bringing his insights to life with engaging narration.

- Suitable for readers who want to revisit key concepts in a different format.

- Provides an immersive experience of learning about habits through storytelling.

This detailed collection of resources in Appendix B ensures that every reader of *Habits Unleashed* has the tools and guidance needed to continue their journey toward habit mastery. Whether you're looking for deeper scientific insights, practical strategies, or inspiration from those who have walked the path before, these recommendations offer a wealth of knowledge to keep you moving forward.

Appendix C: Inspirational Success Stories and Case Studies

Inspirational Success Stories and Case Studies serves as a testament to the transformative power of habit change. This appendix brings together real-life stories and detailed case studies of individuals who have successfully redefined their lives by breaking free from negative habits and building positive, empowering ones. These narratives provide readers with practical insights, motivational boosts, and relatable examples, illustrating that profound change is possible for anyone willing to put in the effort. The stories in this appendix span diverse backgrounds, challenges, and goals, offering a rich tapestry of experiences that inspire and guide readers on their own journeys of transformation.

1. Overcoming Procrastination: The Journey of Jake

Background:

- Jake, a 34-year-old software developer, struggled with chronic procrastination throughout his career. Despite his talent and passion for coding, he found himself constantly delaying important tasks, leading to missed deadlines and a sense of frustration.

Challenge:

- Jake's procrastination stemmed from a fear of failure and a tendency to become overwhelmed by large projects. He often avoided tasks until the last minute, only to rush through them with subpar results.

Strategy for Change:

- Jake began by breaking down his work into smaller, more manageable chunks using a habit called "micro-tasking."

He set a timer for 15 minutes of focused work, gradually increasing the time as he built momentum.

o   He also implemented a reward system, allowing himself a short break after each session of focused work, which helped him associate productivity with positive feelings.

Results:

o   Within six months, Jake's productivity skyrocketed. He no longer felt overwhelmed by large projects and found satisfaction in checking off small tasks each day. His work quality improved, and he regained a sense of pride in his achievements.

Key Takeaway:

o   Jake's story illustrates the power of breaking down overwhelming tasks and using rewards to build momentum. His journey shows that even deeply ingrained habits like procrastination can be transformed with small, consistent changes.

2. Transforming Health Habits: Maria's Path to Fitness

Background:

o   Maria, a 42-year-old accountant, struggled with maintaining a healthy lifestyle due to her demanding job and a lack of time for exercise. She had tried numerous diets and workout plans but often abandoned them after a few weeks.

Challenge:

o   Maria's main challenge was consistency. She would start each new health regimen with enthusiasm, only to lose motivation when results didn't come quickly.

Strategy for Change:

o   Maria shifted her focus from intense, short-term goals to building sustainable habits. She started with a commitment to walking for 20 minutes each morning, gradually incorporating strength training and healthier eating habits.

o   She used a habit tracker app to monitor her progress and joined an online community for support and accountability.

Results:

o   Over a year, Maria lost 30 pounds and, more importantly, developed a daily exercise routine that felt like a natural part of her life. Her energy levels increased, and she found that her improved physical health positively affected her mental well-being.

Key Takeaway:

o   Maria's story highlights the importance of starting small and building consistency before aiming for bigger goals. It shows that gradual changes, when sustained over time, can lead to significant and lasting improvements.

3. Breaking Free from Social Media Addiction: Kevin's Story

Background:

o   Kevin, a 28-year-old marketing manager, found himself spending hours each day scrolling through social media. This habit interfered with his productivity, affected his sleep, and left him feeling disconnected from real-life relationships.

Challenge:

o   Kevin's dependency on social media was rooted in a need for constant stimulation and the fear of missing out (FOMO). He struggled to find ways to relax without reaching for his phone.

Strategy for Change:

o   Kevin implemented a "digital detox" routine, starting with no-phone zones during meals and before bedtime. He also set app limits and used a timer to reduce his social media usage gradually.

o   To fill the void left by reduced screen time, Kevin rediscovered old hobbies like reading and playing guitar, which helped him manage his need for relaxation and distraction.

Results:

o   Within three months, Kevin's screen time decreased by 60%, and he reported better focus, improved sleep, and deeper connections with friends and family. His newfound hobbies became a source of joy and relaxation, replacing his previous need for constant online engagement.

Key Takeaway:

o   Kevin's journey shows that changing a habit isn't just about removal but about finding fulfilling alternatives. His experience demonstrates how creating boundaries with technology can lead to a more balanced and fulfilling life.

4. Building a Gratitude Practice: Anika's Story

Background:

o   Anika, a 39-year-old school teacher, felt overwhelmed by stress and anxiety. Despite having a fulfilling career and a loving family, she often found herself focusing on the negative aspects of her day.

Challenge:

o   Anika's habit of negative thinking was deeply ingrained, leading to feelings of dissatisfaction despite her external achievements. She struggled to break free from the cycle of worry and self-criticism.

Strategy for Change:

o   Anika started a gratitude journal, committing to writing down three things she was grateful for each day. She also practiced gratitude meditation once a week to deepen her sense of appreciation.

o   She set a daily reminder on her phone to prompt her to reflect on positive moments, helping her stay consistent with her practice.

Results:

o   Over time, Anika's perspective shifted. She found herself focusing more on the good moments in her life and became more resilient to stress. Her relationships with colleagues and students improved as she began to express appreciation more openly.

Key Takeaway:

o   Anika's story demonstrates the profound impact of gratitude on mental well-being. It shows how even small daily practices can rewire our thinking patterns, leading to a more positive and balanced outlook on life.

5. Overcoming Negative Self-Talk: Brian's Transformation

Background:

o Brian, a 45-year-old sales executive, struggled with negative self-talk and a lack of self-confidence. He often doubted his abilities and feared taking risks, which held him back professionally and personally.

Challenge:

o Brian's habit of negative self-talk had been with him for decades, making it difficult for him to recognize his achievements and feel satisfied with his progress.

Strategy for Change:

o He began using a cognitive behavioral technique called thought reframing. Whenever he caught himself thinking negatively, he wrote down the thought and countered it with a positive or realistic perspective.

o He also created daily affirmations to reinforce a more positive self-image and used visualization techniques to imagine himself succeeding in challenging situations.

Results:

o Within six months, Brian noticed a significant improvement in his confidence. He became more willing to take on new challenges at work and felt a greater sense of self-worth. His relationships improved as he began to communicate more openly and assertively.

Key Takeaway:

o   Brian's story shows that changing our inner dialogue is possible with consistent effort. It highlights the power of thought reframing and affirmations in transforming a negative mindset into one that fosters self-belief.

6. Replacing Bad Habits with Positive Ones: Emily's Success Story

Background:

o   Emily, a 26-year-old graphic designer, struggled with late-night snacking, which affected her energy levels and concentration during the day. She wanted to break this habit but found it difficult to resist cravings after long workdays.

Challenge:

o   Emily's late-night snacking was tied to her emotional state—she often turned to food for comfort after stressful days. Her challenge was finding healthier ways to manage stress.

Strategy for Change:

o   She substituted her evening snack habit with a new routine: a cup of herbal tea and a short walk around the block. This allowed her to unwind without relying on food.

o   Emily also kept a food and mood journal to track when cravings occurred and identify the emotions that triggered them.

Results:

o   After a few months, Emily's late-night cravings decreased significantly. She found that her new routine of walking and tea not only helped her relax but also improved her sleep. Her energy levels and focus at work improved as a result.

Key Takeaway:

o   Emily's story demonstrates the effectiveness of habit substitution. It shows that by replacing a negative habit with a positive one, it is possible to address the underlying emotional triggers and create healthier routines.

7. Building a Consistent Morning Routine: Priya's Story

Background:

o   Priya, a 31-year-old entrepreneur, struggled with a chaotic morning routine that often left her feeling rushed and unprepared for the day. She wanted to create a more structured morning that included time for exercise, meditation, and planning.

Challenge:

o   Priya had difficulty waking up early and often found herself hitting the snooze button, which led to a frantic start to her mornings.

Strategy for Change:

o   She began by gradually shifting her bedtime and wake-up time by 15 minutes each week. Priya also created a morning checklist that included three non-negotiables: a 10-minute meditation, a short workout, and a quick review of her goals for the day.

o   Priya set up her environment to support her new routine, placing her workout clothes and yoga mat by her bed the night before and using an alarm clock that played gentle nature sounds to wake her up gradually. She also moved her phone away from her bedside to avoid the temptation of the snooze button.

o   To keep herself accountable, she shared her morning routine goals with a friend who also wanted to become an early riser. They checked in with each other each morning, sharing updates on their progress.

Results:

o   Within a few months, Priya's morning routine became second nature. She found that starting her day with mindfulness, exercise, and a clear plan helped her feel more grounded and focused throughout the day. Her productivity improved, and she felt more in control of her time and energy.

o   The accountability check-ins with her friend not only helped her stay committed but also fostered a sense of camaraderie that made the process more enjoyable.

Key Takeaway:

o   Priya's story illustrates the importance of making gradual adjustments and building a supportive environment for habit change. It shows that with consistency and the right strategies, even those who struggle with mornings can transform their routines into empowering rituals.

8. Breaking the Cycle of Stress-Induced Smoking: David's Case Study

Background:

o   David, a 38-year-old financial advisor, had been a smoker for over 15 years. He often reached for a cigarette during stressful situations at work or when dealing with personal challenges. Despite numerous attempts to quit, he found himself returning to the habit whenever stress levels rose.

Challenge:

o   Smoking had become David's default stress-relief mechanism, making it difficult for him to break free from the habit. His challenge was not only the physical addiction to nicotine but also the psychological reliance on smoking as a coping mechanism.

Strategy for Change:

o   David joined a support group for individuals trying to quit smoking, where he learned about healthier stress-management techniques such as deep breathing exercises and progressive muscle relaxation.

o   He also began substituting his smoking breaks with short walks and chewing sugar-free gum. To combat the physical cravings, he used nicotine patches for the first few weeks and gradually reduced the dosage.

o   David kept a journal to track his triggers, noting when and why he felt the urge to smoke. This helped him identify patterns, like the specific times of day when cravings were strongest and the situations that triggered his habit.

Results:

o   Over six months, David's cravings began to diminish, and he successfully quit smoking. He found that the physical activity from his walks and the relaxation techniques helped him manage stress without relying on cigarettes. His journal became a source of motivation, as he could see the progress he had made and how far he had come.

o   David also noticed significant improvements in his physical health, such as better lung capacity, increased energy levels, and a sense of accomplishment from breaking a habit he once thought unchangeable.

Key Takeaway:

o   David's story emphasizes the power of combining physical and psychological strategies for habit change. It shows that replacing a negative habit with positive coping mechanisms and seeking social support can be key to overcoming even long-standing habits.

9. Rebuilding a Relationship with Food: Sophie's Story

Background:

o   Sophie, a 29-year-old graphic designer, had developed an unhealthy relationship with food during her college years, using it as a way to cope with stress and emotions. This led to cycles of binge eating, followed by feelings of guilt and restrictive dieting.

Challenge:

o   Sophie's emotional eating habits were deeply tied to feelings of loneliness and anxiety. She struggled to break the cycle because food had become her primary source of comfort during difficult times.

Strategy for Change:

o   Sophie sought the help of a therapist who specialized in cognitive behavioral therapy (CBT) for eating disorders. Through therapy, she learned to recognize the emotional triggers that led to binge eating and developed strategies for addressing her emotions without turning to food.

o   She started practicing mindful eating, paying attention to her hunger cues and eating slowly to fully experience each meal. Sophie also kept a food and mood diary, where she recorded her meals alongside her emotions, helping her identify patterns in her eating habits.

o   To build a healthier relationship with food, Sophie began exploring cooking as a creative outlet, preparing meals that nourished her body and mind.

Results:

o   Over time, Sophie developed a more balanced approach to food. She learned to enjoy meals without guilt and found new ways to cope with stress, such as journaling, talking to friends, and practicing yoga. Her food and mood diary became a valuable tool in her recovery, helping her track progress and stay mindful of her emotional state.

o   Sophie's weight stabilized, but more importantly, her self-esteem and body image improved. She no longer felt controlled by her cravings and began to appreciate her body for what it could do rather than how it looked.

Key Takeaway:

o   Sophie's story highlights the importance of addressing the underlying emotional issues behind habits. It shows that through therapy, mindfulness, and self-compassion, it is possible to transform even the most complex relationships with food into one of balance and self-care.

10. Building a Creative Habit: Aaron's Artistic Revival

Background:

o   Aaron, a 40-year-old architect, had always dreamed of becoming a painter but struggled to make time for his passion amidst his demanding career and family responsibilities. He often felt that his creativity had taken a backseat to his other obligations.

Challenge:

o   Aaron's challenge was prioritizing his creative pursuits without feeling guilty for taking time away from work and family. He worried that pursuing his hobby would be seen as self-indulgent or that he wouldn't have the time to improve his skills.

Strategy for Change:

o   Aaron committed to a "20 minutes a day" rule, setting aside time each evening to work on his painting, regardless of how tired or busy he felt. He treated this time as non-negotiable, like brushing his teeth or preparing dinner.

o   He also joined a local art group, which provided a sense of community and accountability. Sharing his work and progress with other aspiring artists helped him stay motivated and inspired.

o   Aaron set small goals, such as completing one painting per month and experimenting with different styles and mediums. These incremental targets helped him maintain a sense of progress without feeling overwhelmed.

Results:

o   Aaron's 20-minute rule transformed his relationship with art. What began as a small daily commitment blossomed into a deep passion, and he eventually started participating in local art shows and selling his work online.

o   His daily painting sessions became a form of meditation, allowing him to disconnect from work stress and reconnect with his creative side. The sense of fulfillment he gained from pursuing his passion spilled over into other areas of his life, improving his overall well-being.

Key Takeaway:

o   Aaron's story demonstrates the power of dedicating even small amounts of time to a passion. It shows that by making a consistent commitment and creating a supportive environment, it's possible to integrate creativity into a busy life and reignite the spark of a long-forgotten dream.

Conclusion: The Power of Real-Life Stories in Inspiring Change

Appendix C: Inspirational Success Stories and Case Studies is a testament to the resilience and determination of individuals who have transformed their lives through habit change. Each story offers a unique perspective on the challenges and rewards of building better habits, providing readers with practical insights, motivation, and hope. These case studies remind us that the journey of habit transformation is not linear - it is filled with ups and downs, moments of struggle, and moments of triumph. But through patience, persistence, and the right strategies, it is possible to turn even the most deeply ingrained habits into a source of strength and empowerment. As readers reflect on these stories, they are invited to see themselves in the narratives, knowing that the power to change lies within them as well.

www.ingramcontent.com/pod-product-compliance
Lightning Source LLC
Chambersburg PA
CBHW071358150726
48000CB00001B/69